THE COMPLETE
LICENCE
TO GRILL

CHRIS KNIGHT

McArthur & Company
Toronto

First published in Canada in 2006 by
McArthur & Company
322 King St. West, Suite 402
Toronto, Ontario
M5V 1J2
www.mcarthur-co.com

Library and Archives Canada Cataloguing in Publication

Knight, Chris, 1960-
The complete Licence to grill / Chris Knight.

Includes index.
ISBN 978-1-55278-780-9

1. Barbecue cookery. I. Title.

TX840.B3K547 2009   641.7'6   C2009-901998-1

Design by *Mad Dog Design Inc.*
Front cover author photo courtesy of *Knight Enterprises*
Printed in Canada by *Transcontinental*

The publisher would like to acknowledge the financial support of the Government
of Canada through the Book Publishing Industry Development Program, the
Canada Council for the Arts, and the Ontario Arts Council for our publishing
activities. We also acknowledge the Government of Ontario through the Ontario
Media Development Corporation Ontario Book Initiative.

10 9 8 7 6 5 4 3 2 1

To my son Adam,
to my mother Carolle

Foreword

THIS IS THE LAST BBQ COOKBOOK YOU'LL EVER HAVE TO BUY. What? Bold statement you say? Hey, it's bbq. Bbq IS bold. It's BIG, like this book. It's also big like the great outdoors where we know the bazillion recipes contained herein will bring you and yours much summertime (and wintertime) pleasure for years to come.

After 104 episodes of Licence To Grill, we've pretty much rubbed, marinated, grilled, smoked, charred, basted and infused every imaginable cut of meat, type of veggie and fruit there is, not to mention eggs, waffles, pancakes and a bunch of other stuff you'd never think of doing on the grill. We've picked some of our best recipes for this book with a eye on giving you a nice cross section of ingredients to do on the Q.

But more than just recipes, we think The Complete LTG makes an excellent reference tool for the avid grill jockey, full of tips, tricks, techniques and secrets.

Here now are the LTG 23 Commandments to Exceptional BBQ:

1. WHAT IS BARBECUE ANYWAY?

There are two ways to barbecue.

First you've got your "low-and-slow." This is cooking at low temperature, with or without smoke, using indirect heat with the lid down for a long period of time. Indirect heat means that whatever you are cooking is placed on one side of the grill surface with the burner beneath it turned off. The heat from the other burner(s) (and the smoke, if smoking) fills the cavity of the barbecue (because the lid is down) and cooks whatever it is you've got in there without any direct contact with the flames from the burner. Low-and-slow indirect cooking is generally used for cuts of meat that are tougher and fattier, which need a longer cooking time to break down the fibers or connective tissue, melt the fat and become something wonderfully tender and flavorful.

Then you've got your "high-and-fast." This is cooking at higher temperatures using direct heat with the lid up for shorter periods of time. Now, this is where barbecue aficionados from the Southern US start harrumphing and shaking their heads. They're going to tell you that this is not barbecuing. Barbecue is low-and-slow and that's it that's all. Cooking high-and-fast is grilling which is completely different than barbecuing. Whatever. If you're cooking outdoors on some sort of grill set over some sort of flame, you're barbecuing. High-and-fast is generally used for leaner cuts of meat, fish, and most veggies.

That's pretty much it. Everything else is a variation on these two cooking methods.

2. KNOW YOUR Q – EVERY ONE IS DIFFERENT

Call me crazy, but I'm going to guess that most of you buying a barbecue cookbook already have a barbecue. They come in all sizes and shapes and price points. Some have upper racks for warming, some have infrared back burners for super fast heating and cooking. Some have rotisseries, others have charcoal pits. Some have side burners for pots and pans, others have built in beer fridges and stereo systems (swear to God, it's true). Look, what really matters is that you've got some sort of barbecue-type thing in your backyard and it's summertime and you're outside with a cold beverage in your hand and some good tunes playing and later on your friends come over and you eat and drink and have a few laughs.

Here are some of the things your barbecue should have:

A lid. No lid means no smoking or indirect heat which means you have to do without half the barbecue experience

Wheels. Yes, wheels. If you're going to smoke a pork butt for 3 hours and the prevailing winds change you'll want to move the barbecue around so everyone sitting on the patio doesn't have to inhale clouds of smoke

A temperature gauge. How else are you going to know the temperature inside the barbecue when the lid is down?

A grill surface. There's lots of yakking about how big your grill surface should be. Obviously if you're popular and have lots of people over all the time then you want a bigger grill surface for all the burgers you have to cook. Here's what you have to remember for good barbecue: at a minimum, the distance between any two items on your grill should be at least the width of your thumb. Not an exact science I know, particularly when you consider the thumb size of your average Blackberry addict. The size of your grill dictates how many steaks or fillets or whatever you can cook at any one time. Just don't overcrowd, okay?

Two burners good, three burners better. The more burners you have, the more heat control you have. This is important for rotisserie cooking and indirect heat cooking.

3. CHARCOAL VS. GAS

Diehard barbecue aficionados are going to tell you that the only way to go is charcoal. I've spent more hours reading up on the difference in taste, texture, et cetera between charcoal and gas than I care to think about. Here are my thoughts on the subject:

Charcoal is fine if you've got the time. A great steak house in Chicago or a quality barbecue joint in Memphis will use charcoal because they've got the pits going all the time and it's part of their charm and cachet. You don't have time to coax the coals when you get home from a hard day's work and want to fire up some chicken breasts for the kids.

If there is a difference in taste, then most of us can't tell. It's sort of like two wine snobs sitting around arguing about whether a '78 Petrus is better than an '82 Petrus. Just open the friggin' wine and pour me a glass please.

Most of us barbecue using gas. All the recipes in this book are set up for gas cooking. There, that settles it.

4. OIL YOUR GRILL!

Sounds like something simple enough to remember but it's one of the most important steps to good barbecue. We shot 104 episodes of *License to Grill* with an average of 5 recipes per show and now and then even we'd forget to oil the grill. Oiling the grill ensures that whatever you are cooking doesn't stick to the superheated grill surface. Ever try to lift a nicely cooked salmon steak off an unoiled grill? Not pretty. Canola oil works well because it has a relatively high smoking point. Pour some oil on a paper towel and use tongs to wipe the entire grill surface. You can also use a mister or a spray can but stand back and watch for flare ups.

5. COOKING WITH STEAMBOATS

The grilling recipes (that would be high-and-fast) in this book tell you to set your barbecue to a variety of temperatures. How do you tell if the temperature is right? Hold your hand 2 inches above the grill surface and count steamboats: 7 for low, 5 for medium, 3 for medium high, and 1-geez-that-hurts for high.

6. HOW TO MAKE A SMOKE POUCH

Lots of the low-and-slow recipes will call for smoking the food as well. You can buy tubes and the like to put your wood chips in but it's just as easy to make your own pouch out of foil. Please note that you can also buy wood *pellets*. You make the pouch the same way you would with wood chips, but there's no need for soaking. Quantities vary and you should check the instructions on the packaging. Here's what you need to do to make one with wood chips:

Soak about 2 cups (500 ml) of wood chips in water for about an hour. Drain and squeeze out the excess water.

Spread the wet chips on one side of a large piece of foil. Sprinkle about a cup (250 ml) of dry chips over the wet ones and mix them together. The dry chips acts as kindling to get things going and the wet ones give you a longer smoking time.

Loosely fold the foil over like you're closing a book. Crimp the edges of the foil to seal the pouch.

Use a fork to puncture a few holes on the top and bottom of the pouch to let the smoke escape.

One pouch should give you about 45 minutes to an hour of smoke.

7. HOW TO RUB A RUB

A rub is a combination of dry granular ingredients applied to the surface of some foodstuff to impart additional flavor. Usually it's a bunch of different spices, sugar and/or salt and dried herbs. What you want to do is apply enough pressure when you're rubbing to tear little micro-pockets in the flesh so as to insinuate the ingredients into the meat. Use more pressure for something hardy like a pork butt, less for something delicate like a piece of fish.

8. HOW TO MARINATE WITH A MARINADE

A marinade is a combination of wet ingredients in which some foodstuff soaks so as to impart additional flavor to the dish. The best way to marinate is in some sort of sealable plastic bag. It takes up less room in the fridge and ensures the liquid is covering the entire surface of whatever it is you're marinating.

9. ROOM TEMP YOUR FOOD

Let's say you're marinating something or that you've prepared a dish in advance and you stick it in the fridge 'til dinner time. Make sure you remove it from the fridge well in advance of sticking it on the barbecue. You want the internal temperature of your dish to be at room temperature when it hits the grill otherwise you'll throw all the suggested cooking times off. The recipes will tell you how long in advance to take it out of the fridge.

10. USE A NON-REACTIVE BOWL

A "non-reactive bowl" is one that is non-porous, usually made of stainless steel, glass or ceramic. This is particularly important when using a marinade or dish that involves some sort of acid, as in vinegars, lemon or lime juice or tomatoes.

11. COOK ON THE BONE WHENEVER YOU CAN

There's tons of flavor in them there bones. Any professional chef will tell you that cooking something with the bone in will impart way more flavor. A rib steak is a rib-eye with the bone still attached and I think tastes way better. A chicken breast cooked on the bone might not lie as flat on the grill but looks and tastes way better. Keep the skin on too (unless otherwise directed in the recipe) for a double flavor boost. Dinner guests watching their waistlines can always leave the skin on the side of the plate.

12. TENT YOUR MEAT!

So you throw a steak or a piece of chicken or something on the grill to cook. I won't bore you with all the connective tissue hoo-hah but basically your dinner shrinks a bit while it's cooking. Think of that tenderloin like a sponge that gets squeezed. Release your grip on the sponge and it relaxes and returns to its original size. The same sort of thing happens on the grill. Take the tenderloin off the heat and cover it in foil so it relaxes and the juices return to all parts of the meat making for a better dinner experience.

13. YOU GRILL WITH THE LID UP AND
YOU SMOKE WITH THE LID DOWN

Smoking with the lid down is pretty obvious, but a few words need to be said about grilling with the lid up. There are some guys out there (and I'm not naming names) who grill with the lid down. Wrong. Closing the lid creates a cavity in which the heat from your burners is contained, just like in your kitchen oven. When you grill you're going high-and-fast, so all the heat you need comes from the burner directly beneath the food. By closing the lid, you start cooking the steak or whatever from all sides which in turn throws off all your cooking times. Leave the lid up unless it's snowing.

14. BUY SOME RIB PLIERS

There is a connective membrane that runs along the back of a rack of ribs you need to remove before marinating otherwise the ribs will bunch up on the grill. Buy a pair of pliers and keep them in the kitchen drawer. You can also use them to remove pin bones from fish fillets.

15. GET TO KNOW A BUTCHER
AND A FISHMONGER

This really happened to me the other day. I'm in a big grocery store pushing a shopping cart full of things like canned goods, milk, shaving cream and toilet paper. Suddenly, I get a craving for beef short ribs. I love beef short ribs. So I go the meat section and ask the guy in the white smock and he says: "Sorry dude, our meat comes pre-cut in a box and they've already removed the ribs. We never get them." Seriously, go find someone who sells meat and poultry exclusively for a living. Same for fish and shellfish. Do not buy your salmon from someone who also sells personal hygiene products. At a good butcher and fishmonger the quality and selection will be better, plus they'll be able to give you tips and advice and may do special orders when you want something like a rack of venison or Blue Point oysters.

16. BUY FRESH, BUY LOCAL

The less time it takes for something to get from the farm gate to your plate, the better. Fresh is always best. Plus, when you buy local you're supporting someone from your community and that's always a good thing.

17. DO NOT PEEK

You've gone to all the trouble of marinating the ribs overnight and now you're smoking them on the barbecue. Leave them alone! Do not lift the lid to peek at the food. It's still there, I promise you. No sneaky squirrel came along and snatched them. If you lift the lid you let the smoke out and you lower the temperature inside the barbecue. This is not a good thing. If you have to lift the lid to baste or change the smoke pouch, do it quickly.

18. LEAVE IT ALONE

You're grilling a steak or a piece of chicken. Leave it alone. Resist the urge to move the food around on the grill. Let the barbecue do the work. You'll get nice char marks that way. The only exception is if you get flare ups from dripping fat.

19. READ THE WHOLE RECIPE FROM START TO FINISH. NOW READ IT AGAIN.

Your friends are arriving for dinner in a couple of hours. You've just finished making a killer marinade for tonight's barbecue when you read the line in the recipe that says "and marinate for at least 24 hours." *Read the recipe twice.* Also, when I'm reading a recipe I try to envision myself actually doing the steps – sort of the way an athlete does before the big game – which helps me decide whether it's the sort of dish I'm in the mood to make.

20. BUY YOURSELF SOME DECENT TONGS AND SPATULAS

I hate those barbecue sets with the crappy tongs and the flabby spatulas. Go to a restaurant supply store or a gourmet food store and get real ones that work. They don't need wood paneling to be good.

21. AND RUBBER GLOVES TOO

It's a good idea to have a pair of rubber gloves around for skinning and seeding chili peppers so the natural oils don't come in contact with your skin. Otherwise you're in for a world of pain if you rub your eyes. The gloves are pretty handy when you're peeling beets or pitting cherries to prevent your hands from getting all red from the juices

22. MAKE EXTRA AND EXPERIMENT

When it comes to rubs and sauces and marinades, consider the recipes to be more suggestions than directions. Add more or less garlic, take out the coriander, put in some celery salt, double up on the anchovies or hot peppers. Play with recipes to make a flavor profile that best suits your tastes. And make extra to keep in the fridge for a few days – sauces always taste better when they've mellowed a bit.

23. HAVE FUN

It's barbecue, not brain surgery. It's summertime and it's warm out. Life is good. Have fun.

Contents

CHAPTER ONE

Size Matters After All

Big is not necessarily better when it comes to the size of your grill. When making this potentially expensive purchase, keep in mind the number of people you will be feeding. If you've got ten kids and two sets of grandparents to feed, go for something roomy. However, if you routinely feed a family of four, going smaller is a good idea. It's cheaper to heat and less work to maintain.

Just like every piece of equipment we buy, the barbecue industry has a set of standards, and no, thankfully, a PhD in physics is not required to figure it out. Simply put, the size of a barbecue is measured in terms of "total square inches." How do they come up with that total? Well, here is the "magic" formula:

Primary Square Inches: Is the total number of inches on the main cooking surface. For practical purposes, this is the most important measurement.

Secondary Square Inches: Refers to the size of the warming racks located above the main grilling racks. Not all barbecues come with this feature.

Total Square Inches: Refers to the total square inches of the two rack surfaces combined.

Which Size Do You Need?

Industry standard allocates 50-60 square inches of primary cooking surface for each portion of food cooked. I know that may sound like a lot, but remember you'll need some room to maneuver the food on the cooking surface. For us less technical folks who don't want to take a measuring tape to the barbecue store, the size of your hand is about one portion of food. Two hands will represent a meal consisting of meat and veggies. Think about the largest number of people that you will routinely cook for and aim for that size. Remember though, you want to keep your options open to avoid frustrating cooking experiences.

Can't Stand The Heat?

BTU Who? What? The dreaded BTU, every good barbecue salesperson will be able to tell you that BTU stands for British Thermal Unit. "What is that?" you might ask. (But if you really don't care, skip this part.) A BTU is a scientific measurement of how much energy is expended to raise one pound of water one degree Fahrenheit. What's that got to do "with the price of chicken?!" When referring to barbecues, BTU is the measurement of the maximum output of heat that the barbecue produces with all burners on high.

A consensus among barbecue companies suggest that between 110 to 125 BTUs per square inch is ideal for year-round cooking. This will allow you to pre-heat your barbecue quickly to between 500-600 degrees Fahrenheit within 6 to 9 minutes on an average summer day. Note, a good barbecue with accurate control valves should allow you to lower the temperature for consistent cooking temperature. Be careful with barbecues with a BTU rating of above 125 BTUs per square inch. If the control valves are not of high quality, the temperature will be harder to lower and regulate, thus producing "burnt offerings." If you live in a colder climate and wish to barbecue year round, you'll want a barbecue with a higher BTU rating per square inch to regulate cooking temperatures.

CHAPTER TWO

Gas It Up

Taste Over Convenience?

Myth or fact? You can't get an authentic barbecue flavor from a gas grill. Question: Is charcoal cooking really that cumbersome?

Charcoal Grilling — Only for the Adventurous?

For a nice outer crust on a cut of meat, charcoal grilling is certainly more effective. Very few gas barbecues can reach the level of heat that a charcoal-lit fire can. And for long, slow cooking, tradition has proven that charcoal grilling produces a wonderfully tender, smoke-infused flavor that we all strive for. So if charcoal is so wonderful, then why bother cooking with gas? Well, if you've got 30 minutes to whip up a dinner before soccer practice and you just happen to want to put a chicken breast on your charcoal grill, it's going to take you longer to light the charcoal than it will to cook the chicken!

Come On Baby Light Your Fire

In the "old days" of grilling, people would arrange the charcoal bricks in a pile, douse it with lighter fluid and everyone would "ooh" and "ahh" as the match was struck, the flames shot up to the sky and the roof burnt down. Seriously – the bigger the flame, not necessarily the better the fire and certainly not the better the food! Too much lighter fluid makes the food taste like, well, lighter fluid. We now have the option of self-lighting bricks, with the starter infused in the charcoal.

To avoid using chemicals, try using a flue starter or chimney starter. You can buy these cylindrical-shaped metal chimneys or just make one, by cutting the top and bottom off a large 39-oz can. Using the triangle end of your can opener, punch six holes along the bottom of the can for air vents. Bear in mind, for larger barbecues you will need a starter that is at about 7 inches across and at least 11 inches tall to ensure that it holds enough bricks to spread over the bottom of your grill, thus avoiding having to add cold bricks later, adding to your pre-heating time. Your barbecue salesperson can show you different varieties, sizes and prices to suit your needs. Place the flue starter on the charcoal grate (not the cooking grate). Layer with a fast-igniting dry material, like newspaper. Next, add your charcoal and/or woodchips and light from the bottom. After approximately 15–20 minutes — when the coals are burning to a consistent orangey red color with a thin gray layer of ash on them — remove the cylinder and spread the coals across the bottom of your barbecue.

Probably easiest of all however, is an electric starter. In its basic form, an electric starter is a small exposed element, usually in a ring shape, with a handle. Place the element among the coals, turn it on and wait about 15 minutes. Carefully remove and place on a non-flammable surface to cool before storing away. Voila! Easy; no mess, no hassle, just a bit of time and electricity.

Regardless of the method you use to start your charcoal fire, make sure that there is a fine layer of gray ash on the bricks before you start to cook. The gray ash is a signal that the bricks are hot enough to remain fairly consistent in temperature. Also, don't scrimp on the amount of charcoal you use. More charcoal can mean a longer pre-heat time, but there should be enough to fully cover the bottom of your grill. And don't forget to pre-heat your grilling surface as well. Once the coals are hot and you've spread them out, place the grill on top to heat up – for about 5 minutes. And lastly, don't use the cover for grilling. The off-gassing from the build up of old fumes on the inside of the cover can infuse your food with a bitter chemical taste. If you want to cover or tent your food while cooking, use tinfoil or an aluminum plate.

Take Your Temperature

Because there are no handy-dandy little temperature knobs on a charcoal barbecue to manipulate the temperature of your grill, you'll need to move the hot coals around to create your different temperature zones.

A single layer of charcoal will produce direct heat that is moderate in temperature. This is good for foods that require little cooking time, like a thin fillet of fish, cut veggies or hamburgers. Single layers are also good for longer cooking, called slow roasting.

Two layers of charcoal will bring the coals closer to the food and concentrates more heat in the area that is doubled. This is great for searing meat. Being creative with the layers allows you to have both high and moderate heating surfaces at one time. For instance, for food that needs to cook slowly, thin out the coals from that area of the barbecue. For foods that need to sear, bank the coals at that end of the barbecue, thus producing multiple zones for cooking.

Your barbecue will have side vents along the bottom half. To add more oxygen to the coals, making them hotter, open the vents wider. To cool down the bricks, close the vents accordingly. Be careful though. If you have the lid down and all the vents are closed your fire will die, along with your hopes for a great meal.

To take the temperature of your grill you could buy a cooking thermometer. Or, for us hardy types, judge high heat (roughly 400F), by placing your hand about 4 inches above the grill and counting how many seconds your hand can remain there before you must move it. Should be about 2 seconds. For medium to high heat (375F), about 3 seconds. For medium heat (350F), about 5 seconds and for low heat (250F), about 7 seconds.

Gas It Up

For those of us who want to get the job done quickly and easily, with little mess and preparation, barbecuing with gas is the way to go. You turn a few knobs, ignite, wait 10 minutes and you're cooking with fire. No muss, no fuss.

Even though most gas barbecues don't get as hot as charcoal grills, you can control the temperatures of your cooking surface easier and more accurately than you can with charcoal. No moving coals around and opening and closing vents. And you can cook with the lid down, as there are no noxious fumes from lighter fluid build up on the lid to contaminate your food. This makes searing more efficient and creates even temperatures for long slow roasting. For these reasons, the majority of recipes in this book have instructions for cooking on a gas barbecue.

Want a Light?

When lighting a gas grill, follow the manufacturer's directions. Industry standards require that you light the grill with the lid open. Once lit, close the lid. Leave all burners on high until your desired temperature is reached, then lower accordingly. If your barbecue's automatic igniter is not functional, use a match or barbecue lighter and insert it into the hole in the side of the grill that is provided by the manufacturer for this very purpose. Follow the directions as above.

What's Your Number?

How many burners do you need? In order to cook using indirect heat (for roasting and smoking), you will need a minimum of two burners – one burner that is lit and one burner that is either off or on a low setting. Any more than two depends on how much food you typically cook at one time and how many different temperature zones you might need.

Running Out Of Gas?

Okay, you've got your mother-in-law coming over and five kids jumping up and down for your attention. You've just spent fifty bucks on steaks and you've got that look of determination that comes from needing a good red meat fix. You've got the grill going, the steaks have started searing then suddenly – the flame dies. You've run out of gas! Ways to prevent this:

1) Have a gas line run to the barbecue – you'll NEVER run out!

2) Buy a tank with a gas level gauge on it and always have an extra tank that is full and ready to go. Store extra tanks in a dry, cool environment.

3) If you already have a perfectly usable tank, you can check the gas level by pouring a cup of boiling water down the side of the tank, and then running your

hand along it. Where the tank is empty it will feel warm to the touch. Where the tank is full, it will feel cooler to the touch.

If you've done all that, you have enough gas and your barbecue still won't light, did you remember to turn on the gas tank? If all else fails, check to make sure you're not dealing with a clogged or bent hose that needs to be attended to.

CHAPTER THREE

All Washed Up

When most of us get our barbecues home we discard the maintenance manual faster than yesterday's newspaper. However, maintenance and regular cleaning is of vital importance to the longevity of your grill, affecting not only its performance and safety, but the taste and nutritional value of your food as well.

Rub A Dub Dub

For charcoal grills, it is important to keep the bottom of your grill free of ashes, charcoal bits and grease. This will ensure that the vents at the bottom of the barbecue are clear, providing the coals with the necessary oxygen to keep them lit and hot. Make sure ashes are cool to the touch before disposing of them.

Also, grease build-up on your grill makes it susceptible to grease fire flare-ups and leaves a chemical or acidic taste on your food. For all types of barbecues, remove the racks and wash out the interiors and the grill with warm soapy water. A light scouring pad is fine to use, but must be avoided on painted and stainless steel surfaces, as it will scratch the finish. Check your manufacturer's instructions (which you have kept in a safe place), if warm soapy water is not getting the job done.

Everyone has a different way to clean the grilling racks, from *don't clean them at all because it will remove the flavor* (not great advice!), to *place grills between thicknesses of newspaper, cover with soapy water, let soak all day, then scour and rinse.* The best advice is to clean as you cook. After your grill is lit, and before you start cooking, give your racks a quick scour with a long-handled metal brush, then coat with oil or cooking spray. After your food is cooked and removed from the grill, turn all elements to high heat again. Once heated, turn off the elements and scour the racks with a wire brush. A wide, industrial-strength sponge soaked with water will also work, as it will help steam-clean the racks. Rub clean racks dry and coat with cooking oil. This will aid in preventing rusting. These simple steps, which take up so little time, will prolong the life of your grilling racks, prevent noxious grease build-up and save you from using up too much "elbow grease."

If you're using a gas barbecue, the drip pan under the grill should be cleaned out regularly to avoid ignition. Remove lava rocks from the bottom of the grill, take out any that are broken and covered in grease and replace. Check your burners to make sure the flames emanating from them are consistent and that each has a blue-tipped flame. Clear a clogged burner with an untwisted paper clip, with the barbecue off and cool. Check all connector hoses for bugs and spiders, especially after a period of sitting unused.

Before storing for the winter, after the barbecue is completely cleaned, turn elements on high for 10 minutes to dry out all parts. Oil the racks and store covered in a dry room. Disconnect the gas tank and store it in a well-ventilated area.

CHAPTER FOUR

Tools of the Trade

If you can't stand the heat, get longer oven mitts, tongs and spatulas. Reaching into a hot oven can give you a burn you can do without. It's important to learn which utensils make sense for cooking over an open fire.

Brush Your Grill

We've discussed at length the importance of keeping your grilling racks clean. But which brush cleans the best? A brush with a sturdy, durable and LONG handle of at least 12 inches that feels comfortable in your hand is a must. While there are many kinds of grill brushes with various handles available now, the most durable handle is still one made of wood; quite often "poplar" as a matter of fact. Aluminum and various other metal handles look sturdy and attractive, however they conduct heat very quickly thus making the user wear an oven mitt, which quite frankly makes the whole procedure a slippery affair.

I would recommend two types of brushes for your grill. The first is a brush with brass bristles and are available at most hardware and department stores. The next is a new one on the market that has stainless steel pads instead of bristles. These pads are washable and replaceable and do an excellent job.

Tongs Of Choice

Most of us at one time have purchased the barbecue utensil sets that contained a giant fork. That two-pronged fork is usually the first thing people will use to turn over their hard-earned masterpieces on the grill because it is familiar to our everyday lives. And while the giant fork is indeed very useful for carving meat, be careful. All that time spent searing in juices will be for naught if you're going to go around piercing your food while it is still cooking.

Tongs are the answer. At first tongs can feel a bit awkward to use, but get a strong spring-loaded pair and you'll be purchasing one for the kitchen as well. You'll need a pair that is delicate enough at the ends to grasp fine foods like asparagus. Watch out for serrated edges though; they are often too sharp and can nick the food. Look for tongs with scalloped edges, the surface of which are perfect for just about anything you'll need to maneuver on the grill. Make sure the handle is long enough. Up to 16 inches will allow you to reach to the back of most grills without having to climb in it yourself. A longer handle also needs to be built to last, as it will bend under the weight of a roasted whole chicken for instance. Also, make sure the pincers will spread wide enough to get around something like a drumstick or a small roast.

Spatula Anyone?

Next to your tongs, your spatula will be a workhorse for you. Again, look for something with a long, sturdy handle. I like to use a spatula that is called a "dogleg" or "offset" spatula. That refers to the angle of the blade as compared to the handle. Look for one that has a large lifting surface that will be equally good for lifting a burger as it will a piece of salmon – approximately 3 inches wide by 6 inches long will lift just about everything you need it to. The blade should be thin enough in the front to get under something delicate like a piece of fish, but sturdy enough to ensure that it won't break if you have to scrape something stuck on the grill.

Brushes and A Mop

Not all marinating brushes are created equal and by far the best are the natural boar's hair brushes. Don't be fooled by the nylon varieties. You can almost always detect them because the bristles tend to be transparent and the price is usually cheaper. The boar's hair brush works well, because it stands up to the heat, absorbs liquids at a high rate, doesn't fray and washes well in hot water. The nylon bristles, on the other hand, tend to clump and are not nearly as absorbent as the natural variety. While I do like the feel of a wooden handle, they don't hold up in the dishwasher very well. Look for a brush with a thick plastic handle. You can put it in the dishwasher, making cleaning clingy marinade easier. Choose shorter handled brushes for in the kitchen and smaller jobs on the grill, longer handles for larger cuts of meat and larger quantities of food.

Before purchasing your brush, have a look at the "collar" that attaches the bristles to the handle. You want this collar to be extremely tight. There should be no wiggle room. This will help to avoid getting marinade up into the joint, making it easier to clean and will ensure you lose fewer bristles with use over time.

Also nice, particularly if you're cooking for an audience, is to take a bunch of herbs, such as rosemary, tie it into a bouquet and use that as a brush. Now, don't count on that imparting a whole lot of the flavor on your food, it will a bit, but mainly it looks esthetically pleasing and it's kind of nice for a change. You'll look like you really know what you're doing!

Relatively new to the market are silicone brushes. They don't burn, can be taken apart and put in the dishwasher. Although they aren't absorbent they are still a great option, and the price points are very reasonable in all sizes as they are extremely durable!

Last but certainly by no means least is a "brush" called "The Sauce Mop" or "The Mop" as I call it. This product looks exactly like it sounds, like a floor mop. Not a fancy new one that can power a jet engine by itself, but one of those old fashion kinds that your Grandma used to have in the closet by the back door off the kitchen. Not too appetizing you say? You might change your mind when you taste the results of this marinating tool. It's perfect for a rack of ribs or other big jobs. Made of 100% cotton, it sops up the sop and makes short work of flavoring your short ribs.

Mister

You've spent all that time preparing your prize-winning marinade, diligently brushing it over your butcher's cut of meat with your favorite boar's hair brush, then tragedy strikes. You have a flare up on your grill that is threatening your meal! Quick! Grab a plant mister and spray that fire down. Keep it close at hand and you can't go wrong.

Oil That Grill Grid

Grill pan, grill wok, grill skillet; notice a pattern here? Never has there been an easier time to cook just about anything you can imagine over an open fire. You can pan-fry, stir-fry and grill veggies without the risk of them falling into the fire, now that there is literally some sort of barbecue basket or contraption available for almost everything. The grill grid I've been using is made with a Teflon coating, which keeps the food from sticking to it.

Illicit Kitchen Syringe?

No, you will not get arrested for this injection. If you have a cut of meat that you think might need a bit more flavoring, or you need to preserve moisture during a long roast, you might want to get out the syringe. A syringe in the kitchen you might ask? Dip the syringe in your marinade, pierce the skin to the center and inject! Do this periodically while cooking, making sure to leave enough cooking time at the end to bring the injected marinade up to the appropriate temperature.

Where's The Heat?

My favorite thermometer has a sensor that you sink into the raw meat before you put it on the grill. If you are using a charcoal grill, you snake the wire that attaches to the digital sensor through the vent at the top. If you're using a gas barbecue, simply pull it through to one side of the lid. The sensor sits outside your grill and will tell you when your meat has reached the desired cooking temperature.

Skewed Up

There aren't a whole lot of choices in the marketplace as of yet of viable materials for barbecue skewers. You'll find stainless steel, bamboo or wood (and various combinations of all three). I personally prefer wood or bamboo, but then again, I'm a hands-on kind of cook. I like the organic feel of it, the look of it and they aren't as hot to handle as metal right off the grill. Stainless steel is also a fine choice. As with wood, you have to watch for food sticking to the skewers, but unlike wood, they stay hot for a long time, so care is needed off the grill. They can be pricey if you're serving kebabs to the whole neighborhood and the basketball team thus requiring more than just a few. However that said, they are reusable, where wood is definitely not.

Now obviously the down side with the wood is that it's wood. And wood does tend to burn when over a flame! People will tell you if you soak them they won't catch on fire. Well, that's not exactly true. The truth is, if you soak them they won't catch on fire *as quickly*. I soak mine for about 2 hours. Then I put tin foil under the bare handles on the barbecue to lessen the exposure to direct heat.

Something that is kind of cool is a double skewer. It's shaped like a "U," so you can thread two skewers at a time. This is advantageous because they won't rotate around on themselves making turning them over on the grill easier and allows for more even cooking.

Bag It

Want to know the secret of how to get a perfectly marinated anything, without a whole lot of muss and fuss? Use a sealable plastic bag! It's an "all in one kitchen aid." I pour the ingredients for my rubs and marinades directly in the bag. Then, I add my washed and trimmed meats and throw it in the fridge, freezer or whatever suits at the time. When needed, I take the meat out of the bag and put it directly on the grill – easy – and no mess.

Light The Way

Nothing spoils a romantic night cooking under the stars like serving burnt offerings to your guests. It's necessary to be able to see the grill, and I've found for such occasions a barbecue grill light fits the bill and keeps the party going. These durable all-weather lights mount directly onto your barbecue's handle. The lamp head can pivot for direct-task lighting when needed, but is also strong enough to illuminate the whole grill. They usually run on batteries and the good ones have an automatic shut off mechanism so the batteries are not wasted.

CHAPTER FIVE

History Anyone?

Those of you interested in a little history are in for a treat. Since no one knows for sure exactly where the word "barbecue" came from, there's a theory for everyone. Some experts have said the word may have come from Native American Indians who called their practice of roasting meat over coals "barbacoa." The settlers at the time then turned the word into today's "barbecue." For those of us who like all things French, another theory is that the word came from the whole-hog cooking method called "barbe a queue" which means from "head to tail" or, more precisely, "whiskers to tail" in French. For the more fanciful, according to *Bon Appetit* magazine, the word could have come from an extinct tribe in Guyana who "cheerfully spit-roasted captured enemies." *The Oxford English Dictionary* traces the word back to Haiti, while *Tar Heel* magazine suggests that the word "barbecue" came from an advertisement for a whiskey bar, beer- and pool hall that served roasted pig. This establishment was called the BAR-BEER-CUE-PIG. Depending on how much beer you've shared with your marinade, you could probably come up with a few good origin stories yourself. The spelling of barbecue is interchangeable: barbeque, barbecue, BBQ. I've used the latter two versions throughout.

Not Just For Cowboys

According to *Webster's New World Dictionary*, to barbecue is "to roast or broil over an open fire, often with a highly seasoned sauce." To put that definition in practical terms and apply it to real life, I would add "slow-cook at a low temperature" as well.

We have American cowboys to thank for the slow-cook BBQ method. In 1866, a Texas rancher named Charles Goodnight wanted to drive his herd of 2000 cattle from Texas to Denver. Covering that distance in the summer months required that food be prepared along the way, as there was no refrigeration. Out of sheer necessity, Charles Goodnight and his partner invented the first Chuck Wagon. The wagon became a staple on cattle drives and evolved into more elaborate and detailed "kitchens on wheels" as time went on, often featuring closed shelving, hinged pull-down counters for chopping, storage for bedrolls and, of course, the food.

The food consisted mainly of dried black-eyed peas, corn, cabbage and sourdough bread starter. Because the cowboys were most often fed the less desirable cuts of meat – like the brisket – stews seasoned with onions, garlic and chilies became a staple. They would be left to cook for 6-7 hours over an open fire to tenderize the stringy and tough texture of the meat, making it palatable for the hard-working men. Even today that smokey flavor from the grill conjures up visions of the Wild West, a clear, starry sky and an open fire.

CHAPTER SIX

Smoke Signals

From cave man to modern man, humans have a long history with smoking food. There are so many choices now available that you could literally try a different combination of smoking methods every night for a year and not double up.

Low and Slow

The choice between charcoal or gas, tongs or spatulas, misters or beer, is a fairly modern one. There was a time when food needed to be preserved to last for the days when it was scarce, and I have a feeling that folks then probably weren't overly concerned about marinades and rubs. They were, however, concerned about basic survival. Recorded history tells us that humans have been cooking over an open fire long before we could write about it and smoking meat has been a mainstay.

Smoking meat serves three main purposes: To break down fibrous proteins in order to tenderize it, to impart flavor and to cook or preserve it. Here is where the difference between barbecuing in the traditional sense and grilling should be clear.

Barbecuing, smoking or roasting is the practice of cooking meat at a low temperature, slowly, for long periods of time; anywhere from 1 hour to 20 hours or more on indirect heat. Grilling on the other hand, is high and fast; high heat, cooked quickly.

What Do You Smoke?

Well, thank you for asking. I personally prefer a mixture of hardwoods like apple, cherry, oak or hickory, as they allow for longer, more even burning time. These chips can be any variety of the many readily available at your local hardware store or through barbecue specialty stores. I mix 2 part water-soaked woodchips with 1 part dry woodchips. You can also soak them in beer (notice a theme?) or other spirits and herbs. Really, your imagination is the limit.

You can buy metal smoke boxes made for the barbecue, or make one up yourself in a few minutes. Use a large piece of tin foil, place the wet and dry woodchips on it, and fashion it into a packet. Pierce it with a fork making small holes in the top and bottom for the smoke to escape. Put the packet on the grill, under the grilling racks. Bring your barbecue up to a high heat and watch for the smoke. How long you want the smoke to last will determine how much mixture you need. You may need to make up more than one "packet" if the smoke gets low. A steady stream of smoke around your meat will keep the smoke particles moving and avoid creosote from settling on your food making it taste bitter. Creosote is a by-product of burning wood. It forms a tar that is extremely flammable and not too pleasant to consume. Think of the inside of a fireplace, that's creosote. Would you lick that?

As to what food to smoke, you can smoke anything from ham to cheese, however the more traditional choices are meats like brisket, pork ribs and shoulder. Cuts that you wouldn't normally think to cook in an oven, turn into feasts in a slow barbecue.

It's Getting Hot In Here

Now remember, in order to tenderize, flavor and cook your meat, the temperature has to be low. Controlling the heat on a barbecue is not an exact science, however, so your thermometers come in handy about now - *two* to be exact. Use one for the inside of the barbecue and one for the inside of your meat. For the "low" part of this equation, the external heat of the barbecue or smoker should be at around 220F and the internal temperature of the meat should be no lower than 165F. And for the "slow" part you wait and wait . . . and wait. Seriously, patience and a little care needs to be exercised. If your external temperature is too high, your meat will either dry out or become charred – or both. If it's too low, it won't be safe to eat, nor will it be tender, for that matter. However, you won't care about it being tasty or tender if you're visiting the throne room all night because of under-cooked meat.

Eat Your Veggies!

Life expectancy would grow by leaps and bounds if green vegetables smelled as good as bacon. — DOUG LARSON

Buttermilk Potato Salad
BBQ Beets
Celeriac and Apple Salad
Creamy BBQ Scalloped Taters
Crispy Potato Skins with Bacon
Fire-Roasted Tomatoes
Green Salad with Apricots and Blueberries
Green Salad with Red Wine Vinaigrette
Grilled Beet and Blue Cheese and Bacon Salad
Stuffed Grilled Zucchini
Twice-Grilled Potatoes
Spicy Grilled Potato Skins
Curried Roast Potatoes
Grilled Potatoes with Herbs
Grilled Corn with Chipotle-Maple Glaze
Rosemary Smoked Potatoes
Balsamic Grilled Mushrooms
Mushroom Kebabs
Portobello Cheeseburgers
Stuffed Smoked Onions
Grilled Bacon Onion Wedges
Grilled Onions with Spiced Summer Apricot Mustard Glaze
Cauliflower Kebabs
Charred Stuffed Jalapeno
Grilled Rice Cakes
Grilled Veggie Cornboats
Grilled Vegetables with Garlic Anchovy Dip
Marinated Carrots, Pearl Onions & Radishes
Smoked Corn on the Cob
Smoked Acorn Squash with Maple Spiced Butter
Grilled Fennel with Garlic Anchovy Butter
Grilled Antipasto
Grilled Asparagus and Beets
Grilled Honey-Tarragon Carrots
Grilled Corn Salad
Grilled Pesto Peppers
Grilled Rosemary Baby Potatoes

Grilled Vegetable Gazpacho in Cucumber Cups
Grilled Vegetable Quesadillas
Marinated Grilled Asparagus
Mushroom Rice
Potato and Watercress Salad
Asian Flavored Coleslaw
Baby Arugula Salad with Pine Nuts, Cranberries and Dressing
Big Man Caesar Salad
Chicory Chorizo Salad
Avocado, Grapefruit, Red Onion and Feta Salad
Corn, Red Pepper and Arugula Salad
Fennel & Orange Salad
Tomato & Grilled Bread Salad
Summer Potato Salad
Banana and Spud Salad
Cabage Salad
Carrot Salad
Green Bean Salad
Wild Rice Pecan Salad
Pasta Salad with Grilled Corn & Jalapenos
Couscous Salad with Grilled Vegetables
Rainbow Salad
Roasted Plum Tomatoes
Roasted Vegetable Calzone
Roasted Stuffed Peppers
Rocket Salad with Basil-Oil Mayonnaise Dressing
Smoked Vidalia Onions
Smokey Southwestern Rice
Snow Pea Salad with Lime-Infused Shrimp
Sweet Potatoes with Orange Pecan Butter
Tomatoes Stuffed with Cheese and Vegetables
Tomatoes with Mozzarella Cheese
Watercress Salad with Orange and Tequila Dressing
Yam Potato Tower

They're good for you and over a flame they taste like a treat. Everything from asparagus, to eggplant and zucchini come to life when grilled – honestly!

I've never eaten a vegetable that I didn't like. Well, I guess I should rephrase that. In my adult years, I have never eaten a vegetable that was properly prepared, that I didn't like! Especially when done on the grill. The combination of the smoke, simple seasoning and slight caramelizing really brings the natural flavors up a notch.

How Does Your Garden Grow?

Gardening requires lots of water – most of it in the form of perspiration.
—LOU ERICKSON

While researchers parry back and forth about just how many portions of vegetables one should consume per day, one thing is obvious. Your grandmother was right; vegetables are good for you. Rich in fiber, vitamins and minerals, and beneficial for their high water content, a diet which includes a variety of veggies is simply smart. I would hazard to say that a lot of the fuss with veggies and why people don't like them has to do with the way they are prepared and presented. I wonder if these naysayers have ever had a nice broccoli marinated with a bit of olive oil, balsamic vinegar, salt and pepper lightly grilled on the barbecue? They'd change their mind in a hurry!

There are five elements: earth, air, fire, water and garlic.
—LOUIS DIAT

The word vegetable is actually not a botanical word, but is a culinary term meaning an edible part of a plant that is consumed as sustenance, but which is not a fruit, nut, grain, spice or herb. The practice of growing vegetables for commercial use is a branch of horticulture called "olericulture." (You can thank me for this trivia at your next office party.) Vegetables are usually considered to be savory or non-sweet with the exception of pumpkin and rhubarb. Although I have to say, rhubarb is not something I'd consider sweet on its own! Delicious though it might be with a bit of sugar, in a pie with some strawberries, with a dollop of whipped cream (with a hint of fresh vanilla) on top . . . sorry I digress.

The wonderful thing about vegetables – food from the earth – is the fact that virtually every edible part of a plant is up for consumption and can be divided into five groups:

- *The Flower (Brassicas): cauliflower, broccoli (cruciferous), artichokes*
- *The Seed: corn, peas, beans*
- *Leaf: lettuce, cabbage, spinach*
- *Stalk: celery, asparagus, fennel*
- *Root: carrots, parsnip, turnips*

From there you can sub-categorize and group until you're blue in the face:

- *Shoot Vegetables: asparagus, chicory, bamboo shoot*
- *Onion Family Vegetables: onion, shallot, spring onion*
- *Tubers: potatoes, sweet potatoes, yams*
- *Fruit Vegetables: tomato, cucumber, sweet pepper, avocado*
- *Edible Fungi: mushrooms – all varieties*
- *Seaweeds: Kombu, Wakame, Irish Moss*

Some of the best BBQ veggies

Onions: Spring, Spanish, shallot: you name it, they are all wonderful on the grill. They caramelize beautifully, bringing out their hidden natural sweetness.

Carrots: Cut them to a uniform size, brush with a bit of oil on a medium grill and they'll be sweeter than any carrot you've ever tasted!

Mushrooms: I like all mushrooms, but the Portobello is considered the steak of the mushroom world – sort of like tuna is the steak of the sea! You can eat it straight off the grill on a bun with the same condiments you'd use for your favorite burger.

Corn: Go ahead and leave the husk on! Remove the silk and soak corn in water for about an hour to prevent it from drying out. If you're so inclined you can tie the ends before cooking. Place on a medium grill for 15–20 minutes, turning often to avoid scorching. Delicious!

Yellow squash and zucchini: Those of you who grow zucchini in your garden probably have an overabundance of it! If you can't bribe your neighbors into taking any more and you're looking for a different way to cook it, put it on the grill. Sliced and lightly grilled for 5–10 minutes – it's amazing!

Bell Peppers: The more colors the merrier! Your grill will look like the United Nations. Remove seeds, cut in half lengthwise and grill for about 3–4 minutes. So perfect, so easy!

Potatoes: In jackets, out of jackets, mashed, crushed, whole, sliced, diced – potatoes are wonderful. The carbohydrate-conscious folks have shied away from the lowly tuber, yet sweet potatoes have fewer carbs than the white variety and still offer a great potato "feel." The key to cooking potatoes on the grill is to cook the inside while not burning the outside. Either steamed in foil or sliced on the grill, they are the perfect BBQ food. I love to slice a whole potato in half lengthwise, place the pieces on a large sheet of foil, sprinkle each half with a bit of salt and pepper, add onion slices and a bit of butter. Seal it up in the foil and cook on medium heat, turning regularly for 20–30 minutes. Great with a steak!

I could go on and on and on about veggies, but really give yourself permission to explore. Turnips, radicchio, fennel, parsnips, broccoli, cauliflower – "it's all good!" And best of all, if you have fussy eaters in your midst, grilling disguises some veggies both in taste and appearance. Your resident fusspot might not know that he or she is eating a dreaded broccoli stem! Remember, cook on a medium- to medium-high heat and remove before they turn to mush or ashes.

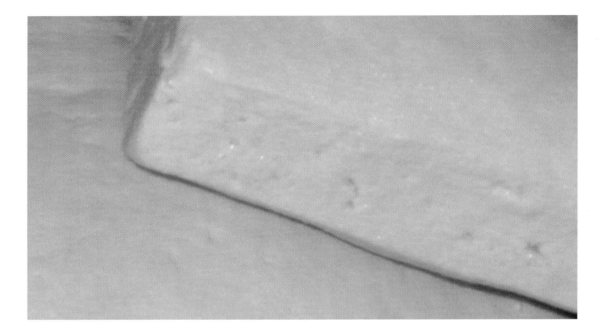

One last thing, for those of us who enjoy a bit of tofu now and again – and for those of us who don't – tofu can also be a great addition to your grilling repertoire. You'll want to look for firm or extra-firm tofu. The silken varieties are great for pureeing, but will not hold up on the grill. Press out excess moisture by weighing tofu down under a plate on paper towels for about 30–60 minutes. Discard remaining liquid. You can then soak the tofu in your favorite marinades, or simply brush with it a bit of oil and seasonings. Soy sauce and sesame oil are wonderful on tofu. Grill on medium heat until browned, about 5 minutes per side. Make sure you oil the grill generously before flipping.

Tip – Freezing tofu will give it a chewier texture and will help it absorb marinades like a sponge. Freeze for at least 36 hours to get the full effect. It's wonderful, I promise!

BUTTERMILK POTATO SALAD

Potato salad: a staple at any family cook-out. But wait until you see how one different ingredient – buttermilk – can improve this tried-and-true.

6 medium baking potatoes, peeled

1/4 red bell pepper, sliced

1/4 yellow bell pepper, sliced

5 hardboiled eggs

1/3 cup chopped sweet pickles (75mL)

2 tbsp sweet pickle juice (30mL)

5 sliced green onions

1 1/2 tsp chives (7.5mL)

1 tsp garlic salt (5mL)

1 tsp freshly ground black pepper (5mL)

Salt to taste

Dressing

1/4 cup sour cream (50mL)

1/2 cup buttermilk (125mL)

2 tbsp chopped fresh chives (30mL)

1 tbsp prepared mustard (15mL)

Directions:

- In a large pot of boiling salted water, cook potatoes for 15–20 minutes or until they are tender. Remove from heat and let stand until cool.

- Combine sliced bell peppers with chopped eggs, pickles, pickle juice and green onions in a bowl.

- Chop cooled potatoes into bite-size pieces. Add potato and chives to bowl, mixing lightly.

Dressing Directions:

- In a separate bowl, combine dressing ingredients and mix well. Add to salad and let stand in the refrigerator for at least 2 hours before serving.

Serves 6

BBQ BEETS

Make sure you wear rubber gloves when you peel the beets! This recipe is so simple and puts a lot of colour and taste on the plate.

4 medium beets, rinsed and trimmed

6 tbsp bottled raspberry vinaigrette (90mL)

1 tsp fresh tarragon, minced (5mL)

1 tbsp olive oil (15mL)

Directions:

- Partially boil the beets in a pot of boiling water (for approximately 15 minutes). They should be a bit firm. Cool, peel and slice the beets into 1-inch thick rounds and set aside.

- Pour the raspberry vinaigrette into a bowl and mix in the fresh tarragon.

- Preheat the barbecue to low heat 250F (125C).

- Using a brush, apply the raspberry dressing to the beets.

- Oil the grill. Place the beets on the grill. Cook for 2 minutes per side, serve and enjoy!

Serves 4

CELERIAC AND APPLE SALAD

Celeriac (also known as celery root) is a special kind of celery grown for its big knobby root. It's mild in taste—think of a cross between celery and parsley—and pairs up nicely with crisp tart Granny Smith apples.

1/3 cup mustard vinaigrette (75mL)

   (see recipe below)

1 celery root, 14–16 ounces (400–500g)

Juice of 1/2 an orange

1/2 cup carrots, sliced into matchsticks (125mL)

1 large Granny Smith apple, cored, quartered

and sliced into matchsticks

3 tbsp chopped hazelnuts (45mL)

Mustard Vinaigrette

2 tbsp red wine vinegar (30mL)

2 shallots, finely diced

1 garlic clove, minced

Pinch of salt and pepper

1 tbsp Dijon mustard (15mL)

1/3 cup hazelnut oil (75mL)

2 tbsp chopped chives (30mL)

1 tbsp chopped parsley (15mL)

Directions:

- Peel the celery root as you would an orange, then cut into 1/2-inch (1 cm) thick disks and cut again into matchstick-sized pieces. Place the celery root in a bowl of acidulated water (water with orange juice added) to prevent browning while preparing the remaining ingredients.

- Once dressing has been prepared, strain the celery root matchsticks and toss into large bowl. Add the apple and carrot and mix together.

- Pour dressing on salad just before serving and garnish with chopped hazelnuts.

Mustard Vinaigrette Directions:

- For the vinaigrette, blend the Dijon, red wine vinegar, minced garlic, and diced shallots. Add hazelnut oil until thick. Pour into a bowl and stir in some chopped parsley and chives.

Serves 4

CREAMY BBQ SCALLOPED TATERS

Asiago cheese is the secret to this dish. It's a semi-firm Italian cheese with a sweet nutty flavor and plays nicely off the nip from the cheddar. With two types of cheese, butter AND whipping cream, this is obviously not a diet dish, but worth the splurge.

2 1/2 lbs baking potatoes, sliced (1.2kg)

1 large white onion, sliced

2 tbsp butter (30mL)

1/2 cup asiago cheese, shredded (125mL)

1/2 cup white cheddar, grated (125mL)

1 tablespoon fresh rosemary, chopped (15mL)

1 tablespoon chopped garlic (15mL)

1/2 cup whipping cream (125mL)

Salt to taste

Freshly ground black pepper to taste

Directions:

- Cut the potatoes into 1/4-inch thin slices. Slice onion thinly. Place butter in a saucepan over low to heat to melt.

- Brush some melted butter over a 24-inch square of heavy-duty aluminum foil. Arrange half of the potatoes and half the onion in a single layer (potatoes underneath and onions on top). Brush the layer generously with melted butter and season with salt and pepper.

- Sprinkle the layer with the cheddar and asiago cheeses. Add the remaining onions. Sprinkle freshly chopped rosemary and garlic on top of the onions. Add the last layer of potatoes and brush with more butter.

- Fold the sides of the foil up and carefully pour in the cream. Seal the foil closed with a double fold.

- Preheat the barbecue to medium-high heat 350F (175C). Place the potato package directly over the heat source and cook for 25–30 minutes. Serve as a scrumptious side dish.

Serves 4

CRISPY POTATO SKINS WITH BACON

A spin on a pub favorite. The provolone, along with the bacon, makes it melt in your mouth! By the way, this is a good way to get your kids to eat potato skins, which are loaded with fiber!

6 large russet potatoes (baked for 1 hour
    at 400F (200C) and cooled)
1 cup bacon, cooked and chopped (250mL)
1 tbsp olive oil (15mL)
2 cups provolone cheese, shredded (500mL)
1/4 cup green onions, chopped (60mL)
Salt and pepper to taste

Directions:

- Cut baked potatoes in half, lengthwise

- Scoop flesh from potatoes leaving 1/4 inch in each potato.

- Drizzle potato skins with olive oil. Add salt and pepper to taste

- Sprinkle with green onions, bacon and cheese.

- Preheat barbecue to 220F (104C) or medium-high. Place potatoes over well-oiled grill.

- Cook for 4–5 minutes with lid closed or until cheese has melted and bottoms of potatoes are crispy. Serve with sour cream.

Serves 6

FIRE-ROASTED TOMATOES

Roasting tomatoes brings out their natural sugars and makes them sweet, sweet, sweet. Keep an eye on them though, leave them on the grill too long and you end up with mush!

10 large beefeater tomatoes, halved

4 garlic cloves, finely sliced

2 tsp lavender honey (10mL)

2 tbsp balsamic vinegar (30mL) plus
*   1 tbsp to drizzle (15mL)*

1 tbsp olive oil (15mL) plus 1 tablespoon
*   to drizzle (15mL)*

Salt and black pepper to taste

1 tbsp flat-leaf parsley, chopped (15mL)

Directions:

- Preheat barbecue to 300F (150C) or medium-low heat.

- Place tomato halves cut-side-up on a baking sheet or perforated barbecue tray. Divide garlic slices between the tomatoes and place on top of each tomato half. Drizzle with honey, vinegar and oil. Season the tomatoes with salt and pepper.

- Place the tray of tomatoes on the grill. Roast the tomatoes until very soft and lightly charred (about 30 minutes). Remove tomatoes from the grill and place on a serving platter. Sprinkle with parsley and drizzle with remaining olive oil and balsamic vinegar.

- Serve chilled or at room temperature.

Serves 6

GREEN SALAD WITH APRICOTS AND BLUEBERRIES

I put all kinds of berries in my salads when summer comes around. Arugula is my favourite leaf with a pungent peppery taste and is a classic match for sweet apricots and blueberries.

2 cups white wine vinegar, warmed (500mL)

1 Vidalia onion

1 tbsp coarse salt (15mL)

1/4 cup fresh basil, chopped (60mL)

Juice of 1 lemon

2 tablespoons olive oil (30mL)

1 cup fresh or frozen blueberries (250mL)

1/2 cup sugar (125mL)

4 fresh apricots, sliced 1/4-inch thick

2 bunches arugula, washed

1/3 cup vegetable oil (75mL)

1 lemon

4 wooden skewers soaked in water for 1 hour

Directions:

- Pour the white wine vinegar into a pot over low heat to warm through. Remove from heat.

- Add blueberries, sugar and lemon to warmed vinegar. Let sit for 20 minutes then strain blueberries from flavored vinegar and discard. Whisk in olive oil and season with salt and pepper.

- Cut the onion into paper-thin slices and place them in a shallow baking dish. Sprinkle salt on the onion slices, chop the fresh basil and add it to the dish. Squeeze the lemon juice over the onion and drizzle with 2 tablespoons of olive oil. Cover the dish with plastic wrap and place in the refrigerator for approximately two hours.

- Thread apricot slices onto skewers.

- Preheat the grill to low heat, approximately 300F (150C). Oil the grill and place the apricots skewers on it. Cook for 2 minutes on each side and remove.

- Remove the onions from the refrigerator and pour them into a serving bowl. Add the apricots and arugula and toss.

- Whisk together 1/2 cup of the blueberry dressing with vegetable oil. Pour over salad and toss.

Serves 6

GREEN SALAD WITH RED WINE VINAIGRETTE

Go down to your local farmer's market and bring home a bunch of whatever greens are
out there—chickory, romaine, bib, arugula, whatever . . . and don't forget herbs . . .
throw in some herbs!

10 cups assorted fresh summer greens (2.5L)

1/3 cup red onion, thinly sliced (75mL)

1/2 cup julienned red pepper (125mL)

1/2 cup julienned yellow pepper (125mL)

8 oz goat cheese (227g)

1/2 cup toasted pine nuts (125mL)

Dressing

1/2 cup red wine (125mL)

3 tbsp grapeseed oil (45mL)

2 tbsp balsamic vinegar (30mL)

1 tbsp Dijon mustard (15mL)

2 tbsp fresh basil, torn or chopped (30mL)

1/2 tsp salt (2.5mL)

1 tsp cracked pepper (5mL)

1 tsp honey (5mL)

Directions:

- In a medium bowl combine Dijon mustard, red wine and vinegars and whisk, then add remaining ingredients and blend. Taste and adjust seasoning if necessary.

- Place the greens, onions and peppers in a large serving bowl and toss gently.

- Drizzle with one third of the dressing. Top the salad with crumbled goat cheese and toasted pine nuts. Add remainder of dressing, toss and serve immediately.

Serves 6

GRILLED BEET AND BLUE CHEESE AND BACON SALAD

2 large red beets

2 cups watercress cleaned(500ml)

1/2 cup of blue cheese, crumbled(125ml)

1/4 cup chopped roasted walnuts(60ml)

4 strips cooked bacon

1 tablespoons of olive oil(15ml)

1 tablespoon of chopped chives(15ml)

1 tablespoon of chopped tarragon(15ml)

1 tablespoon of chopped dill(15ml)

1 tablespoon of balsamic vinegar(15ml)

salt and pepper

2 table spoons good quality olive oil (30ml)

Directions:

- Place beets in a pot of cool water over medium high heat. Bring to a boil. Reduce heat to low and allow to simmer until beets are 3/4 way cooked. Parboil beets until tender but still firm in the centre, approximately 15 minutes. Peel beets & slice into 1/4" rounds. Drizzle with 1 tablespoon olive oil and season with salt and pepper.

- Prepare barbecue for direct grilling. Preheat grill to medium heat. Oil grill and place beets on the grill for 1-2 minutes per side. Remove.

- Assemble salad. Toss beets with herbs. Place on platter top with watercress. Top with cheese, nuts, bacon, then drizzle with balsamic vinegar, olive oil. Season with salt and pepper.

STUFFED GRILLED ZUCCHINI

There are all sorts of "zukes" out there. For this recipe go for the ones that are about 6 inches long. Check the outer skin and make sure it's free of nicks and blemishes. Zucchini holds up nicely on the grill. No, you can't use dried herbs instead of fresh for this one . . .

1 tbsp extra-virgin olive oil (15ml)

1 cup finely chopped red onion (250ml)

1 tsp minced garlic (5ml)

1/2 cup dried bread crumbs (125ml)

1 tbsp finely chopped fresh oregano (15ml)

1 tbsp finely chopped chives (15ml)

1/2 tsp kosher salt (2.5 ml)

1/2 tsp fresh cracked pepper (2.5 ml)

3 medium zucchinis, trimmed and cut
    in half lengthwise

2 tbsp olive oil (30ml)

1 tbsp lemon zest (15ml)

1 cup grated mozzarella cheese (250ml)

1/4 cup freshly grated Parmigiano
    Reggiano cheese (125ml)

1/2 cup chopped red pepper (125ml)

Salt and pepper to taste

Directions:

- In a sauté pan set over medium heat, heat the oil.

- Add the onion and garlic. Sauté until translucent but not browned, about 3 to 4 minutes. Remove from heat and add bread crumbs, herbs, salt and pepper. Mix until combined. Place in a bowl to cool.

- Season zucchinis with salt and pepper and drizzle with oil.

- Prepare barbecue for direct grilling at a medium-high heat.

- Oil grill and place the zucchinis flesh-side down on grill for 3 minutes or until nicely charred. Remove.

- Allow zucchinis to cool slightly.

- Use a melon baller to scoop out centers, leaving a 1/2-inch border.

- Chop the zucchini flesh and add it to the bowl of onions and breadcrumbs. Mix well. Add cheese and diced red pepper to mixture.

- Add the filling back into the zucchini shells.

- Oil the grill and place zucchinis stuffing-side up on grill to cook for 8 minutes with the lid down or until filling is warm and cheese has turned golden brown.

Serves 6

TWICE-GRILLED POTATOES

We love grilling potatoes so much, we do it *twice* in the same recipe. Har har.
Actually the reason for the double grilling is to soften up the spud enough to scoop
the flesh out, then mix with all the great stuff below and then return to the barbecue
to warm through. This is a killer side with steak or chicken.

4 russet potatoes, cleaned

2 tbsp vegetable oil (30ml)

Salt and pepper

Directions:

- Wash the potatoes, pat dry with paper towel and cut in half lengthwise.

- Rub with oil and season with salt and pepper.

Stuffing

1/2 cup whipped cream (125ml)

1/2 cup grated provolone cheese (125ml)

1/2 cup grated Parmesan cheese (125ml)

3 tbsp chopped chives in 1" pieces (45ml)

1/2 cup cooked bacon (125ml)

2 tbsp Dijon mustard (30ml)

Salt and pepper to taste

1/2 cup sour cream to garnish (125ml)

- Prepare barbecue for direct grilling at low heat. Oil the grill well and place the potatoes flesh-side down. Close the barbecue lid and cook for 30 minutes, turning once until soft and flesh side is caramelized. Remove from grill and cool slightly.

- Scoop out the insides leaving a 1/2-inch (1.75 cm) border all around the potato so that it won't fall apart on the grill.

- Place the scooped potato in a bowl and add whip cream and half of the cheese.

- Add the chives, bacon, Dijon, salt and pepper. Mix the stuffing until well combined, but still chunky.

- Fill the potatoes with stuffing and top with the remaining cheese.

- Place back on grill at medium low heat.

- Cook until warmed through and cheese has caramelized. Approximately 7 – 10 minutes. Remove and top with sour cream. Enjoy!

Yield: 8 halves

SPICY GRILLED POTATO SKINS

I've got to be honest with you, I'm not a big fan of potato skins but everyone else seems to love them and all the flavor *is* in the skin after all and not so much the flesh. Here's our take on the roadhouse standby. Enjoy.

6 baking potatoes (4–6 oz each /113g –170g)

1 tbsp vegetable oil (15ml)

3/4 cup bottled salsa (180ml)

1 cup sour cream (250ml)

1 tbsp finely chopped jalapeno (15ml)

1 tbsp roasted garlic (15ml)

1 cup grated cheddar (250ml)

1/4 cup chives cut into 1 inch (16cm)
    pieces to garnish (60ml)

Directions:

- Wash potatoes well and pat dry with paper towel.

- Using the tines of a fork, prick potatoes all over. Wrap potatoes in aluminum foil.

- Preheat barbecue to 300F/150C and cook potatoes with the lid down for 40 minutes or until tender.

- Remove the spuds from the grill. Unwrap the foil and slice them in half.

- Scoop the flesh out of the potatoes leaving approximately 1/2 an inch (1.27cm) of the flesh around the sides. Allow to cool. Brush the skins with oil and season with salt and pepper.

- Place the skins on well oiled preheated medium-high grill for 8 minutes flesh-side down or until golden and crispy. Remove.

- Lay the potato skins out in a row and drop a dollop of bottled salsa in each, followed by sour cream and then chopped jalapeno and roasted garlic.

- Add grated cheddar and top with chopped chives.

- Serve right away

Serves 6

CURRIED ROAST POTATOES

I do love potatoes on the barbecue. Technically you could do these on the stove but hey, it's too hot in the summer, so get outside and fire up the grill.

1 large vidalia onion cut into large wedges

2 tsp ground coriander (10ml)

2 tsp ground cumin (10ml)

1/2 tsp cayenne pepper (2ml)

3 tsp curry powder (15ml)

1 tsp turmeric (5ml)

3 tsp freshly grated ginger (15ml)

1 1/2 tsp crushed garlic (7ml)

Salt and pepper to taste

3 cups chicken broth (750ml)

6 potatoes unpeeled, washed and quartered

2 limes quartered

1 tbsp vegetable oil (30ml)

Directions:

- Preheat the grill to medium high.

- Place a large cast iron skillet on the grill to heat up for 3 or 4 minutes.

- Add the onions and cook without oil and without stirring for 8 minutes or until the onions begin to brown.

- Add spices, ginger, garlic, salt and pepper and cook until fragrant, maybe 2 or 3 minutes longer.

- Add 1 1/2 cups (450ml) of chicken stock and stir, picking up the onion bits from the bottom of the pan. Simmer over low heat for approximately 10–15 minutes until the mixture gets thick and the stock reduces.

- Add the potatoes to the mixture and toss to coat.

- Add the remaining stock.

- Place the skillet uncovered on the grill and close the lid.

- Cook for 30 minutes adding water/stock as necessary or until potatoes are tender.

Serves 6

GRILLED POTATOES WITH HERBS

Obviously you can play with the type of herbs you want to use in this recipe.
The trick is not to cut the spuds too thick or they will burn on the grill before
cooking all the way through.

3 Yukon Gold potatoes

3 tbsp olive oil (45ml)

1 tsp dried thyme (5ml)

2 tsp dried oregano (10ml)

Salt and pepper to taste

Directions:

- Slice potatoes 1/2-inch thick and place into a
  sealable plastic bag. Add oil, dried thyme, oregano,
  salt and pepper. Seal the bag and toss the
  potatoes to ensure they are well coated. Set aside.

- Preheat barbecue to medium-low heat.

- Oil the grill liberally. Remove the potatoes from the
  bag and place them directly over the heat. Cook for
  approximately 8 minutes per side or until golden
  brown, crispy and cooked through.

Serves 4

GRILLED CORN WITH CHIPOTLE-MAPLE GLAZE

1/4 cup unsalted butter (60ml)

1/2 cup pure maple syrup (125ml)

1 tsp fresh minced garlic (5ml)

1 tsp onion salt (5ml)

1 tsp freshly ground black pepper (5ml)

*1 tbsp minced canned chipotle chilies in
     adobo sauce (15ml)*

6 ears fresh corn, husked

Directions:

- In a saucepan combine butter, maple syrup, garlic, onion salt, pepper and chipotle and bring to a simmer over low heat for 5 minutes, stirring occasionally.

- Place the corn on a baking sheet and brush with chipotle-maple glaze.

- Preheat the grill to medium heat.

- Oil the grill and add the corn. Grill for about 2 minutes.

- Baste and turn the corn to grill for a further 2 or 3 minutes.

- Remove from the grill and serve immediately.

Makes 6 cobs

ROSEMARY SMOKED POTATOES

If you want even more flavor, parboil the spuds in chicken stock instead of water. Parboil just means boiling them 'til they soften up a bit as opposed to all the way through (otherwise they might fall apart on the grill).

15 small red skinned baby potatoes

8 rosemary stalks, soaked in water for
*   30 minutes*

2 tbsp garlic, chopped (30ml)

1/4 cup oil (60ml)

Salt and pepper to taste

Directions:

- Parboil the potatoes whole in salted water for 10 minutes. Allow to cool and drain.

- Halve the potatoes and place in a plastic bag. Drizzle with oil and chopped garlic. Seal bag and let marinate at room temperature for 20 minutes.

- Soak the rosemary sprigs in water.

- Preheat barbecue to 325F/162C

- Remove the potatoes from marinade; discard any excess marinade.

- Season the potatoes with salt and pepper.

- Place the soaked rosemary on the grate. Place the potatoes on top of the rosemary. Close the lid and leave to smoke for 15 minutes.

- Remove the potatoes and discard the charred rosemary.

Serves 6

BALSAMIC GRILLED MUSHROOMS

'Shrooms and balsamic are a classic combo. This side works well with chicken or steak. Bit too much for fish though.

2 lbs button mushrooms, cleaned

3 tbsp balsamic vinegar

1/4 cup olive oil

Salt and pepper to taste

Directions:

- Place a grill basket on the barbecue and heat on high for 15 minutes with the lid closed.

- Toss all of the ingredients into a large bowl to coat.

- Place the mushrooms directly into the hot grill basket.

- Toss and turn the mushrooms every 2 minutes until they are golden brown and evenly cooked.

Serves 6

MUSHROOM KEBABS

Don't marinate for more than 20 minutes or the 'shrooms will go moosh. Make sure the mushrooms are all about the same size to ensure even cooking time.

1 lb of whole button mushrooms, cleaned and stems trimmed (450g)

12 bamboo skewers, soaked in water for a minimum of 30 minutes

Marinade

1/2 cup dry red wine (125ml)

1/4 cup olive oil (62ml)

1 tbsp lemon juice (15ml)

2 large cloves garlic, minced

3 tsp dried thyme

1 tsp sea or kosher salt (5ml)

1 tsp freshly cracked black pepper (5ml)

Directions:

- Place the mushrooms in a large plastic bag.

- Combine all of the marinade ingredients and pour over the mushrooms. Seal the bag and marinate for 20 minutes at room temperature.

- Preheat the grill to high heat.

- Remove the mushrooms from the bag and discard the marinade.

- Skewer the mushrooms and place them onto the grill.

- Grill for approximately 7–10 minutes with the lid up and turning on a regular basis to ensure even cooking.

Serves 6

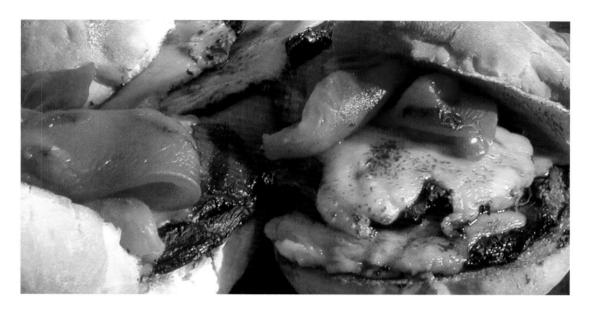

PORTOBELLO CHEESEBURGERS

"Portobello" seems to be Italian for "really nice door you have there." Apparently some marketing whiz came up with the name in the 1980s to help sell these big mother 'shrooms. Looks like it worked. Portobellos hold up really well on the grill because of their size and density. Enjoy.

4 large portobello mushroom caps, cleaned

1/4 cup balsamic vinegar (62ml)

2 tbsp olive oil (30ml)

1 tsp dried basil (5ml)

1 tsp dried oregano (5ml)

1 tbsp minced garlic (15ml)

Salt and pepper to taste

4 slices mozzarella cheese

Directions:

- Place the mushrooms in a large plastic bag.

- Add the balsamic vinegar, olive oil, basil, oregano, garlic and salt and pepper.

- Marinate at room temperature for 15 minutes

- Preheat the grill to high heat.

- Oil the grill and place the mushrooms top-side down on the grill and cook for 2 minutes. Flip and cook for another 2 minutes.

- Flip again and add a slice of cheese to each mushroom.

- Continue to cook for another 2–3 minutes until the cheese is melted and the mushrooms are tender and cooked through.

Serves 4

STUFFED SMOKED ONIONS

Get vidalia onions if they're in season. They are sweeter and milder but a good Spanish onion will do just as well.

6 large Spanish or vidalia onions (8oz ea)

1 cup bread crumbs (250ml)

2/3 cup chicken broth (175 ml)

1 lb fresh veal sausage

1 tsp dried oregano (5ml)

1 tsp dried sage (5ml)

1/2 tsp dried cumin (2ml)

3 tbsp pine nuts (45ml)

Make a smoke pouch (see page 5)

3 cups apple wood chips

3 sprigs fresh thyme

Directions:

- Leave the outer papery skin on the onions, wash and rinse.

- Trim the root end off onion to make a flat bottom. Cut tops off and reserve.

- Hollow out the centers leaving two or three outer layers in tact. Reserve center for other use.

- In a bowl, mix remaining ingredients. Toss gently to combine. Fill onions with equal amounts of sausage mix. Place tops on onions.

- Place each onion upright in center of a piece of heavy-duty aluminum foil and bring edges up to seal. Seal loosely to allow steam to escape.

- Prepare the barbecue for indirect grilling. Crank the heat on one side and place the smoke pouch directly on the burner. Close the lid and wait for smoke. Once barbecue is smoking, reduce the heat to 220F/110C

- Place the onion parcels upright on the unlit side, close the lid and cook for an hour or until very tender.

- Remove the onions from foil and carefully remove the outermost skin. Whoa baby, that's hot! Watch your fingers.

- Reserve cooking juices and drizzle over the onions.

Serves 6

GRILLED BACON ONION WEDGES

Another cool variation on this recipe is to wrap the onion wedges in prosciutto
instead of regular bacon.

2 large sweet onions, cut into wedges

8 thick slices bacon

2 tbsp balsamic vinegar (30ml)

2 tbsp brown sugar (30ml)

1 tbsp molasses (15ml)

Bamboo skewers soaked in water

Directions:

- Wrap the onion wedges in bacon and fasten them on with soaked bamboo skewers. Place them into a large sealable plastic bag. Add balsamic, sugar and molasses and toss gently to coat.

- Marinate for 30 minutes or so at room temperature.

- Preheat barbecue to medium-high heat and oil grill

- Remove the onions from the marinade. Pat dry with paper towels.

- Place them on the grill to barbecue for approximately 8–10 minutes per side. Keep an eye on them as you'll probably get flare ups as the bacon begins to cook and the fat drips so you'll have to move them around. No problem here as you're not going for nice char marks.

Serves 6

GRILLED ONIONS WITH SPICED SUMMER APRICOT MUSTARD GLAZE

A nice Spanish onion will do in a pinch if vidalia onions are out of season.
The Dijon, lemon juice and vinegar add tartness to the sweet apricot jelly.

3 medium sweet vidalia onions

1 tbsp olive oil (15ml)

Apricot Mustard Glaze

2 cups apricot jelly (500ml)

2 tbsp Dijon mustard (30ml)

Juice of 3 lemons

1 tbsp rice wine vinegar (15ml)

1 shallot, chopped fine

Directions:

- Peel and slice the onion into approximately 1/4-inch-thick slices, brush both sides with olive oil. Place them on a baking sheet, ready for grill.

- Prepare barbecue for direct grilling. Preheat grill to medium heat.

- Oil grill and place onions on to cook for 3 minutes.

- Flip the onions over and baste with the apricot glaze and continue to cook a further 2–3 minutes.

Apricot Mustard Glaze Directions:

- Combine ingredients in a saucepan set over low heat.

- Simmer on low heat for 5 minutes and remove.

- Reserve half for a dipping sauce.

Serves 6–8

CAULIFLOWER KEBABS

Red curry paste has an amazingly deep and complex taste along with some great heat. Once you've tried this recipe you'll never think of cauliflower the same way again. Perfect as a side to a nicely grilled bit of salmon or tuna.

A head of cauliflower

2 tsp salt (5ml)

2 tsp red curry paste (10ml)

1 tsp sugar (5ml)

1/2 cup coconut milk (125ml)

Juice of 1 lime

6 10-inch (25cm) wooden bamboo skewers
soaked in cool water 1 hour prior to grilling

Aluminum foil

Directions:

- Using a small pairing knife, cut the cauliflower from its core into 2-inch (5cm) florets.

- In a large pot set over high heat, boil 10 cups (2.5L) of salted water.

- Add the cauliflower to boiling water and cook for 3 minutes.

- Strain cauliflower in a colander and immediately plunge into an ice bath. This is done to prevent further cooking and to keep the cauliflower crisp. Once cool, strain from ice water bath and pat dry.

- In a small bowl mix red curry paste, sugar, coconut milk and the lime juice.

- Skewer the cauliflower florets on wooden skewers. Brush with the sauce.

- Preheat grill to medium high.

- Oil the grill and place a 4-inch (10cm) by 10-inch (25cm) piece of aluminum foil in the center of barbecue.

- Place the cauliflower directly on the grill with the ends of the skewers directly over foil. (This is to prevent burning of skewers.)

- Cook the florets while basting with sauce for 5 minutes or until golden brown char marks are achieved.

Yield: 6 kebabs

CHARRED STUFFED JALAPENO

Look for jalapenos clear of nicks and blemishes. This recipe requires you to "pipe" the stuffing into the charred pepper. If you don't have a piping bag, then put the cream cheese stuffing into a sturdy plastic bag and cut off one of the corners. Voila. Instant piping bag.

14 large jalapenos

1 tbsp olive oil (15ml)

1 package cream cheese (250g),
*   room temperature*

4 slices of bacon, fried crisp and crumbled

1 tbsp fresh oregano (15ml)

1/2 cup fresh chives, minced fine (125ml)

2 green onion, minced fine

Zest of 1 lemon

Salt and pepper to taste

Directions:

- Using a sharp knife, cut along the length of the jalapeno (being careful not to cut through to the other side) to create a pocket. Leave tops intact.

- Using the knife carefully devein and remove seeds from the chilies.

- Toss the jalapenos with olive oil.

- Preheat barbecue to medium-high heat.

- Place the chilies on grill and char on the outside for about 3 minutes turning constantly with tongs. Remove from grill and cool.

- When peppers are cool remove the charred skins and discard. You might want to wear rubber gloves for this part or at least remember: *do not* rub your eyes.

- In a medium bowl combine the cream cheese with the remaining ingredients and mix well. Place the mixture in a piping bag. Pipe the mixture into the peeled peppers.

- Preheat barbecue to 400F/204C or high heat. Place peppers on warming rack and allow the filling in peppers to get warm and gooey.

- Remove and let cool slightly before serving.

Yield: 14 peppers

GRILLED RICE CAKES

Tired of potatoes as a side dish? Check this one out. Grilled rice cakes go really well with fish or a nicely grilled pork tenderloin. No ring molds? Go to your local hardware store and get the guy to cut you some different widths of PVC pipe. Instant ring molds.

3 cups sushi rice, cooked following

   package instructions

1/4 cup rice wine vinegar (60ml)

1 tbsp sugar (15ml)

1 tsp salt (5ml)

1/4 cup chopped fresh basil (60ml)

3 tbsp lightly toasted pine nuts (45ml)

2 tbsp peanut oil for brushing (30ml)

Directions:

- Placed cooked warm rice in a bowl.

- In another bowl, mix together the rice wine vinegar, sugar and salt. Stir to dissolve.

- Pour the mixture over the rice and gently toss.

- Add the basil and pine nuts and mix until evenly distributed.

- Mold the rice into a 3-inch ring mold until it is about 3/4 inch in height. Gently pack in until a nice firm disk is achieved.

- *Tip: To stop rice from sticking to your hands, dip your hands in cold water before handling the rice.*

- Remove from the ring and place on a well-oiled baking sheet. Repeat and brush the cakes with the peanut oil.

- Preheat the barbecue to medium heat.

- Oil the grill and place the rice cakes on direct heat.

- Grill for approximately 3 minutes per side or until nice golden crispy char marks are achieved.

- Remove from heat. Plate and serve.

Makes 8 cakes

GRILLED VEGGIE CORNBOATS

This looks way more complicated than it really is. I promise that once you've tried it, this will become a favorite side. Try adding different veggies depending on your personal tastes. Smoked gouda is a great cheese that doesn't get as big a workout as some of the more popular types.

6 cobs of corn

2 red peppers

2 yellow peppers

20 asparagus stems, woody part
   of stem removed

Directions:

• Preheat the grill to high.

• Pull the husks back from the cob without tearing them off. Remove the silk from the corn.

• Using a paring knife, carefully remove the cob of corn from the husks which should remain intact and attached by the end of the cob. Place the husks into a pot of water to soak.

10 cloves garlic with the skin on

2 red onions, cut into wedges

1/2 lb smoked gouda, grated

1/2 cup cilantro, freshly chopped

Bamboo skewers, soaked in water

- Cut all the vegetables into equal medium sized pieces. Place the red onion and garlic onto the bamboo skewers.

- Drizzle the vegetables and skewers with oil and season with salt and pepper.

- Oil the grill and place the corn, skewers and veggies on the grill. Grill the corn for approximately 5 minutes turning often until tender.

- Continue to cook the vegetables and skewers for another 10 minutes or so until lightly charred and tender.

- Leave the grilled vegetables and corn to cool. Once cool, use a sharp knife to cut the corn from the cob. Place in a bowl. Cut the remaining vegetables into bite-sized pieces and add to the bowl.

- Add the grated cheese and cilantro.

- Remove the corn husks from the water and pat dry with paper towels.

- Place a healthy scoop of the vegetable mix into the middle of the husk. Close the husk over and tie the loose end so it sort of looks like a weird corn husk canoe filled with veggies.

- 10 minutes before serving, place the corn boats on the top rack of the barbecue at medium high heat. Close the lid. This will melt the cheese and heat the vegetables up again. Serve warm.

Serves 6

GRILLED VEGETABLES WITH GARLIC ANCHOVY DIP

This is our take on an old Italian favorite called "bagna cauda." This is an excellent sit-around-the-backyard-and-have-a-drink-and-a-few-laughs kind of starter to a Saturday night dinner party. The recipe calls for just one whole bulb of garlic but go ahead and add more if you don't plan on kissing anyone. You can also roast the garlic in the oven in advance to save time.

Dip

1 large bulb of garlic

Freshly ground cracked black pepper

3 sprigs of fresh thyme

1 tbsp of olive oil (15ml)

2 1/2 ounces of drained anchovy fillets, chopped (65g)

2 tbsp of unsalted butter, melted (30 ml)

1 cup of extra virgin olive oil (250ml)

Vegetables

3 red peppers

12 cherry tomatoes

6 small sweet potatoes (11/2 lbs)

6 carrots (375 g)

2 lbs of asparagus, trimmed (1000 g)

4 tbsp of extra virgin olive oil (60ml)

Salt and ground pepper to taste

Directions:

- Preheat the grill to medium-high heat.

- To make the dip first roast the garlic. Cut the top off of the garlic bulb. Using a fork, poke holes in the exposed garlic. Rub with olive oil and season with cracked black pepper. Add a few sprigs of thyme and wrap it all in tin foil. Place on the grill for approximately 1/2 hour.

- When the garlic has completely roasted, squish the bulbs from the skin into a blender. Add the chopped anchovies and butter and whiz. Season with freshly ground pepper.

- Pour the garlic anchovy mixture into the cup of olive oil. They should remain separated with the anchovy mixture sitting at the bottom of the oil.

- For the vegetables, cut the sweet potatoes, carrots, and red peppers lengthwise into large even pieces (thirds or quarters) and place them in a large glass bowl. Add the cherry tomatoes and asparagus. Add the olive oil and season generously. Toss the vegetables.

- Arrange the vegetables on the grill and cook for approximately 1 1/2 minutes per side with lid up.

- While the veggies are grilling, pour the dip into a pot and set on the grill to warm through. The aromas are insane.

- Serve warm with the dip on the side.

Serves 6

MARINATED CARROTS, PEARL ONIONS & RADISHES

Okay, so you don't actually barbecue this recipe. Marinated veggies as a starter with some nice cheese (like a brie or not-so-stinky Camembert) and good bread works great on a warm summer's night.

3/4 lb very young carrots, peeled and trimmed (340g)

1 cup pearl onions, skins removed (250ml)

1 cup radish, cleaned and stems removed (250ml)

3 cups water (750ml)

6 tbsp dry white wine (90ml)

Directions:

- In a medium size non-reactive saucepan, bring the water, wine, vinegar and olive oil to a boil with the garlic, parsley, thyme, oregano, sugar, salt, and cayenne.

- Reduce heat to medium and add the carrots, radish and onions. Cook for 5 minutes. Let cool in the saucepan.

6 tbsp white wine vinegar (90ml)

1/4 cup extra-virgin olive oil (60ml)

1 large garlic clove, crushed

1 small bunch fresh parsley

1 small bunch fresh thyme

1 small bunch fresh oregano

2 tbsp sugar (30ml)

1 tsp kosher salt

1 tsp cayenne pepper (5ml)

1 tsp Dijon mustard (5ml)

2 tbsp finely chopped fresh basil
    leaves (30ml)

- Pour the liquid and vegetables in a serving jar and refrigerate overnight.

- Next day, strain vegetables, reserving 2 cups of the poaching liquid. (500ml).

- Strain the liquid into a saucepan. Reduce over high heat to 1 cup (250ml). Stir in the mustard; cool.

- When ready to serve drizzle reduced sauce over vegetables and sprinkle with fresh chopped basil.

Makes 4 cups (1L) of vegetables servings

SMOKED CORN ON THE COB

The nice thing about corn is that it comes in its own grill container, namely the husk. Smoking adds a nice depth of flavor to the natural sugars in the corn. The bacon will melt and crisp up adding even more taste. Pretty easy, huh?

6 ears of corn with their husks, silks removed

Salt and pepper to taste

1 tbsp garlic powder (15ml)

1 tbsp cayenne pepper (15ml)

6 slices bacon

Wood chips for smoking

Directions:

- Pull back the husks of the corn keeping the base in tact. Remove all of the corn silk. Place the corn tip-down in a large stock pot of cold water to soak for an hour. You want to plump the corn up with water before smoking.

- Make a smoke pouch (see page 5).

- Prepare the barbecue for indirect grilling. Crank the heat on one side and place the first smoke pouch directly on the burner. Close the lid and wait for smoke. Once barbecue is smoking, reduce the heat to 220F/110C.

- Drain the corn and pat dry. Season each cob with salt and pepper, garlic powder and a pinch of cayenne.

- Wrap a slice of bacon around each cob. If necessary, use a water-soaked toothpick to secure the bacon to the cob.

- Pull the husks back over the cobs and place them on the unlit side of the grill.

- Close the lid and let the corn smoke for 1 hour.

Makes 6 cobs

SMOKED ACORN SQUASH WITH MAPLE SPICED BUTTER

They call it acorn squash because it sort of looks like a giant mutant acorn. Inside is a nice orange flesh that works incredibly well with the maple butter and the cranberries. Serve this as a side with chicken.

Maple Spiced Butter

3/4 cup unsalted butter, softened (185ml)

3 tbsp maple syrup (45ml)

1 tsp cinnamon (5ml)

1/2 tsp nutmeg (2.5ml)

Directions:

- Place all the Maple Spiced Butter ingredients into a small saucepan and simmer over low heat for 5 minutes.

- Brush inside cavity of the squash with 1/2 of the maple butter. Wrap the base of the squash in foil.

- Make a smoke pouch (see page ?).

Smoked Acorn Squash

3 acorn squash, cut in half, seeds and fibers
  removed – about 1lb each (454g)
1 cup dried cranberries (250ml)
1/2 cup slivered almonds, toasted (125ml)

Apple or cherry wood chips.

- Prepare the barbecue for indirect smoking. Crank the heat on one side and place the smoke pouch directly on the burner. Close the lid and wait for smoke. Once the barbecue is smoking, reduce the heat to 220F/110C.

- Add acorn squash to unlit side, close the lid and smoke the squash for 1 hour or until soft and slightly caramelized (check for doneness with a fork).

- Remove from grill. Place acorn squash on a large serving platter. Cut the halves into thirds. Sprinkle with cranberries and toasted almonds.

- Top with a dollop of reserved room temperature maple butter.

Serves 6

GRILLED FENNEL WITH GARLIC ANCHOVY BUTTER

2 fennel bulbs

1 tbsp of extra virgin olive oil (15ml)

Garlic Anchovy Butter

5 tbsp butter, at room temperature (75 ml)

4 large garlic cloves

5 anchovy fillets

Juice from 1 lemon

1 tbsp of freshly chopped cilantro (15ml)

1 tsp of freshly ground black pepper (5ml)

Directions:

- Trim the fennel bulbs of their leafy tops.

- Cut the bulb into 3/4-inch wedges, being sure to leave the root end intact so that they don't fall apart on the grill.

- Preheat barbecue to medium high and oil the grill.

- Place the soft butter in a large bowl.

- Crush the garlic and add it to the bowl.

- Rinse the anchovy fillets and dice them. Add the diced anchovy, lemon juice, cilantro and pepper to the bowl and mix.

- Drizzle the fennel wedges with the olive oil. Grill the fennel for about 5 minutes a side with the lid up. Watch for flare ups and shift the vegetable if they persist.

- Serve hot with garlic anchovy butter melting on top.

Serves 4

GRILLED ANTIPASTO

Antipasto is Italian for "before the pasta" and refers to any sort of hors d'oeuvre which is French for "outside the work" and refers to small nibbles served before a meal. Kind of got a United Nations thing going on here, but all you need to know is this is a delicious way to start a dinner when everyone is sort of standing around in the backyard having a drink and listening to tunes. Got to love summer nights.

2/3 cup balsamic vinegar (150ml)

2 6-oz jar artichoke hearts (350ml)

2 medium sweet red peppers sliced
*   into 1-inch pieces*

2 medium sweet yellow peppers sliced
*   into 1-inch pieces*

16 small whole or 8 medium halved cipollini
*   or 16 pearl onions*

16 large crimini or button mushrooms caps

4 ounces of feta cheese sliced into thin,
*   short strips (125ml)*

1/4 cup black olives (60ml)

1/3 cup fresh parsley (75ml)

1/3 cup fresh basil (75 ml)

Salt and pepper - to taste

8 long metal skewers

Directions:

- In a saucepan, bring the balsamic vinegar to boil. Let simmer for 5 minutes uncovered or until the vinegar reduced to 6 tbsp (90ml), and set aside to cool.

- Drain the artichokes, reserving 4 tbsp (60ml) of artichoke juice and set aside.

- Skewer the red and yellow peppers, cipollini and mushroom, leaving a 1/4-inch space between each vegetable.

- In a small bowl, combine the reserved balsamic vinegar with the artichoke juice. Brush half of the vinegar mixture evenly over the vegetable skewers.

- Preheat the barbecue to medium, oil the grill.

- Grill the skewers directly over the heat with lid closed for 4–5 minutes or until vegetables are tender.

- Turn once, brushing with the remaining vinegar mixture. Continue grilling for another 4–5 minutes.

- Once vegetables are grilled, remove from the skewers and place in a large salad bowl.

- Add drained artichoke, cheese, black olives, basil, parsley and season with salt and pepper, toss gently to combine all ingredients.

- Serve on crackers, grilled bread or endive spears

Serves 10–12

GRILLED ASPARAGUS AND BEETS

Beets come in all sorts of colors and sizes. Go for the ones a bit smaller than the size of a tennis ball. The asparagus should be about as think as your pinky. Make sure you put on rubber gloves to slice the beets or you'll end up with red hands.

2 lbs summer beets, mixed colors (1kg)

2 lbs asparagus

2 tbsp olive oil (30ml)

1 tbsp balsamic vinegar (15ml)

Salt and pepper to taste

1/4 cup fresh basil, chopped roughly (60ml)

Directions:

- Add summer beets to a pot of boiling water and cook for about 7 minutes or until the beets are tender. The exact time will vary depending on how big your beets are. You should be able to poke a fork through to the middle.

- Drain the beets under cold running water.

- Skin the beets, then slice them 1/3-inch thick and place them on a baking sheet.

- Next, snap the woody ends off the asparagus and place them on the baking sheet with the beets.

- Drizzle the asparagus and beets with oil, balsamic vinegar, salt and pepper.

- Preheat the barbecue to high heat and oil the grill

- Grill the beet slices for about 2 minutes

- Flip the beets and add the asparagus. Grill for another 2 minutes

- Remove from the grill and serve right away, topped with the basil

Serves 6–8

GRILLED HONEY-TARRAGON CARROTS

Tarragon is an underused herb with sort of a lemony-licorice kick to it. It goes so well with honey, which goes so well with carrots. Don't use the big honkin' telephone pole carrots, instead go for ones about as thick as your thumb. This side goes nicely with chicken, pork tenderloin or some grilled fish.

14 fresh carrots

3 tbsp sesame oil (45ml)

3 tbsp honey (45ml)

3 tsp chopped ginger (45ml)

4 tarragon sprigs, torn

3 tbsp vegetable oil (45ml)

Salt and pepper to taste

Directions:

- Cut the leafy tops off the carrots leaving only half an inch at the root.

- Wash and peel the carrots and cut them in half lengthwise.

- Put them into a sealable plastic bag and drizzle with sesame oil, honey, ginger and tarragon.

- Toss to coat and marinate at room temperature for about 30 minutes.

- Preheat the barbecue to medium heat.

- Oil the grill. Place carrots flat-side down over direct heat and cook for 3 minutes or so depending on how thick the carrots are.

- Flip and continue grilling for a minute or two.

- Remove from the heat and serve warm.

Serves 7

GRILLED CORN SALAD

Served cold or at room temperature, this salad is fantastic! The buttery texture of the avocado combined with the crunchy sweet corn makes your mouth sing.

8 fresh cobs of corn, cleaned, with husks
    pulled back but not removed

5 tbsp fresh lime juice (75mL)

5 tbsp of cooking oil (15mL)

5 tsp garlic salt (25mL)

2 tsp chili powder (10mL)

2 small avocado, peeled, pitted and chopped

1/2 cup chopped red pepper (125mL)

1/2 cup chopped yellow pepper (125mL)

1/3 cup snipped fresh parsley (75mL)

1/2 tsp of salt (2.5mL)

Directions:

- Preheat grill to a medium heat

- In a bowl, combine lime juice, oil and garlic salt. Brush corn lightly with mixture and sprinkle with chili powder. Set remaining mixture aside. Fold the husks back up around the corn.

- Place corn on grill racks and grill for approximately 8–12 minutes (with lid closed) or until corn is tender, turning every few minutes.

- Meanwhile, add avocado, peppers, parsley and salt to remaining lime juice mixture.

- Cut corn kernels from the finished cobs and add to salad and toss to coat evenly. Serve at room temperature or chill and enjoy!

Serves 8

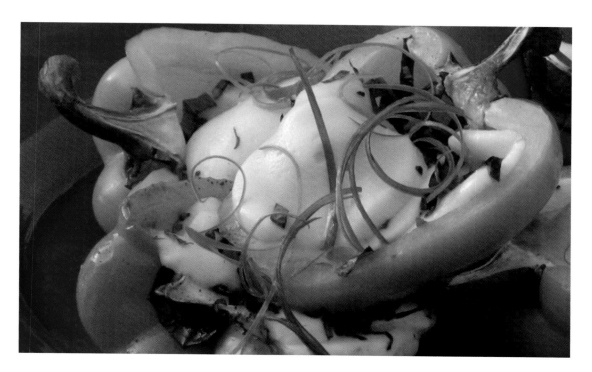

GRILLED PESTO PEPPERS

Store bought pesto is okay, but try making your own this summer when there's lots of inexpensive fresh basil for sale. Nothing in a jar or a bottle tastes as good as what you make at home yourself.

4 red or yellow peppers

2 large garlic cloves, minced

1/4 cup olive oil (6omL)

8 tbsp pesto (45mL)

Salt and freshly ground pepper

Freshly grated buffalo mozzarella

1/2 cup Panko breadcrumbs (Japanese breadcrumbs, which are larger and stay crisp longer than traditional breadcrumbs)

Directions:

- Cut peppers in half lengthways. Scrape out and discard the cores and seeds. Drizzle olive oil, season with salt and pepper and add a few slivers of garlic into the cavity of each pepper.

- Preheat the grill to 375°F/200°C or medium high heat

- Place the peppers on the grill, cavity side up, until charred (approximately 3 minutes)

- Add a spoonful of pesto into each of the peppers and sprinkle with breadcrumbs and cheese.

- Continue to cook peppers until cheese is melted (approximately 3 minutes).

GRILLED ROSEMARY BABY POTATOES

The combination of white and red baby potatoes look great on the plate with those nice grill marks running across the flesh, specked with chopped rosemary. Perfect with steak or chicken.

1 lb baby white potatoes (1kg)

1 lb baby red potatoes (1kg)

1/4 cup olive oil (60mL)

2 tbsp dried rosemary (30mL)

Salt and pepper to taste

Directions:

- Preheat barbecue to 300F.

- Slice potatoes in half. Place in a sealable plastic bag and add remaining ingredients. Place in refrigerator for 1 hour.

- Place on preheated barbecue, either directly on grate or in grill basket and cook for 15–20 minutes or until golden brown and crispy. Serve and enjoy!

Serves 8

GRILLED VEGETABLE GAZPACHO IN CUCUMBER CUPS

Grilling the veggies before making the soup gives this dish a more profound and layered taste (comes from the natural sugars in the veggies caramelizing on the barbecue). Back off on the vodka if you're going to give this one to the kids though . . .

1 Spanish hot banana pepper, diced into
    small pieces

2 cups chopped yellow tomato, peeled
    and seeded (500mL)

1 yellow pepper, small dice

3 green onions, split and diced

3 cucumbers

2 tbsp fresh basil, chopped (30mL)

1 tbsp tarragon (15mL)

1 cup vegetable stock (250mL)
    or chicken stock (250mL)

1/2 tsp salt (2.5mL)

1/2 tsp white pepper (2.5mL)

2 tsp Worcestershire (10mL)

A few splashes hot sauce

1 tbsp sherry vinegar (15mL)

1/4 cup vodka or to taste (60mL) (optional)

Directions:

- Prepare cucumber by cutting into 2-inch rounds. Scoop out the seeds and flesh in the center of the cucumber using a melon baller or spoon. Be careful not to go all the way through the cup. (Place scooped cucumber into a bowl.) Carve out enough of the cucumber to leave a 1/2 inch (8 mm) border, along sides and bottom. You should have 10–12 mini cups.

- Place all of the remaining ingredients in a food processor including the reserved cucumber. Puree until smooth. Adjust seasoning to taste. Add vodka and strain through a colander.

- Chill for 1 hour and up to overnight to develop flavor.

- Pour puree into cucumber cups and serve immediately.

Serves 5-6 appetizer portions

GRILLED VEGETABLE QUESADILLAS

Zucchini and summer squashes can get lost in the grill. One way to prevent that is to cut your zucchinis lengthwise into long, thin slices. These longer slices are not only visually appealing – think grill marks here – but easier to flip and control on the grill.

6 bell peppers, red, green and yellow,
    quartered and seeded

1 Japanese eggplant, sliced into 1-inch
    thick rounds

2 red onions cut into wedges with root intact

2 zucchini, sliced into 1-inch thick rounds

8 tbsp of olive oil (120mL)

14 oz block Monterey Jack cheese (400grams)

2 chipotle peppers, seeded and sliced
    into rounds

1 tbsp of commercial or homemade salsa
    (15mL)

8 soft corn or wheat tortillas

Salt and pepper to taste

Directions:

- Preheat barbecue to a medium heat.

- Toss bell peppers with onions, zucchini and eggplant in a large bowl and drizzle with oil, coating the vegetables well.

- Place peppers, skin side down on preheated grill and cook until seared and browned underneath. Then grill onions, zucchini and eggplants until they have softened slightly and are branded with brown grill marks. Toss all cooked veggies into a bowl.

- Cut cheese into 20 slices and add to roasted vegetables. Add chipotle peppers and mix in salsa, season with salt and pepper to taste.

- Grill tortillas on one side only. Flip, and pile vegetable mixture into the centers of 4 tortillas. When the tortilla browns underneath, put another tortilla on top, cooked side down. Carefully turn the quesadilla over using a wide pizza server with tubular handles and continue to cook until cheese begins to melt.

- Remove from grill with pizza server, serve immediately and enjoy!

Serves 4

MARINATED GRILLED ASPARAGUS

Rosemary and oregano go together like ribs and marinade. They are a perfect combination, and provide a great way to liven up an underappreciated vegetable!

2 lb fresh asparagus with thick stalks (1kg)

1/4 cup of olive oil

2 teaspoons of fresh oregano (10mL)

2 sprigs of fresh rosemary, stems removed

Salt and pepper to taste

Juice of 1 lemon

Directions:

- Preheat the grill for 15 minutes on high

- Wash the asparagus in cold water and pat dry. Snap the tough bottom portion of the fresh asparagus off and discard. Place asparagus stalks into a large, sealable plastic bag. Add the oil and the remaining ingredients to cover asparagus. Let the vegetables marinate for 10-15 minutes.

- Turn one burner off and turn the burners down to medium.

- Drain the marinade and reserve for dipping sauce. Place the asparagus in a foil pouch and seal. Place the pouch on the grill and cook with the lid closed for 10 minutes, turning at least twice.

- Serve the asparagus warm off the grill. Drizzle with fresh lemon juice and season to taste.

Serves 6

MUSHROOM RICE

Think of dried mushrooms as you would tea leaves in that they infuse the vegetable stock with their musty, woodsy flavor. Twenty bucks gets you an amazing rice-cooker that does away with any rice-sticking-to-the-bottom-of-the-pot issues.

3 cups converted rice (750mL)

6 cups vegetable stock (1500mL)

1 tbsp salt (15mL)

1 tsp pepper (5mL)

1/4 cup dried porcini mushrooms (62mL)

1 cup frozen peas (250mL)

Directions:

- Bring all the ingredients except for the peas to a boil and cover. Reduce the temperature and simmer for approximately 15 minutes until light and fluffy.

- Add peas after 10 minutes.

- Keep warm until ready to serve.

Serves 8

POTATO AND WATERCRESS SALAD

Another simple summer salad that emphasizes fresh ingredients and contrasting textures.

1 lb new red and white potatoes (500g)

2 large bunches watercress

Juice of 2 lemons

2 cloves minced garlic

1/2 cup extra virgin olive oil (125mL)

Salt and freshly ground black pepper to taste

Directions:

- Rinse and scrub potatoes and trim stems from watercress.

- Place potatoes in a large saucepan with enough water to cover completely and bring to a boil over high heat. Reduce heat and boil until potatoes are cooked through – about 25 minutes in total. Drain potatoes and set aside to cool.

- Place watercress in a large salad bowl and set aside. In a separate bowl, combine lemon juice, garlic, olive oil and seasonings and whisk together to create vinaigrette.

- Once potatoes are cool enough to handle cut them into quarters and add to watercress. Pour vinaigrette over potatoes and watercress, mix well and serve immediately.

Serves 4

ASIAN FLAVORED COLESLAW

What *doesn't* coleslaw go with? Okay, maybe French Toast…and birthday cake…it would probably suck with birthday cake. But it goes with pretty much anything that comes off the barbecue. We throw an Asian curve by including sesame seeds, ginger, sesame oil, and rice vinegar. Try this next to a sandwich and some fries.

1 tsp sesame seeds (5ml)

4 cups (1L) thinly sliced Napa cabbage
   (about 1/2 large head)

1/2 red pepper, thinly sliced

1/2 yellow pepper, thinly sliced

1/2 cup thinly sliced green onions (125ml)

Asian Dressing

3 tbsp rice vinegar (50ml)

2 tbsp peanut oil (30ml)

1 tbsp minced fresh ginger (15ml)

1 tsp sesame oil (5ml)

1 tsp sugar (5ml)

2 tsp Asian hot sauce (10ml)

Directions:

- Stir sesame seeds in a dry non-stick skillet over medium heat until golden (about 3 minutes), then set aside

- Combine cabbage, red and yellow peppers and green onions in a large bowl.

- In a separate bowl mix together dressing ingredients to combine. Toss with cabbage mixture and season to taste with salt and pepper.

- Sprinkle with seeds and serve

Serves 6

BABY ARUGULA SALAD WITH PINE NUTS, PEACHES AND DRESSING

Arugula is far and away my most favorite salad green. I could eat it every night. The baby leaves are more tender than the grown-up variety (kind of like people, really). Arugula has a nice sort of peppery taste, so Parmesan (salty) and peaches (sweet) go really well with this salad green.

Salad

3 tbsp pine nuts (45ml)

4 cups organic baby arugula (500g or 1 litre)

2 fresh peaches cut into 1/4-inch thick wedges

1/2 cup coarsely shredded Parmesan cheese
    (125ml)

Dressing

4 tbsp olive oil (60ml)

3 tbsp raspberry vinegar (45ml)

Juice of 1 lime

1 shallot, diced

Salt and pepper to taste

Pinch of sugar to taste

Directions:

- Place pine nuts in a non-stick skillet and roast over low heat until golden brown.

- Divide the baby arugula between four salad plates. Top with peach wedges and roasted pine nuts and sprinkle with shredded Parmesan.

- In a separate bowl, combine olive oil, raspberry vinegar, lime juice, diced shallot and salt and pepper. Whisk ingredients together. Taste and adjust acidity with sugar.

- Drizzle dressing over salads and serve. Not too much dressing! You don't want to drown out the other flavors on the plate.

Serves 4

BIG MAN CAESAR SALAD

I swear there are more ways to make a Caesar than just about any other salad. Some people like to add the Parmesan to the dressing, others like it on top. If you're going to make this salad on a regular basis then it's worth investing in a wooden bowl that you don't use for anything else, because after a while the garlic will permeate the wood of the bowl and affect the taste of anything else you put in there.

Caesar Salad Dressing

2 cloves garlic

Salt and cracked black pepper

2 tsp Dijon or dry mustard (10ml)

2 egg yolks

4 tsp of anchovy paste (20ml)

2 lemons, juiced

2 tbsp Worcestershire sauce (30ml)

1 cup olive oil (250ml)

2 romaine lettuces heads

5 slices bacon, cooked to crispy

1/4 cup shaved Parmesan cheese (62ml)

1 cup croutons (250ml)

Directions:

- Crush the garlic cloves in a wooden salad bowl and add a pinch of salt.

- Add the cracked pepper, mustard, egg yolks, anchovy paste, lemon juice and Worcestershire sauce. Stir vigorously.

- Add the olive oil in a steady stream and stir until emulsified. Add salt to taste.

- Shred the cleaned romaine lettuce leaves and add to the salad bowl. Mix until salad is well coated with the dressing.

- Top with bacon, Parmesan and croutons.

- Serve and enjoy!

Serves 6–8

CHICORY CHORIZO SALAD

Chorizo is a Spanish pork sausage heavy on the garlic, paprika and spices. Very delicious. Chicory is a peppery and bitter green. Also delicious. Asiago is a semi-soft Italian cheese with a nice nutty taste. Mucho delicious. Put them all together in a bowl with some tomatoes and roast garlic dressing and BOOM, you've got yourself an amazing salad.

1/2-lb chorizo sausage

4 cups chicory, washed and cleaned (1 liter)

1/2 cup cilantro, chopped (125ml)

2 medium tomatoes cut into eighths

1 cup roasted garlic vinaigrette (250ml),
   store bought

1/4-lb Asiago cheese, finely shaved

Directions:

- Grill the sausage in a skillet over medium-low heat for 10 minutes to render fat.

- Remove from pan, drain on paper towels. Slice into thin discs and set aside.

- Place chopped chicory and cilantro into large bowl, add tomatoes and toss.

- Add Asiago cheese and cooled sausage.

- Drizzle the roasted garlic vinaigrette on the salad just before serving.

Serves 4

AVOCADO, GRAPEFRUIT, RED ONION AND FETA SALAD

I love a salad now and then that isn't just all greens with a bit of dressing. Peppery arugula, creamy avocado, tart grapefruit, salty feta and nippy onion make for a nice change with a great piece of fish and some good, crisp white wine.

2 large bunches arugula, washed and trimmed

2 large avocados, halved, pit removed,
*   peeled, sliced lengthwise*

1 large red or pink grapefruit, peeled and
*   sectioned, any juice reserved*

1 medium size red onion, thinly sliced

3 oz feta cheese, crumbled (about 1/2 cup)

1/2 cup best-quality plain yogurt (125ml)

3 tbsp honey (45ml)

1/3 cup fresh orange juice (83ml)

Salt and freshly ground black pepper to taste

Directions:

- In a bowl gently toss the arugula, avocado, grapefruit, onions and feta cheese.

- In a separate bowl combine yogurt, honey, grapefruit juice, orange juice, salt and pepper.

- Just before serving, spoon some of this dressing over the salad and toss until well coated.

Serves 6

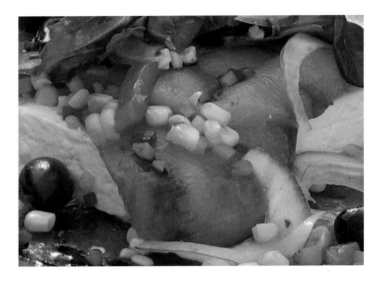

CORN, RED PEPPER AND ARUGULA SALAD

I'm a nut for arugula. Come summertime you can get the baby variety in most decent green grocers. If you go for the grown-up arugula, just remove the spines from some of the bigger leaves.

3 ears of corn, husks and silks removed

2 red bell peppers

1 yellow bell pepper

6 tbsp extra-virgin olive oil (90 ml)

4 cups arugula, washed and dried

1/2 cup sliced red onion (125 ml)

1/2 cup feta cheese, crumbled (125 ml)

2 tbsp balsamic vinegar (30ml)

Salt and pepper to taste

Directions:

- Crank barbecue to medium high and oil the grill.

- Drizzle the corn and peppers with 2 tbsp (30ml) of olive oil.

- Place the peppers on grill and cook for 7–8 minutes, turning every now and then, until peppers are charred and blistered. Remove and let cool.

- Place corn on grill for 4–5 minutes. Rotate the corn when the color turns vibrant yellow and slightly charred. Remove and let cool.

- Peel the skins and remove the seeds from the peppers and roughly dice (the pepper, not the seeds). Place the peppers in a large bowl. Strip the kernels from cobs and add to bowl.

- Add the arugula, red onion and feta.

- Before serving, drizzle balsamic vinegar and remaining olive oil over the salad and toss.

Serves 6

FENNEL & ORANGE SALAD

Fennel has a very mild sort of licorice flavor to it which plays off nicely against the sweet orange and peppery watercress in this salad. Normally I say load on the garlic but don't go too crazy here or you'll drown out the other flavors.

Dressing

1/2 cup fresh orange juice (125ml)

2/3 cup olive oil (150ml)

Splash of hot sauce

4 cloves garlic, minced

4 tbsp fresh flat leaf parsley, chopped (60ml)

Salt and pepper to taste

3 fennel bulbs, thinly sliced with core intact

3 oranges

1 large bunch of watercress, tough stems
    removed

1/2 cup honey-roasted macadamia
    nuts (125ml)

Directions:

- In a glass bowl, mix the dressing ingredients.

- Place thinly sliced fennel in a sealable plastic bag or a ceramic dish. Pour two-thirds of the dressing over the fennel and set the rest of the dressing aside. Seal the bag and place in the fridge for at least 5 hours. Remove from the fridge a good 30 minutes before grilling.

- Using a knife, trim the skin off of the oranges and segment the slices.

- Preheat the grill to medium high. Oil the grill and cook the fennel, lid up, for 3 minutes per side (depending on how thick you sliced it).

- Add orange slices to grill for last minute of grilling.

- Toss grilled fennel and orange with the watercress and honey-roasted macadamia nuts. Drizzle with the reserved marinade and serve while still warm.

Serves 6

TOMATO & GRILLED BREAD SALAD

This salad has been around probably as long as bread has. You can leave out the jalapeno and load up on the basil if you prefer.

3 1-inch thick slices of French bread

2 tbsp olive oil (30ml)

4 large vine-ripened tomatoes, cut in wedges

1/2 red onion, sliced thin

1 small jalapeno pepper, diced

2 cloves garlic

1/2 cup chopped chives (125ml)

3 tbsp basil, leaves torn (45ml)

1/4 cup balsamic vinegar (62ml)

1 tsp salt and pepper (5ml)

Directions:

- Preheat the grill to medium high.

- Rub olive oil on both sides of the sliced bread.

- Oil the grill and toast the bread until very crisp. Leave the slices to cool then cut them into 1 inch squares.

- Combine the remaining ingredients in a bowl and toss gently. Add bread cubes and toss again. Cover and let sit for 10 minutes before serving.

Serves 4

SUMMER POTATO SALAD

Hey, what's barbecue without potato salad, right? There's a whole lot of flavors and textures going on in this one with the cilantro, olives, celery and gherkins.

2 lbs small red or white new potatoes, scrubbed (907g)

1/3 cup fresh chopped parsley (80ml)

1/4 cup fresh chopped cilantro (60ml)

2 cups canned or jarred artichoke hearts, drained and quartered (500ml)

1 cup black kalamata olives, pitted (250ml)

2 large ribs celery, diced small

4 small gherkins, chopped fine

3 cloves garlic, minced

1/4 cup fresh lemon juice (60ml)

1 tsp salt (5ml)

1 tsp fresh black pepper (5ml)

1 tsp cumin (5ml)

1/2 tsp cayenne pepper (2.5ml)

1 tsp sugar (5ml)

1/2 tsp paprika (2.5ml)

1/2 cup olive oil (125ml)

Additional salt and pepper to taste

Directions:

- Place potatoes in a large uncovered pot of boiling salted water. Let potatoes boil for 5–7 minutes.

- Strain potatoes in a colander and run under cold water to stop the cooking process.

- When the potatoes are cooled, slice each in half. Place in a large bowl.

- Combine the potatoes with the parsley, cilantro, artichoke hearts, olives, chopped gherkins and celery ribs.

- Place garlic in a food processor and puree. Add the lemon juice, salt, pepper, cumin, cayenne, paprika and sugar. Blitz and slowly add the olive oil, processing until the dressing is thickened and emulsified.

- Mix the dressing with the salad and refrigerate for 30 minutes to infuse flavors.

- Add salt and pepper to taste.

Serves 6–8

BANANA AND SPUD SALAD

No we're not crazy. Okay, we are crazy *but* bananas and spuds really work in this off-the-wall play on the traditional potato salad. Make sure the bananas are a bit green so they hold up to the boiling water you're going to dunk them in.

2 lbs red or white baby potatoes (1kg)

1 1/2 lbs greenish bananas (4 or 5)

1 red onion, sliced thin

1 red bell pepper, sliced thin

1/4 cup capers, drained (60ml)

4 tbsp olive oil (60ml)

2 tbsp white wine vinegar (30ml)

1 tbsp Dijon mustard (15ml)

2 1/2 tsp salt (12.5ml)

1 tsp cracked black pepper (5ml)

3 tbsp chives (15ml)

Directions:

- Wash the potatoes with the skins on.

- Place the spuds in a pot of boiling water for 7 minutes, or until just cooked.

- Drain and run under cool water in a colander to stop the cooking process.

- Cool and cut into halves

- Bring another pot of water to a boil.

- Working quickly, peel bananas and begin slicing into boiling water to cook for just 30 seconds.

- Once cooked, drain the bananas in a colander.

- Place potatoes and bananas into bowl and add sliced onion, red pepper and capers.

- In a separate bowl whisk together olive oil vinegar, mustard, salt, pepper and chives. Pour over top and toss.

- Into the refrigerator to cool.

Serves 6–8

CABBAGE SALAD

1/2 head green cabbage, grated or sliced thin

1/2 head red cabbage, grated or slice thin

3 carrots cut into matchsticks

1 red pepper, sliced into strips

2 jalapeno, chopped

4 green onions, chopped

Dressing

1 cup sour cream (250ml)

3 tbsp mayonnaise (45ml)

2 tbsp apple cider vinegar (45ml)

2 tbsp smoked chipotle pepper,
*   chopped (45ml)*

1 tsp celery salt (5ml)

2 tbsp molasses (30ml)

Directions:

- Mix all ingredients for dressing in a large bowl.

- Add the fresh vegetables and toss.

- Place in the refrigerator for at least 2 hours for flavors to blend.

Serves 6

CARROT SALAD

Another way of doing this is to slice the carrots lengthwise and grill them 'til nicely charred, then toss with the dressing and serve as a side dish with salmon or chicken.

6 carrots, peeled, cut on a 1/4-inch bias

1 tbsp olive oil (15ml)

Salt and pepper to taste

1 cup sliced snow peas (250ml)

1 cup green pea shoots or salad greens (250ml)

Bamboo skewers soaked in water for 1 hour

Dressing

Juice of 2 oranges

Juice of 1 lime

1 tsp honey (5ml)

1 tsp chopped ginger (5ml)

1 tsp sugar (5ml)

Pinch of salt

Pinch of pepper

2 tbsp olive oil (30ml)

Directions:

- To prepare dressing, whisk together all ingredients in a medium sized bowl.

- Preheat the barbecue to medium high.

- Skewer the carrot strips onto soaked bamboo skewers.

- Place skewered carrots on grill for 1–2 minutes per side or until lightly charred.

- Remove carrots from grill and toss into a large salad bowl with snow peas, greens and salad dressing.

- Serve immediately.

Serves 4

GREEN BEAN SALAD

You can either serve this on its own as a starter or as a side dish with chicken or pork.

1 lb green beans (450 g)

3 cloves garlic

1/4 cup extra virgin olive oil (60ml)

2 tsp honey (10ml)

2 tbsp red wine vinegar (30ml)

1/2 cup hazelnuts, crushed (125ml)

1 cup shallots, thinly sliced (250ml)

1/2 cup pitted kalamata olives (125ml)

1 tsp salt (5ml)

1/2 tsp black pepper, freshly ground (2.5ml)

Directions:

- Bring water to a boil in a large pot, add the beans and cook for 2 minutes. Immediately strain and plunge the beans into a bowl full of ice water to stop the cooking process.

- Fine dice the garlic and add to a small bowl. Using a whisk add olive oil, honey and red wine vinegar.

- Pour mixture over beans add nuts, shallots, olives, and salt and pepper to taste.

- Toss and chill well before serving.

Serves 4

WILD RICE PECAN SALAD

Wild rice isn't actually a rice (it's a grain) and it has a nice bite and a great nutty flavor. Combined with the 'shrooms and cranberries this is a great side dish for steak or lamb or pork.

1 1/2 cups uncooked wild rice (375ml)

6 ounces wild mushrooms, cut into small
   thin slices

1/2 cup dried cranberries (125 ml)

3 green onions, minced

Zest of 1 orange

Dressing

2 tbsp olive oil (30ml)

Juice of 1 orange

1/2 tsp prepared horseradish (2.5ml)

Salt to season

1/2 cup pecan pieces toasted (125ml)

Directions:

- Cook the wild rice according the package instructions and pour the finished rice into a bowl to cool to room temperature.

- Add mushrooms, cranberries, green onion and orange zest.

- Whisk the ingredients for the dressing together in another bowl. Pour the dressing over the salad and mix it well.

- Cover the salad with plastic wrap and refrigerate for 1 hour to 24 hours.

- Place pecans on a tray and place on grill to toast.

- Stir the pecans into the salad and serve chilled.

Serves 6

PASTA SALAD WITH GRILLED CORN & JALAPENOS

For some reason, revenge and pasta salad are two dishes best served cold. *Al dente* is Italian for "to the tooth" and means cooking the pasta 'til it has a bit of resistance when you bite into it, maybe 2 minutes less than you normally would (depending on the pasta). There are a lot of steps here but it's a pretty easy recipe.

11 oz short pasta such as penne (453g)

4 ears fresh corn, shucked and silks removed

4 jalapeno chili peppers

1 large white onion, cut in 1/2-inch-thick rounds

Olive oil for drizzling

8 medium tomatoes

3 tbsp chopped fresh basil (45ml)

Directions:

• Lay corn, jalapenos and onion on baking sheet. Drizzle vegetables with olive oil.

• Preheat the barbecue to medium-high heat on one side and medium-low heat on the other.

• Oil the grill and add the onions to the medium-low side first, then add the corn and jalapenos to the medium-high heat side.

3 tbsp chopped fresh oregano (45ml)

3 tbsp chopped fresh cilantro (45ml)

1/3 cup green (hulled) pumpkin seeds (80ml)

1/4 cup olive oil (60ml)

4 cloves garlic, minced

1 tsp ground cumin (5ml)

Salt and pepper to taste

1 1/2 cups crumbled feta cheese (250 ml)

Garnish: fresh cilantro leaves

- Grill the onions to char, about 5 minutes.

- Grill the corn and jalapenos to char for about 2–3 minutes, turning to prevent burning.

- Remove the vegetables from grill and let cool to room temperature.

- Remove skins and seeds from jalapenos and place cleaned peppers into a bowl.

- Cut the corn off the cob and into the bowl.

- Chop the onion and quarter the tomatoes and then into the bowl.

- Add basil, oregano and cilantro.

- Meanwhile, cook pasta in a pot of boiling water, following instructions for al dente. Once cooked, place in colander to rinse under cold water. Shake off excess water and add to bowl. Drizzle with some olive oil.

- Next, in a non-stick skillet, toast the pumpkin seeds over low heat until lightly browned. Add to salad ingredients in bowl.

- In another non-stick skillet heat oil, add garlic and cumin. Cook for 3 minutes stirring with wooden spoon over medium-low heat. Add the flavored oil to the salad, toss, season with salt and pepper, refrigerate.

Serves 6–8

COUSCOUS SALAD WITH GRILLED VEGETABLES

Couscous looks like a little grain but is really granular semolina. A staple of North African cuisine, couscous cooks in no time and absorbs the flavor of whatever you add to it. It's a great, quick alternative when the family is tired of pasta. For added flavor use chicken or veggie stock instead of water for the couscous.

1 red onion cut into 3-inch wedges

2 medium zucchini, each cut lengthwise
 into 4 wedges

3 large leeks, (white and pale green parts
 only) quartered lengthwise

1 red bell pepper, cut into 3-inch strips

1/4 cup plus 4 tbsp of olive oil

2 1/2 cups water

1 tsp salt

1 10-oz box of couscous

3 tbsp balsamic vinegar

2 tbsp chopped fresh thyme

2 tbsp chopped fresh rosemary

2 tbsp chopped fresh oregano

4 tbsp thinly sliced fresh basil

6 tbsp fresh lemon juice

1 cup pitted and halved kalamata olives

4 tbsp drained capers

Directions:

- Preheat grill to medium high.

- Cut all of the vegetables into roughly the same size and place on a large platter. Drizzle with 4 tbsp of olive oil and ensure that everything is well coated.

- Season the vegetables generously with salt and pepper.

- Oil the grill and add the vegetable wedges. Grill for about 2–4 minutes per side, or until cooked through with nice grill marks. Remove and cool.

- In a large pot, bring the water to a boil. Place the dry couscous in a large bowl. Pour the boiling water overtop and cover in plastic wrap. Leave to sit for 5 minutes.

- Meanwhile, chop the grilled vegetables up into bite-sized pieces. When the couscous is ready, stir to fluff it up and mix in the vegetables.

- Add the remaining olive oil, herbs, lemon juice, olives and capers and mix.

- Cover again with plastic wrap and let sit at room temperature until ready to serve.

Serves 6

RAINBOW SALAD

All the colours of the rainbow in one salad bowl, plus lots of great flavors and contrasting textures. This is a salad with a big crunch.

1 yellow tomato, cut into 8 wedges

2 red tomatoes cut into 8 wedges

1 cucumber peeled, quartered
    lengthwise, seeded and chopped

1 red bell pepper, seeded and julienned

1 yellow bell pepper, julienned

1 small red onion, cut into thin wedges

1 stalk of celery, halved lengthwise
    and chopped

6 x radishes, cleaned and cut into disks

1 x jalapeno pepper, seeded and minced

Directions:

- Combine all of the salad ingredients into a large bowl.

- Drizzle with dressing of your choice and serve.

ROASTED PLUM TOMATOES

Plum tomatoes are also known as Italian tomatoes. They have a nice firm flesh which makes them excellent for grilling, then dicing up as a topping on bruschetta.

8 ripe plum tomatoes stem end removed
and cut in half lengthwise
1 tbsp extra virgin olive oil (15mL)
1 tbsp balsamic vinegar (15mL)
Salt and fresh ground pepper to taste

Directions:

- Prepare barbecue for grilling with indirect heat by preheating one side of the grill to 200F (100C) or medium-low heat and leaving the other side of the grill off.

- Drizzle olive oil on tomatoes and season with salt and pepper.

- Place tomatoes on non-heated side of grill and cook for 1 hour.

- Remove tomatoes and drizzle with balsamic vinegar.

- Serve with crusty bread or with a salad.

Serves 8

ROASTED VEGETABLE CALZONE

2 pre-made pizza dough

2 leeks white part only, cleaned and cut into 4 inch pieces (6.5cm)

2 red peppers cleaned and cut into 1 inch slices (1.6cm)

2 cups button mushrooms cleaned (500ml)

6 cloves of garlic with skins in tack

2 cups spinach cleaned (500ml)

3/4 cup goat cheese (185ml)

2 cups grated provolone cheese (500ml)

1/2 cup chopped sun dried tomatoes (125ml)

1/2 cup fresh basil chopped

2 tablespoons olive oil (30ml)

2 bamboo skewers soaked in water for 1 hour

Olive Crust

1/2 cup black kalamata olives pitted and halved (125ml)

1 teaspoon capers

6 cloves of roasted garlic

1/4 cup olive oil (60 ml)

The juice of 1 lemon

Egg Wash

1 egg

2 tablespoons water (30 ml)

Flour for dusting

Cornmeal for dusting

Pizza paddle

Directions:

- To prepare vegetables, cut leeks to size and leave the top root attached. Soak leeks standing up in a large container of cold water root side up. (Note leeks have a large amount of dirt between leaves; by soaking up side down the dirt will fall to the bottom of the container.

- You may have to repeat several times to remove all grit and dirt.

- Clean mushrooms by lightly brushing with a dry cloth or mushroom brush.

- Cut and remove seeds and veins from peppers.

- Place all vegetables in a large bowl.

- Toss vegetable with olive oil and season with salt and pepper.

- Place garlic cloves with skins in tack on soaked bamboo skewers.

- Preheat barbeque to 375°F/190°C or medium high heat.

- Oil preheated barbeque grate.

- Place leeks and garlic skewers on grill first and cook for 4 minutes. Flip leeks and add the mushrooms and peppers. Cook the mushrooms and peppers for 2 minutes per side (The vegetables should still be tender- crisp as you will be cooking them again later in the calzone). Remove all the vegetables. Place in tray and let cool.

- Peel the skins from garlic and set aside.

- Once vegetables are cool chop all into bite sized pieces and set aside.

- In a food processor combine olives, roasted garlic, lemon juice and capers, blend lightly with the pulse button of the blender. The mixture will be slightly chunky.

- Roll pizza dough into 2 x 12 inch rounds (2 x 19.6cm) on a large cutting board lightly dusted with flour and cornmeal.

- Smear olive mixture on half of the pizza dough. Leave a 1 inch (2.5cm) border around the outside. Repeat with the other rolled pizza dough. Place cheeses on top of ½ the olive crust then top with spinach, chopped vegetables and sun dried tomatoes. Sprinkle with freshly chopped basil.

- Make egg wash by whisking together egg with water in a small bowl. Using a pastry brush, brush egg wash over the empty half of the pizza dough's border. Carefully fold the crust over top the vegetable cheese mixture to form a half moon shape. Using your fingers or a fork press both edges together. You should have ½ moon shaped calzone. Repeat with the second olive crust.

- Place calzone on a cornmeal dusted pizza paddle.

- Preheat one side of the barbeque to 350°F/176°C or medium heat and the other side to 250°F/137°C or low heat .

- Place calzone on medium heat side for 3 minutes or until crust is hard and can calzone can be easily be moved.

- Move calzone over to low heat side and close lid on barbeque.

- Cook with lid down for 20 minutes or until crust is golden brown and crisp. The calzone will puff up to form what looks like a pillow.

- Remove calzone from grill with the pizza paddle.

- Cut in wedges and serve.

Serves 8 large wedges

ROASTED STUFFED PEPPERS

These roasted peppers are a main course in themselves or make for the perfect appetizer at a casual backyard dinner party. Nice thing is you can do all prep work in advance and hang out with your guests.

6 medium red, yellow and green bell peppers

1/4 cup unsalted butter (60mL)

3 tbsp corn oil (45mL)

3 cups corn kernels fresh or frozen (750mL)

1 large white onion chopped fine

1 small jalapeno pepper, chopped fine

1 small eggplant, chopped

1 medium zucchini, chopped

1 tsp white pepper (5mL)

Salt to taste

1 1/2 cups low sodium chicken stock (375mL)

1/2 cup 10% cream (125mL)

1 tsp hot sauce (5mL)

2 cups of dry cornbread crumbs (500mL)

1 egg, lightly beaten

1/4 cup fresh basil, chopped (60mL)

Directions:

- Slice the tops off of the peppers about a 1/2 inch (8 mm) from stems. Remove seeds and cores carefully. Cut a thin slice off of the bottom of each pepper without cutting into the cavity — this will allow them to stand without wobbling.

- Melt butter and oil in a medium size skillet over medium high heat. Add the corn, onion, jalapeno, chopped eggplant and zucchini. Season with salt and pepper. Sauté until fragrant and onions have become slightly translucent; about 5 minutes.

- Add the cream, stock and hot sauce. Cook the vegetable mixture until slightly thickened; about 7 minutes. Remove filling from heat and let cool.

- Stir cornbread crumbs into cooked filling mixture.

- Whisk the egg lightly in a bowl and stir into the filling until well distributed.

- Place peppers on tray and stuff each pepper equally with filling.

- Replace the tops to the peppers and secure with toothpicks.

- Preheat barbecue to 300F (148C) or medium-low.

- Place peppers on the upper bun rack of the grill and allow the peppers to cook for 40–45 minutes. Remove from heat and serve immediately.

Serves 6

ROCKET SALAD WITH
BASIL-OIL MAYONNAISE DRESSING

"Rocket" is another word for "arugula." Both are pretty cool names for this peppery tasting lettuce. The leftover basil oil can be used with pizza, pasta, grilled fish or grilled shrimp.

Basil Oil Mayonnaise Dressing

1 1/2 cups basil leaves stripped from
    their stock (375mL)

3/4 cup of sunflower oil (175mL)

4 tbsp of olive oil (60mL)

1/2 cup mayonnaise (125mL)

1/2 tsp Dijon mustard (2.5mL)

1 tsp lemon juice (5mL)

Salt and white pepper to taste

2 small handfuls of arugula

1/4 cup shallots, thinly sliced (60mL)

1/4 cup dried cranberries (60mL)

Directions:

- For basil oil, place basil leaves in a bowl and pour boiling water over them, leave for approximately 30 seconds until they turn a brighter green. Drain and refresh under cold running water, drain again and squeeze dry with paper towel. Place in a food processor and add both oils and process to a puree.

- Line sieve with cheese cloth and set it over a deep bowl. Pour basil oil puree and leave undisturbed for 1 hour, or until all the oil has filtered through into the bowl. The solids left behind in the sieve can now be discarded.

- Combine mayonnaise with a splash of basil oil. Add Dijon mustard, lemon juice and salt and pepper to taste. Cover well and chill until needed.

- Place cleaned arugula in a salad bowl and add shallots and cranberries. Just before serving toss salad with 1 tablespoon of basil oil mayonnaise dressing. Serve and enjoy!

SMOKED VIDALIA ONIONS

Cola on onions? You bet! It takes caramelizing to another level! Vidalias are one of the sweetest onions around and are worth watching for. Try this recipe with a nice Spanish onion or mini cippollinos when the Vidalia is out of season.

3 large Vidalia onions

Olive oil

1 can of cola

1 cup apple woodchips

Directions:

- Soak apple woodchips in cold water for 30 minutes

- If using a charcoal grill, arrange coals to heat only one side of the grill. If using a gas grill, use only one burner, leaving one side of the barbecue cool. Preheat barbecue to 220F (110C). Drain apple woodchips, place them in a foil pouch, pierce it with holes, and place on the hot side of the grill.

- Slice each onion in half and peel the outer layer. Cut down to, but not through, the base of each onion half in crisscross directions to make an onion "flower."

- Rub a thin coat of oil over the onions and wrap each half in foil. Transfer onions to barbecue, close cover and smoke for 30 minutes.

- Open foil from the top of onions and drizzle with oil and pour cola over top; this will caramelize the onion and give it an amazing taste. Seal foil, close lid and smoke for another 30 minutes or until onion is tender.

Serves 6

SMOKEY SOUTHWESTERN RICE

If you want to add an extra smokey kick to this dish, then get yourself a bottle of liquid hickory smoke and add it to the water you boil the rice in. Excellent!

2 tbsp of cooking oil (30mL)

4 strips bacon, cut into 1/4-inch slivers

1 medium onion, finely chopped

1 medium green bell pepper, stemmed seeded and finely chopped

5 cloves garlic, minced

2 tsp dried basil (10mL)

2 tsp fresh thyme (10mL)

Salt to taste

1 tsp freshly ground black pepper (5mL)

3 tbsp tomato paste (45mL)

1/2 tsp sugar (2.5mL)

5 1/2 cups water (or more if needed) (1375mL)

3 cups long grained rice (375mL)

2 tbsp fresh lime juice (30mL)

1 can cooked kidney beans (15oz)

Directions:

- Heat the oil in a large heavy pot over a medium heat. Add bacon and cook until crispy. Add onion, bell pepper, basil, thyme, salt and pepper and cook until onion is golden brown.

- Stir in tomato paste and sugar and cook for approximately 2 minutes.

- Add water and bring to boil.

- Reduce heat to low. Add rice and lime juice and cover and return to a boil. Cook for approximately 15 minutes or until rice is tender. Add a few tablespoons of water if rice needs to continue cooking.

- Stir in kidney beans during the last 3 minutes of cooking. Remove pot from heat and let stand for 5 minutes.

- Just before serving fluff rice and beans with fork and correct seasoning, adding salt and or black pepper as needed.

Serves 8

SNOW PEA SALAD WITH LIME-INFUSED SHRIMP

The biggest mistake most people make in marinating seafood is in the timing. Marinades have an acidic component (in this recipe it's rice vinegar and lime juice) that "cooks" the seafood while it's marinating. Too long and you get rubbery seafood.

18 large tiger prawns (21–25/lb),
    peeled and deveined
6 bamboo skewers soaked in water for 1 hour

Shrimp Marinade

Juice of 1 lime

1 tbsp rice vinegar (15mL)

2 tbsp honey (30mL)

Pinch cilantro, chopped (60mL)

1 tsp jalapeno pepper, finely chopped (5mL)

1/4 cup peanut oil (60mL)

3 kaffir lime leaves, finely chopped

Directions:

- Combine marinade ingredients for shrimp. Place shrimp in a sealable plastic bag. Pour marinade over shrimp, seal plastic bag and refrigerate for 30 minutes.

- Preheat barbecue to 400F (200C) or high heat, and oil grill.

- Remove shrimp from marinade. Discard the leftover marinade.

- Place 3 shrimp on each skewer.

- Season shrimp with salt and pepper

- Oil grill and place the shrimp on the barbecue for 1–1 1/2 minutes per side or until cooked through.

- Serve with Snow Pea Salad

Snow Pea Salad

4 cups snow peas, cleaned and sliced
   into strips (1L)

1 red pepper, sliced thin

1 yellow pepper, sliced thin

1 red onion, sliced thin

Dressing

1 tbsp peeled and minced ginger (15mL)

2 large garlic cloves, minced

1/4 cup rice vinegar (60mL)

1 tbsp brown sugar (15mL)

1/4 cup vegetable oil (125mL)

Juice of 2 limes

3 tbsp soy sauce (45mL)

4 tbsp dark sesame oil (60mL)

1/4 cup toasted sesame seeds (60mL)

Pepper to taste

Snow Pea Salad Directions:

- Place sliced snow peas in a large bowl. Add peppers and onions.

Dressing Directions:

- Combine the ginger, garlic, vinegar, sugar, oil, lime juice and soy sauce in a small bowl.

- Whisking vigorously, add the sesame oil and pepper to taste.

- Lightly toss the dressing over salad and sprinkle with sesame seeds.

- Serve with Lime-Infused Shrimp

Serves 6

SWEET POTATOES WITH ORANGE PECAN BUTTER

Sweet potatoes have fewer calories than the regular variety of spud. Feel better? Okay, you're going to love this dish, especially the way the honey plays off the orange juice with a kick from the chilis at the end.

6 small sweet potatoes

1/4 cup vegetable oil (60mL)

Orange Pecan Butter

1/2 cup unsalted softened butter (125mL)

2 tsp liquid honey (10mL)

Juice and zest of 2 oranges

1/4 cup chopped roasted pecans (60mL)

1/2 tsp dry mustard (2.5mL)

1/2 tsp dried chili (2.5mL)

Salt and pepper to taste

Directions:

- Preheat barbecue to 220F (104C) or medium heat.

- Scrub sweet potatoes clean and prick all over with a fork. Rub with oil and season with salt and pepper. Wrap with aluminum foil.

- Place the wrapped potatoes on the grill and allow to cook for 2 hours or until potatoes are fork tender.

- Meanwhile, prepare Orange Pecan Butter. Combine ingredients in a small saucepan and cook over low heat for 1 minute.

- Remove potatoes from grill and carefully peel back the foil.

- Slice potatoes lengthways and drizzle with Orange Pecan Butter before serving.

Serves 6

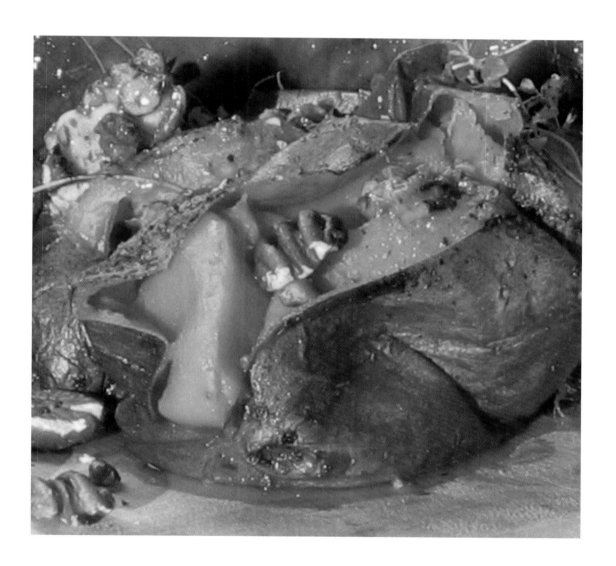

TOMATOES STUFFED WITH CHEESE AND VEGETABLES

Look for big round beefsteak tomatoes that have enough body to act as a bowl for all the other good stuff in this recipe. Slippery, fall-through-the grill onions? Put them on a skewer. Make sure to slice onions about 1/2-inch thick. Push skewer through and thread as many as your skewer will hold. Makes turning them with tongs a snap!

4 large ripe tomatoes

Kosher salt

Stuffing

1 medium red onion, cut crosswise into
  1/3-inch slices

1/2 medium red bell pepper and green
  pepper, stem and seeds removed,
  cut into flat pieces

1 medium zucchini cut lengthways in
  1/3-inch slices.

1 cucumber, cut crosswise 1/3-inch slices

2 tablespoons extra virgin olive oil (30mL)

3/4 cup goat cheese (190mL)

1 tablespoon finely chopped fresh
  basil (15 mL)

1 teaspoon balsamic vinegar (5 mL)

Salt and pepper to taste

Directions:

- Cut a 1/2 inch slice off the top of each tomato. Scoop out the center. Discard.

- Lightly salt the inside of tomatoes and tip upside down over paper towels.

- Preheat grill with one side on medium heat and the other side on medium high.

- Season the onions, peppers and zucchini with salt and pepper and drizzle with oil.

- Place the onions over the medium heat side and grill for 3–4 minute per side, or until nice char marks are achieved.

- Place the zucchini and peppers on the medium high side and grill for 2 minutes per side or until nice char marks are achieved.

- Let cool and cut into 1/2 inch small pieces. Combine the chopped grilled vegetables, cucumber, cheese, basil, and vinegar into a bowl and stir.

- Spoon the vegetable stuffing into the tomatoes.

- Grill the tomatoes on the top warming rack of barbecue until cheese is melted.

Serves 4

TOMATOES WITH MOZZARELLA CHEESE

Garlic and oregano infusing gooey melted mozzarella cheese inside a piping hot sweet fleshy tomato? How do you spell summer eats? To roast garlic, cut the top third off of a whole clove of garlic so that each clove is exposed. Pour a bit of olive oil over it and sprinkle with salt. Loosley wrap it up in tin foil and place on the grill (indirect heat) for about 30 minutes. To remove cloves, squeeze the root.

8 medium tomatoes

4 cloves garlic, thinly sliced

8 tbsp shredded or small chunks of
   mozzarella cheese (1 tbsp per tomato)
   (120 mL)

8 tsp extra virgin olive oil (40mL)

Salt and fresh-ground black pepper

1-2 tbsp of minced fresh oregano (155mL)

Directions:

- Preheat grill for 10– 15 minutes, with all burners on high.

- Remove and save the top of each tomato (top 1/4 of the tomato). Remove 1/2 of the core from each tomato and discard, leaving a hollowed-out tomato with the base intact.

- Place half of a garlic slice and 1 tbsp of mozzarella cheese into each tomato cavity. Drizzle with olive oil and sprinkle with salt, pepper and oregano.

- Replace tomato tops and grill the tomatoes in a grill plate/basket or on a tray with the cut side of the tomato up. BBQ for 10 minutes or until tomatoes are soft to touch. Serve and enjoy! Great with roasted garlic.

Serves 8

WATERCRESS SALAD WITH ORANGE & TEQUILA DRESSING

Jicama is also known as a "Mexican potato" and can now be found in most major grocery stores. It has a sweet nutty flesh that chops up pretty easily. In this dish it gets matched up with tart tangerine and peppery watercress.

Salad

3 large bunches watercress with
   tough stems removed

2 tangerines with membrane removed
   and sectioned

3/4 cup diced jicama (175mL)

1/2 cup of mild red radishes thinly
   sliced (125mL)

1/4 cup sliced green onions (60mL)

Dressing

1/4 cup fresh orange juice (60mL)

1/4 cup vegetable oil (60mL)

2 tbsp tequila (30mL)

2 tbsp of lime juice (30mL)

2 tsp of honey (10mL)

1 clove of garlic

Directions:

- Combine salad ingredients in a salad bowl, and toss.

- For dressing, combine ingredients in a blender and pulse until mixture is smooth.

- Drizzle the dressing over salad, toss and enjoy!

Serves 4

YAM POTATO TOWER

4 large yams sliced 1/2-inch thick on an angle

Salt and pepper to taste

2 tbsp olive oil (30mL)

Filling

1 cup crumbled goat cheese (250mL)

3 tbsp basil (45mL)

Salt to taste

Pepper to taste

1/2 cup toasted pecans, crumbled (125mL)

Zest of one lemon

Directions:

- Preheat grill to 375F (190C) or medium-high heat.

- Drizzle yams with olive oil, salt and pepper.

- Sear on medium-high heat 1–2 minutes per side or until slightly softened.

- Remove from grill and allow to cool.

- Reduce grill temperature to 325F (162C) or medium-low heat.

- On a tray layer one disk of yam with filling and top with another yam disk. Layer more cheese and top with a third yam disk. Repeat until you have 6 yam towers.

- Place foil on grill and then place yam towers on foil.

- Grill with lid closed for 4–5 minutes or until fully warmed. Serve and enjoy.

Serves 6

What's Your Beef?

Apple-Stuffed Veal with Minty Rub

Beef Brisket

Beef Short Ribs

Cherry wood-Smoked Veal Chops with
Apple Brandy Sauce

Hickory Smoked Veal and Spinach Stuffed
Beef Butt Roast

Mushroom Pecan Veal Chops

Papaya-Glazed Veal Ribs

Seared Beef on Thyme Crostini with
Cranberry Chutney

Sirloin Steak with Onion-Garlic Mustard
Sauce

Slow-Smoked Beef Ribs

Spicy Grilled Beef Short Ribs

Chicago Pizza Burgers

Korean Beef Ribs

Rotisserie Prime Rib with Mashed Roast
Sweet Potatoes

Five-spice Beef Kebab

Grilled Filet Mignon with Stuffed Pears

Grilled Rib Steak with Wine Sauce

Hamburgers with Homemade Ketchup

Texas Beef Sandwiches with Barbecue
Sauce

Smoked Beef Brisket

Smoked Hot Dogs

Southwestern Veal Shoulder

Tuscan Grilled Veal Chops

Smoked Veal Loaf

Seafood Stuffed Veal Tenderloin

Mushroom and Nut Crusted Veal Chops

Rotisserie Veal Roast with Pesto Cream
Sauce

Prosciutto-Wrapped Veal

Jerk Mango-Glazed Veal Ribs

Spicy Beef Skewers with Sour Cream

Veal Chops with a Port and Red Wine Glaze

No, Buffalo wings don't come from buffalos, and "chicken of the sea" isn't chicken at all, for that matter. Confusing? Well, when it comes to beef, there are so many different cuts of meat that are perfect for the grill, that it too can be a bit overwhelming. Learn the basic cuts to diversify your repertoire and beef up your palate.

A Little On The Chewy Side

There is a reason why beef is such a popular choice for the grill, as opposed to say, cottage cheese. First, the animal itself offers an abundance of choices – eight primal cuts (areas of the cow) in all. And of course once you've mastered the art of preparing the many different cuts, the chews you choose will be less chewy to chew (forgive me, I couldn't help myself). Here's a quick – very quick – overview:

Chuck/shoulder: Located right near the neck section of the cow along the side and top running to the fifth rib. Meat from this section tends to be a bit on the fatty side, but flavorful. As it has a lot of connective tissue, it's a popular choice for hamburgers. If not ground, it will need a low-and-slow method for cooking in order to tenderize it.

Rib: The rib cut section sits next to the chuck towards the back of the animal. It starts at the sixth rib and extends to the twelfth. This area produces meat that has a robust beefy flavor with some tenderness to it. Prime rib and rib-eye steaks come from this area.

Short Loin (or loin): The short loin cut comprises of the last rib to the end of the midsection of the animal. Several wonderful choices come from this area. The tenderloin, also known as filet mignon is the most tender cut on the cow and has an extremely mild flavor. Strip steaks, also known as shell steaks, come from here, as do T-bone and porterhouse steaks. The T-Bone and porterhouse both contain a bit of the tenderloin and make for a feast.

Sirloin: Still following along the top sections of the cow, the sirloin contains cuts of meat that are relatively inexpensive. These cuts also tend to be a bit on the tougher side and are suitable for low-and-slow roasting. Top sirloin is usually the suggested choice here.

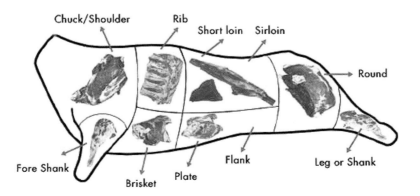

Tip – a little secret is the tri-tip, also called a triangle roast, which comes from the bottom part of the sirloin. It is triangular in shape and usually weighs about 1 1/2 –2 pounds. It can be roasted whole, cut into steaks, or into cubes for kebabs and stir fries. There is only one per cow, so butchers in the past have usually ground it, as there weren't enough for a whole display. Great full taste, but very lean, so it can be dry if not properly marinated or cooked carefully.

Round: Taking up the rear, these cuts are fairly low in fat but can be quite fibrous. Top round is the best of the bunch and with some practice can be seared, then roasted quite nicely.

Flank / Plate / Brisket/Shank: Continuing back to front, these areas make up the smaller underside sections of the animal, where boneless cuts usually on the thicker side are found. The brisket is used a lot in the low-and-slow roasting methods. The plate is usually not sold on a commercial level but rather used in the production of deli meats like pastrami. Flank steak however, is a wonderful choice on the grill – it is meaty flavored and tender.

Whatcha Lookin' At?

You've been standing in the beef section of your grocery store for ten minutes. There's a shopping-cart traffic jam around you and people are giving you dirty looks as they try to squeeze by. What are you looking at? Staring into the display, visions of the perfect barbecue swirl through your head; your family gathered around you gazing up at you adoringly – even your mother-in-law is in awe of your cooking prowess – and then it happens. You break out into a cold sweat as you suddenly realize you don't have a clue which of the dozens of packages to buy.

Choosing fresh, high-quality beef is not as confusing as it would appear. Besides, the government has already very kindly narrowed down most of the choices in quality for us. This is a voluntary program on the part of the meat packers and for our purposes we'll focus on three of the eight grades available.

"**Prime**" cuts are heavily marbled and therefore very moist, if cooked properly. These cuts are mostly sold to restaurants, butchers and high-end grocers. "**Choice**" cuts are most readily available to the public and have varied levels of marbling. And finally, there are "**Select**" cuts. They have very little marbling and tend to be slightly tougher than the other two grades.

Marbling: Look for meat that is slightly marbled in texture. It helps to impart a rich, robust, distinctly beef flavor. By marbled I mean thin white streaks of fat spread throughout the meat. Avoid big clumps of fat, as it doesn't break down evenly and can be quite tough and unpleasant to eat. Marbling will help the meat stay tender, infusing it with an almost "buttery" feel.

Color: A piece of meat that is a bit older and perhaps tougher in texture tends to be darker in color – a burgundy/brown. Look for brighter reds that are uniform in color throughout.

Purge: The meat should hold water and liquid. If you notice a lot of red juice (blood and water) in the package, it is called purge. This is either the result of freezing that wasn't done properly (perhaps frozen and thawed twice), or meat that is just old. Purged meat will not be as juicy as it should be when cooked.

Smell: If you're buying meat from a butcher, have a quick smell. It should smell mild and non-offensive. If it smells gamey and tweaks your nose even a bit, ask for a different cut.

Firmness: The meat should have a firm feel to it, with a slight spring. If it feels either too hard or too soft, avoid it. It will be either tough and/or flavorless.

I know this seems like a lot to go through for a bit of beef, so if you live in an area with a butcher you trust, either in the grocery store or the shop down the street, I suggest you buy your meat there. You'll be dealing with people who handle the cuts on a regular basis and know what it is you're buying. They'll be able to steer you in the right direction.

The Maillard Reaction (no, not a duck allergy)

Is there anything more appetizing than a steak that is perfectly browned on the outside, especially with those "professional-looking" grill marks that you see in commercials? Still warm, with a shiny buttery look to it – mmm! Well, that browning effect is so desired that it actually has a name. It's called the Maillard Reaction, so named after the French chemist who discovered it a hundred years ago.

The Maillard Reaction occurs when the amino acids, or proteins, mix with the naturally occurring sugars in the meat and together come in contact with high heat. They start a reaction, which turns the meat brown, helping to form a crust on the outside. Almost every self respecting meat eater loves that crust! If your heat is too low, the meat will tend to steam and won't have that brown color to it. Not only is that not as appetizing, but it's also not as flavorful.

Are You Done Yet?

How do you tell if your meat is done? Well, if you're a fourth-generation barbecuer who was born with a silver tong in your hand, you probably go by instinct and experience. But if you're like the rest of us and want a more accurate method, I'd suggest the good old "instant read thermometer." Insert the thermometer into the center of your meat and compare:

Rare 125F (51C)
Medium-Rare 130F (54C)
Medium 140F (60C)

Medium-Well 150F (65.5C)
Well-Done 160F (71C)

Health guidelines suggest that cooking meat to 160F will ensure that all bacteria and pathogens are killed off. Now, although that is very important indeed, the more the meat is cooked, the more the fibers contract and release their juice, which results in a drier piece of meat. Let personal preferences along with the guidelines become your standard.

A Tent In The Kitchen?

A tent in the kitchen? You bet! I know you've been paying attention to everything I've written thus far, so your meat, when it's ready to come off the grill is going to look like sheer perfection. You're going to be hungry and ready to dive in. Hold on a minute, though! Erect a tent I say. That's right, put a piece of foil, or a bowl, or some kind of lid over that piece of art you've just created and wait 5–10 minutes.

As meat is exposed to heat and cooks it coagulates, and the juices from the outside move toward the cooler center of the meat. If you cut your meat right away while it's still piping hot, all the juices from the center will come out onto your plate. Give the meat a rest and let it sit. This will allow some of the fibers to re-absorb the juices and help the meat to be more uniformly juicy. Enjoy!

I am a great eater of beef, and I believe that does harm to my wit.
–WILLIAM SHAKESPEARE

APPLE-STUFFED VEAL WITH MINTY RUB

Apple is a classic combo with veal or pork (you can substitute a nice pork roast for the veal if you'd like). Ask your butcher for the double smoked bacon—it's worth the trip to go and get it.

4 lb boneless veal loin roast (2 kg)

Dry Rub

1/3 cup dried mint (75mL)

1 tbsp fresh rosemary, chopped (15mL)

1/4 teaspoon freshly ground black
*   pepper (1mL)*

2 tsp garlic powder (10mL)

2 tsp kosher salt (10mL)

Stuffing

1 tbsp olive oil (15mL)

1 large Granny Smith apple, peeled and diced

1/2 lb double smoked bacon, cooked
*   and crumbled (250g)*

1 tsp lemon juice (5mL)

1 tsp fresh lemon thyme, chopped (5mL)

2 cups sweet apple cider (500mL)

2 rosemary sprigs

Small bunch fresh mint leaves

Directions:

- Combine dry rub ingredients in a small bowl. Toss to mix well.

- Place the veal in a large sealable plastic bag. Add the rub and shake well, coating the veal loin. Remove the veal from the bag and set aside.

- In a non-stick skillet, heat olive oil on medium-high heat. Cook apples for 10 minutes or until softened. Let cool. In a bowl combine the apple, bacon, lemon juice and lemon thyme. Mix well.

- Cut a wide, deep slit into the side of the roast. Stuff the pocket with the apple mixture. Tie the roast at 1-inch (2.5 cm) intervals with heavy string.

- Place a drip pan under the grill of the barbecue, pour in the cider and add the rosemary sprigs and mint leaves. Preheat the barbecue to high heat 325°F/160°C. Leave one burner off. Place roast over grill with no heat. Cook over indirect heat for 2 hours.

- Take veal off the barbecue and let rest for 10 minutes before serving.

Serves 6–8

BEEF BRISKET

Okay, this one takes a bit of effort. But c'mon . . . you get to do your own brisket! As always, experiment with the rub ingredients and come up with your own secret mix.

8 lb beef brisket with 1/2-inch fat cap (4kg)

12 cups apple woodchips

Meat injector needle

Dry Rub

1/2 cup brown sugar (125mL)

2 tbsp chili flakes (30mL)

1 tsp nutmeg (5mL)

1 tsp dried thyme (5mL)

1 tsp oregano (5mL)

2 tsp ground cinnamon (10mL)

1 tsp ground ginger (5mL)

1 tsp coriander (5mL)

2 tsp dry mustard (10mL)

1 tbsp ground black pepper (30mL)

Marinade

1/4 cup apple cider (60mL)

1 tbsp cider vinegar (15mL)

1/4 cup beef broth (60mL)

1 tsp hot sauce (5mL)

1 tsp dried mustard (5mL)

2 tsp pepper (10mL)

1 tsp onion powder (5mL)

1/4 cup melted butter (60mL)

Directions:

- Combine dry rub ingredients and rub into brisket.

- Combine marinade ingredients in a large measuring cup.

- Fill meat injector needle with marinade and inject the rub-covered beef brisket throughout (follow manufacturer's instructions).

- Cover with plastic wrap and refrigerate overnight or up to 24 hours

- Soak 8 cups of apple woodchips in water.

- Build a smoke pouch by squeezing the excess water from 2 cups (500mL) of wet woodchips and place on a large piece of aluminum foil. Place 1 cup (250mL) of dry woodchips on top and mix them together. Close foil around chips to make a sealed package. Using a fork, puncture holes in both sides of the pack to allow smoke to flow through and infuse the meat. Make a total of 4 foil pouches.

- Place drip pan underneath one side of grill. Place smoke pouch on the opposite side. Turn heat on under the smoke pouch to 350F (175C). Close lid and wait for smoke.

- Place brisket on cool side of grill over the drip pan. Close lid. Allow brisket to slowly smoke for 8 hours, change smoke pouches when smoke dissipates (approximately every 2 hours).

- Remove beef brisket from heat, cover with aluminum foil and allow to rest for 15 minutes. Carve against the grain and serve on crusty buns with mustard & pickles.

Serves 8

BEEF SHORT RIBS

Once upon a time, beef short ribs were cheap, cheap, cheap. Not so much any more because everyone wants to do them now. But they are SO worth the effort.

4 beef short ribs, bone in

Dry Rub

1 tbsp Five Spice Powder

1/3 cup of brown sugar (83mL)

3 tbsp of garlic salt (45mL)

3 tbsp celery salt (45mL)

Five Spice Powder

1 tbsp cinnamon

1 tsp ground cloves

1 tbsp ground star anise

1 tbsp freshly ground pepper

2 tsp onion powder

3 cups of woodchips (cherry or apple)
    (750mL)

Directions:

- Combine all of the rub ingredients in a large bowl. Rub half of the rub mixture into the ribs and reserve the other half of the rub for use the next day. Place the ribs in a large plastic bag and refrigerate overnight.

- A half hour before you plan to put the ribs on the grill, remove them from the plastic bag and apply the remaining rub from the night before, leaving approximately 2 tablespoons to sprinkle on the ribs while they smoke.

- Let the ribs stand for half an hour to come to room temperature. This will ensure that they cook evenly on the grill.

- Place 1 cup of the woodchips in cold water to soak for half an hour.

- If your grill has several grates, remove one on the far side and set it aside. Preheat the grill to high heat – approximately 400–450 F (200–225C).

- Squeeze the excess water from the soaking woodchips and place in the center of a large piece of tin foil. Add the remaining 2 cups of dry woodchips. Fold the aluminum foil around the chips to create a sealed pouch. Using a fork, poke holes in the package on both sides to allow the smoke to filter through.

- Place the smoke package directly over the flame on the far side where the grate has been removed. Close the lid and wait for smoke to start building in the barbecue.

- Once smoking has begun, lower the heat under the woodchip pouch and turn the heat off on the other portions of the grill. Wait for the temperature to reach approximately 200F (100C).

- Place the ribs on the grates where the heat is off. Close the lid and leave to smoke with indirect heat for approximately 4 hours. After 11/2– 2 hours flip the ribs and sprinkle with remaining rub mixture.

- After 4 hours, the ribs should have a crispy, delicious exterior and the meat should be almost falling off the bone.

Serves 4

CHERRY WOOD-SMOKED VEAL CHOPS WITH APPLE BRANDY GLAZE

Make sure you get a nice smoke going and have extra packs of woodchips ready to go. Low and slow is the order of this day!

10 veal loin chops, 1-inch thick (16mm)

Marinade

1/2 cup Calvados (125mL)

5 cloves garlic, crushed

4 tbsp olive oil (45mL)

1 tbsp fresh oregano (15mL)

1 tsp fresh thyme, chopped (2.5mL)

1/4 tsp freshly ground pepper (1.25mL)

1/2 fennel bulb, sliced thinly, divided in two

6 cups (1L) cherry woodchips

Directions:

- Combine all the marinade ingredients into a bowl and mix to combine. Slice the fennel and add half to the marinade. Reserve the other half for the smoking pouch. Place the veal in a sealable plastic bag and pour marinade over top. Seal the bag and toss to ensure the veal is well coated with marinade. Refrigerate for 6 hours or overnight.

- Remove the veal from the marinade and allow the meat to come to room temperature.

- Place 4 cups (750 mL) of cherry woodchips (for a gas grill or all the woodchips if using a charcoal grill) into water to soak for 1 hour.

- Prepare the barbecue for smoking. Preheat the barbecue to 400F (200C) or high heat on one side, leaving the other side off. Remove barbecue grate on heat side.

- To make a smoke pouch, squeeze the excess water from the woodchips and place 2 cups in the center of a large piece of foil. Add 1 cup dry chips, the remainder of the sliced fennel and mix (makes 2 pouches). Close the foil around the chips sealing the package. Using a fork, poke holes in both sides of the package. Place 1 smoke pouch directly over high heat source of the grill, close the lid and wait for smoke. If using charcoal, squeeze the excess water from the chips and sprinkle the chips directly into the fire bed.

- When the smoke has filled the cavity of the barbecue, open the lid and place the veal over the "off" side of the grill. Close the lid.

- Smoke the veal for 1 hour and 15 minutes, changing the smoke pouch half way through cooking or when necessary. Remove veal and loosely cover with foil. Let meat rest 5 minutes before serving.

Serves 6

HICKORY SMOKED VEAL AND SPINACH STUFFED BEEF BUTT ROAST

1 pound ground veal (454g)

5 strips double smoked bacon

1 medium onion fine dice

2 cloves of garlic fine dice

2 tablespoons fresh chopped basil (30ml)

2 tablespoons olive oil (30ml)

1 tablespoon Dijon mustard (15ml)

2 teaspoons chili powder (10ml)

Salt and Pepper

4 cups spinach, blanched and refreshed (1 litre)

8 slices of Beef Butt Roast, sliced into 1/16"

slices approx 3" x 4" (ask your butcher)

2 lemons

3 cups hickory wood chips (350ml)

Directions:

- Prepare smoke pouch. Place 2 cups (500ml) of hickory wood chips into a bowl of cold water to soak for 1 hour. Reserve 1 cup (250ml) dry wood chips.

- In a sauté pan set over medium heat cook bacon until crisp. Remove bacon & drain on paper towels. Drain off bacon fat leaving 1 tablespoon in the pan. Over medium heat sauté onions, garlic & chilli powder until soft. Remove, allow to cool , then place in a bowl. Add bacon, Dijon, veal, and basil. Mix to combine and season with salt & pepper.

- Cut Beef Butt Roast into ½ inch thick slices. Season with salt and pepper. Cover with spinach and drizzle with lemon juice. Place cooled veal mixture over the spinach and roll into individual beef cigars and place on a tray. Use a toothpick to secure if necessary. Drizzle outside with oil and season with salt and pepper.

- To build a smoke pouch, drain 2 cups (500ml) of the wet wood chips and squeeze excess water out. Spread wet wood chips on a large piece of aluminum foil. Place 1 cup (250ml) of dry wood chips on top and mix them together. Close the foil around the chips to make a sealed foil package. Use a fork to puncture holes in the top and bottom of the foil pack to allow the smoke to flow through and infuse the meat.

- Prepare barbecue for direct grilling to sear the beef. Preheat the grill to medium-high heat. Oil the grill and place the beef on turning onto all sides to achieve nice char marks, about 1 minute per side.

- Switch the BBQ to indirect grilling by switching one side off and reducing the heat on the other side to 220ºF/110ºC. Place the smoke pouch directly over the heat source. Close the lid and wait for smoke. Once BBQ is smoking, place the beef on the side of the BBQ without direct heat. Smoke the beef over indirect heat for 45.

- Remove and let rest for 5 minutes before serving.

MUSHROOM PECAN VEAL CHOPS

These chops are even better if you let them marinate overnight. Ask your butcher to cut the chops for you "bone on". It looks better when they hit the plate.

4 veal chops, 1-inch-thick each, about

12 ounces (350g)

Marinade

1/2 cup white wine (125mL)

Juice of 1 lemon

3 sprigs sage, chopped

Splash of walnut oil

Pepper to taste

Pecan and Mushroom Dry Rub

1/2 cup dried wild mushrooms (125mL)

1/2 cup pecans (125mL)

2 tbsp dried oregano (30mL)

Salt and pepper to taste

Directions:

- Combine marinade ingredients in a small bowl. Place the veal into a sealable plastic bag, pour the marinade over top, make sure the meat is covered entirely and refrigerate for at least 1 1/2 hours.

- To prepare the rub, in a blender or a coffee grinder, grind the mushrooms to fine dust. Let the dust settle a bit and add the remaining ingredients to the blender or grinder. Combine long enough to make a coarse meal out of the pecans. Pour into a small bowl and rub onto the veal.

- Grill at 350F (175C) for 8 minutes on each side. Serve and enjoy!

Serves 4

PAPAYA-GLAZED VEAL RIBS

Yes, veal ribs. You don't see them very often but they are amazing. Watch your butcher's face light up when you ask for them. He'll know you're a real BBQ god. If you can't find papaya purée, then papaya juice will do just as well.

2 x 5 lb racks of veal ribs (2 x 2.5 kg)

9 cups apple woodchips (2 litres)

Marinade

6 whole green onions

3 tbsp fresh thyme leaves (45mL)

1/2 tsp ground allspice (2.5mL)

1 tsp salt (5mL)

1 1/2 tsp ground black pepper (7.5mL)

1 tsp nutmeg (5mL)

1 tsp cinnamon (5mL)

4 cloves garlic, finely minced

2 tbsp finely minced ginger (30mL)

1 scotch bonnet pepper, finely minced,
*   seeds removed*

1 cup papaya purée (250mL)

4 tbsp light soy sauce (60mL)

2 tbsp cider vinegar (30mL)

1/2 cup vegetable oil (125mL)

1/2 cup dark rum (125mL)

Juice of 1 lime

Directions:

- In a food processor combine all marinade ingredients and process until a smooth paste is achieved. Set aside 1/2 cup (125mL) of the marinade for basting.

- Place veal ribs on a large, non-reactive tray and pour marinade over top. Turn veal to ensure all meat is covered.

- Cover with plastic wrap and place veal in the refrigerator to marinate overnight.

- Place 6 cups (1.5L) of the woodchips to soak for 1 hour.

- Build three smoke pouches: lay out 3 sheets of aluminum foil. Build a smoke pouch by squeezing the excess water from 2 cups (500mL) of wet woodchips and place on a large piece of aluminum foil. Sprinkle some rum over wet chips. Place 1 cup (250mL) of dry woodchips on top and mix them together. Wrap the foil up loosely to create a square pouch. Using a fork, poke holes in the foil to allow the smoke to escape.

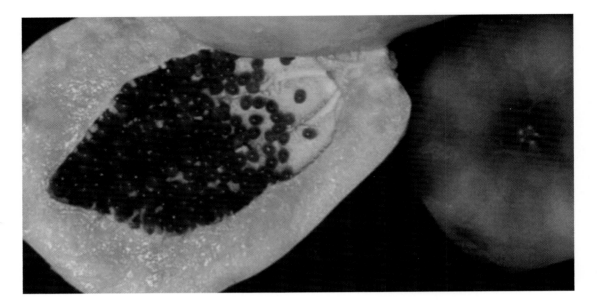

- Remove barbecue grill rack from one side of the barbecue. Insert the smoke pouch and turn the heat under the smoke pouch to 400F (200C) or high heat and close lid. Leave the other side of the barbecue off. Wait for smoke.

- Once the cavity of the barbecue is filled with smoke, reduce heat to 220F (104C) or low heat.

- Remove the ribs from the marinade and pat dry.

- Place ribs on cool side of barbecue, opposite the smoke pouch. Close lid on barbecue and check temperature; it should read 220F (104C). Allow the ribs to smoke for 3 hours. You will have to change the smoke pouch every hour.

- Baste with reserved marinade every 30 minutes.

- Once ribs are fork-tender, baste again with remaining marinade. Place ribs on a tray and tent loosely with foil and allow the ribs to rest for 15 minutes before slicing.

Serves 6–8

SEARED BEEF ON THYME CROSTINI
WITH CRANBERRY CHUTNEY

This is an elegant combination of flavors – cranberries and fresh thyme!
Great for any dinner party. Pass this around with drinks before everyone sits down
for the main event.

1 center-cut beef tenderloin, sliced into
  1/2-inch portions (8mm)
Salt and pepper
1 tsp dried basil (5mL)
2 tbsp olive oil (30mL)
Cranberry Chutney (recipe follows)

Crostini

1 French stick sliced into 1/2-inch slices (8mm)
1/4 cup of softened butter (60mL)
2 tbsp fresh thyme, chopped (30mL)
Salt and pepper to taste

Cranberry Chutney

3/4 cup sundried cranberries, chopped
  (175mL)
2 tbsp chopped shallot (30mL)
1 tsp crushed tomato (5mL)
4 cloves roasted garlic
1/4 cup honey (60mL)
1 tbsp balsamic vinegar (15mL)

Directions:

- To make crostini, mix butter, thyme, salt and pepper together in a small bowl

- Slice bread into 1/2-inch (8mm) slices and spread evenly with butter mixture. Place on tray.

- To prepare beef, sprinkle slices with salt, pepper and dried basil. Drizzle with olive oil to coat.

- Preheat barbecue to medium-high heat 375F (190C). Oil grill.

- Place the tenderloin slices on grill and cook for 1 minute. Flip and continue to cook for 1 minute or until desired doneness. Remove from grill, loosely cover with foil and let rest 4 minutes.

- Place bread slices on bun rack and cook for 2 minutes until warm and slightly crisp.

- Place beef on bread slices and top with cherry chutney.

Cranberry Chutney Directions:

- In a small bowl mix together all ingredients until well combined.

- Refrigerate for 1–2 hours.

Serves 16 appetizer portions

SIRLOIN STEAK WITH ONION-GARLIC MUSTARD SAUCE

BIG TIP: Always cook your meats with the bone in whenever you can. There's tons of flavor in that bone that insinuates itself into meat as it cooks. And remember, your marinade is only as good as the ingredients you use, so don't cheap out on the wine.

Remember to sear your meat quickly on either side, then turn down the heat and let it cook through to your predetermined temperature. If you're using your instant-read therm-ometer and it's telling you that your steaks are good only for the garbage pail, I can help:

- Insert the tip of the sensor of your thermometer through the SIDE of the meat NOT from the top. The sensor might not be located directly at the tip of the thermometer; therefore the sensor won't be in the center of your meat.

- Ensure your sensor isn't resting against the bone. You won't get an accurate reading.

- Be sure to check each steak – not all are created equal!

1 x 3 lb sirloin steak, bone-in

2 tbsp olive oil (30mL)

Salt and pepper to taste

Marinade

1 cup red wine (250mL)

1 tbsp cracked black pepper (15mL)

2 rosemary sprigs, coarsely chopped

3 cloves garlic, coarsely chopped

1/4 cup olive oil (60mL)

Directions:

- Place marinade ingredients into bowl and mix well. Place the steak in a sealable plastic bag and pour the marinade over steaks to coat. Seal the bag and refrigerate for 3 hours.

- Pre-heat barbecue to 375F (190C) or medium-high.

- Remove steak from marinade and pat dry. Allow steak to come to room temperature. Drizzle with olive oil and sprinkle with salt and pepper.

- Oil the barbecue grill. Cook steak for 6 minutes, turn 45 degrees and cook for another 6 minutes.

Onion-Garlic Mustard Sauce

2 medium onions, chopped

4 cloves garlic, minced

1/2 lb double-smoked bacon (250mL)

2 tbsp cider vinegar (30mL)

2 tbsp grainy mustard (30mL)

1 tbsp pure maple syrup (15mL)

*1/2 tsp jalapeno, chopped, seeds
    removed (5mL)*

Salt and pepper to taste

1 tsp Tabasco sauce (5mL)

- Flip steak and cook for an additional 6 minutes, turn steak 45 degrees and finish cooking for 6 more minutes (for medium-rare).

- Remove steak and cover with aluminum foil. Let rest for 5 minutes.

- Slice steak into desired portion-sizes and serve with Onion-Garlic Mustard Sauce.

Onion-Garlic Mustard Sauce:

- In a medium skillet, sauté double-smoked bacon, garlic and onions over medium-high heat. Sauté until bacon is crisp and onions are dark brown.

- Add cider vinegar and cook for 40 seconds, reduce heat to low, add the remaining ingredients, and allow sauce to simmer for 15 minutes.

Serves 4

SLOW SMOKED BEEF RIBS

More juicy, tender beef ribs. Have your butcher separate the ribs for you (as opposed to a whole rack) and go to town. The sauce recipe below is really basic, so go through the fridge, pantry, and liquor cabinet and throw in anything else you think will taste great.

2 racks of beef ribs

9 cups hickory woodchips (2L)

Dry Rub

1 tbsp Cajun spice (30mL)

1 tsp thyme (5mL)

3 tbsp brown sugar (45mL)

1 tbsp dry mustard (15mL)

1 tbsp ground ginger (15mL)

2 tbsp onion powder (10mL)

2 tsp garlic powder (10mL)

1 tbsp kosher salt (15mL)

2 tbsp cracked black pepper (10mL)

Beef Rib Sauce

1 bottle commercial BBQ sauce

1 tbsp Worcestershire sauce (15mL)

1 tbsp Dijon mustard (15mL)

1 tsp chili powder (5mL)

1 tbsp lemon juice (15mL)

Splash of hot sauce

Directions:

- Combine rub ingredients in a small bowl. Rub the mixture vigorously and evenly over beef ribs. Place beef ribs in a large, sealable plastic bag and place in fridge for 5 hours or overnight.

- Prepare rib sauce by mixing ingredients in a bowl. Cover and refrigerate until needed.

- Place 6 cups of the woodchips in water and soak for 1 hour.

- Build a smoke pouch by squeezing the excess water from 2 cups (500mL) of wet woodchips and place on a large piece of aluminum foil. Place 1 cup (250mL) of dry woodchips on top and mix them together. Close the foil around the chips to make a sealed foil package. Using a fork, puncture holes in both sides of the foil pack to allow the smoke to flow through and infuse the meat. Repeat twice more to make a total of three pouches.

- Remove one side of the grill grate and insert one smoke pouch.

- Prepare barbecue for grilling with indirect heat by preheating one side of the grill to 400F (200C) or high heat and leaving the other side of the grill off.

- Close lid and wait for smoke. Once you have smoke, lower heat under smoke pouch to 250F (120C) or medium-low heat.

- Place beef ribs on cool side of grill, opposite from the smoke pouch. Close lid and leave to smoke for 2 1/2 hours or until meat is tender enough to fall off the bone. Change smoke pouch every 45 minutes.

- During the last 20 minutes of cooking, baste with rib sauce. Serve with any remaining sauce.

Serves 8

SPICY GRILLED BEEF SHORT RIBS

I remember not so long ago when beef ribs were cheap cheap cheap. Not so much anymore. Everyone seems to have cottoned on to the wonders of the beef rib. Lots of fat and cooking on the bone make these ribs perfect for slow cooking on the barbecue. This is a very simple recipe with lots of flavor at the end. Serve it up with your favorite barbecue sauce and some potato salad. You can ask your butcher to cut the ribs in half width-wise if you'd like.

4 beef short ribs, bone in

Rub

1/3 cup five-spice powder (83ml)

1/3 cup brown sugar (83ml)

3 tbsp garlic salt (45ml)

3 tbsp celery salt (45ml)

Wood chips (cherry or apple) for smoking

Directions:

- Combine all of the rub ingredients in a large bowl. Rub half of the mixture into the ribs and reserve the other half of the rub for use at cooking time.

- Place the ribs in a large plastic bag and into the fridge to set up overnight.

- A half hour before you plan to put the ribs on the grill, remove them from the fridge. Remove them from the plastic bag and apply the remaining rub from the night before, leaving approximately 2 tbsp to sprinkle on the ribs while they smoke.

- Let the ribs stand for half an hour to come to room temperature. This will ensure even cooking on grill.

- Make 4 smoke pouches (see page 5).

- Prepare the barbecue for indirect grilling. Crank heat on one side and place first smoke pouch directly on burner. Close lid and wait for smoke. Once barbecue is smoking, reduce heat to 220F/110C.

- Place the ribs on the cool side of the grill.

- Close the lid and leave to smoke with indirect heat for approximately 4 hours, changing the smoke pouch about once an hour.

- After 2 hours, flip the ribs and sprinkle with remaining rub mixture.

- After 4 hours, the ribs should have a crispy delicious exterior and the meat should be almost falling off of the bone.

Serves 4

CHICAGO PIZZA BURGERS

2 pounds ground sirloin

1 cup chopped pepperoni (250ml)

1/3 cup grated Parmesan cheese (75ml)

2 tablespoons canned pizza sauce (30ml)

8 slices 1/8 inch thick Provolone cheese

Salt and pepper to taste

8 onion cheese buns

Directions:

- Place sirloin, pepperoni, Parmesan cheese and pizza sauce into a large bowl. Mix ingredients until well combined.

- Using your hands form 8 burger patties. Place burgers on a tray.

- Preheat barbeque to 375°F/190°C or medium high heat.

- Preheat barbeque to 325F/162C.

- Oil the grill.

- Drizzle burgers with oil and season with salt and pepper.

- Place burgers on grill and cook for 5 minutes on each side.

- Place a slice of cheese on each burger for final minute of cooking.

- Place buns on grill for 1 minute or until toasted. Close lid and allow cheese to melt.

- Remove burgers and serve on toasted buns.

Serves 8

KOREAN BEEF RIBS

We here in North America tend to think we corner the market on barbecue. Wrong. Lots of cultures, lots of countries, have some sort of outdoor grilling or smoking as part of their indigenous culinary repertoire. They just might not call it barbecue that's all. Case in point is Korea. The marinade combines sugar, vinegar, sesame oil and five-spice powder (yeah, I know it's called Chinese five-spice, but whatever) for a distinctly Asian take on the short rib.

3 lbs short beef ribs, cut into 2-inch lengths

Marinade

1/3 cup soy sauce (80ml)

3 tbsp light brown sugar (45ml)

2 tbsp rice vinegar (30ml)

1/4 cup peanut oil (60ml)

2 minced green onion

2 tsp minced garlic (10ml)

2 tsp sesame oil (10ml)

2 tsp grated fresh ginger (10ml)

1/2 tsp hot sauce (2.5ml)

Salt and pepper to taste

1/2 tsp five-spice (2.5ml)

Directions:

- In a bowl combine soy, brown sugar, rice vinegar, oil, green onion garlic, sesame oil, peel and grate in some ginger, hot sauce, salt and pepper, five-spice.

- Add ribs and marinade to a sealable plastic bag. Turn to coat ribs evenly and then into the refrigerator overnight.

- Remove from refrigerator and place on baking sheet 30 minutes before cooking.

- Discard the marinade.

- Pat and dry the ribs and oil, season with pepper.

- Prepare the barbecue for direct grilling. Preheat the grill to medium-high heat.

- Oil the grill and add the ribs. Cook for 7– 8 minutes per side.

- Remove from grill allow to rest 10 minutes covered in foil.

Serves 6

ROTISSERIE PRIME RIB WITH MASHED ROAST SWEET POTATOES

Prime Rib is an expensive cut of meat so *please* read the recipe a couple of times before diving into this one, okay? The nice thing about prime rib is how well it's marbled with fat, which melts over the long cooking process and infuses the meat with tons of flavor. This simple rub allows the rich beef taste to take center stage.

8-lb prime rib roast with fat cap and
   bone in (3.63kg)

1 tbsp black pepper (15ml)

1 tbsp garlic salt (15ml)

2 tsp onion powder (10ml)

2 tsp dry thyme (10ml)

1 tbsp dried mustard (15ml)

1 bottle white wine (750 ml)

4 sprigs fresh rosemary

Directions:

- In large mixing bowl combine pepper, garlic salt, onion powder, dry thyme and dried mustard.

- Completely cover prime rib with rub.

- Cover with plastic wrap and set aside for 60 minutes.

- Preheat barbeque to 325F/162C.

- Push rotisserie spit through the roast. Make sure you balance roast in the middle of the spit so you don't get the "wobbles" when it begins to rotate.

- Heat both sides of barbecue leaving the middle burner off and place the drip pan in middle. Pour white wine into drip pan and add the rosemary.

- Place roast on rotisserie and start it up.

- Close the lid and roast for about 3 hours, adding more wine if required.

- Remove the roast from the rotisserie and insert a meat thermometer – should be 125F/51C for medium rare – and tent with aluminum foil.

- Let stand for 20 minutes before serving.

Mashed Sweet Potatoes

4 medium sweet potatoes

1/2 cup butter (125ml)

2 tbsp olive oil (30ml)

Salt and pepper to taste

Mashed Sweet Potato Directions:

- Preheat grill to medium low 375F/190C. Wash sweet potatoes and prick the all over with a fork. Rub the sweet potatoes with olive oil and salt and pepper. Wrap in aluminum foil. Place on barbecue to cook for 40 minutes. Remove from the grill and allow to cool for 10 minutes. Completely remove the skin. Place peeled sweet potatoes in large bowl. Mash potatoes with a potato masher. Stir in butter and season to taste with salt and pepper.

Serves 6–8

FIVE-SPICE BEEF KEBAB

Chinese five-spice powder is a combination of cinnamon, cloves, fennel, star anise
and peppercorns and is used extensively in Asian cuisine. This combination of flavors
is pretty unique and once you try it, you might find yourself adding it to soups and
sauces and other non-barbecue stuff. This recipe calls for sirloin because you're just
grilling for a few minutes a side.

3 lbs sirloin steak cut into 1 inch cubes

Marinade

3 tsp sesame seeds, toasted (45ml)

3 cloves garlic, finely chopped

1 tsp dried chili flakes (5ml)

2 tsp grated fresh ginger (10ml)

1/3 cup light soy sauce (80ml)

1/4 cup white sugar (60ml)

1/4 cup dry sherry (60ml)

2 tsp five-spice powder (10ml)

2 tbsp peanut oil (30ml)

12 bamboo skewers or disposable wooden
 chop sticks soaked in cool water for 1 hour

Directions:

- Mix together the marinade ingredients. Set aside
  1/4 cup (60ml) of marinade for basting. Pour the
  remaining marinade over cubed beef and
  refrigerate for 5 hours.

- Remove the beef from the fridge 30 minutes before
  grilling. Remove from the marinade, pat dry and
  thread the beef on skewers.

- Preheat barbecue grill to medium high.

- Place beef on well oiled grill.

- Grill beef for approximately 2 minutes per side
  (for medium rare) or until desired doneness.

- Remove from grill and lightly tent with foil. Allow
  meat to rest 5 minutes.

Serves: 6

GRILLED FILET MIGNON WITH STUFFED PEARS

There's not a whole lot you have to do to beef tenderloin and it doesn't take very long to grill. The combination of grilled pears stuffed with a nice blue cheese (you can go stinky if you'd like), crunchy nuts and chewy sweet cranberries is the perfect side to this slab 'o beef.

1 beef tenderloin, 12 inches in length

Olive oil

1 tsp salt (5 ml)

1 tsp freshly ground black pepper (5 ml)

Stuffed Pears

4 medium-firm pears, cored and halved

3 oz. mild, soft blue cheese

1 tbsp shelled hazelnuts (15 ml)

1 tbsp chopped fresh chives (15 ml)

1 tbsp dried cranberries (15 ml)

Directions:

- Cut the beef tenderloin into 8 1-inch portions. Rub each steak with olive oil and salt and pepper. Place the steaks on a baking sheet and set aside.

- Prepare the stuffing by crumbling blue cheese into a medium bowl. Fold the nuts into a towel and hit with a hard object to crush (not your head). Add nuts to the blue cheese. Snip the chives into the bowl using scissors and add the dried cranberries. Mix well. Stuff the pear halves and add them to the baking sheet with the steaks.

- Preheat the barbecue to medium high.

- Oil the grill. The filet mignon will cook over direct heat with the lid up for a total of 8 minutes (4 minutes per side for medium-rare). After 2 minutes of grilling turn the steak 1/4-turn to produce cross char marks. Repeat after turning steaks.

- Add the pears to the grill after the first 5 minutes.

- Take the steaks off the grill and tent with aluminum foil. Let the meat rest for at least 5 minutes.

- Leave the pears on the grill, turn the barbecue off, and close the lid for a couple minutes longer. The cheese should be soft and melted.

- Serve immediately.

Serves 8

GRILLED RIB STEAK WITH WINE SAUCE

What's a rib steak? Stack a bunch of them together and you've got yourself a Prime Rib. Cut the bone away and you have a rib-eye. I prefer the rib steak to the rib-eye because cooking on the bone is always better. "Herbes de Provence" originates in Provence, France and is a combination of dried basil, fennel, lavender (you should see the lavender fields in Provence), marjoram, rosemary, sage, savory, and thyme. You'll find it at any decent grocer or specialty food store.

The steaks don't take long to cook, so start the wine sauce first.

Rib Steaks

4 rib steaks – approximately 1-inch thick

4 tbsp olive oil (60ml)

2 tsp herbes de Provence

Salt and pepper to taste

Mushroom and Red Wine Sauce

1/2 small onion, diced (1/4-inch)

2 small carrots, diced (1/4-inch)

2 celery stalks, diced (1/4-inch)

2 garlic cloves minced

2 tsp olive oil (10ml)

1 tsp herbes de Provence (5ml)

2 cups red wine (500ml)

2 cups beef stock (500ml)

1/2 cup dried wild mushrooms (125ml)

1 tbsp cold butter, cut into cubes (15ml)

1 tbsp olive oil

Directions:

- Preheat barbecue to high heat

- Pat rib steaks with paper towel. Drizzle them with olive oil and season with salt, pepper and the herbes de Provence.

- Oil the grill liberally. Place steaks on the grill. For medium-rare steaks cook meat for 2–3 minutes. Turn the steaks 60 degrees and allow them to cook for another 3–4 min. Flip and repeat. Extend or reduce the cooking time as necessary to result in a well done or rare steak.

- Remove the steaks from grill and cover with aluminum foil. Let stand for 10 minutes before serving with sauce.

Mushroom and Red Wine Sauce Directions:

- Add the oil to a skillet set over medium high heat.

- Add the onion, carrots, celery and garlic to the skillet with the herbes de Provence.

- Sauté over medium heat for 3 minutes until tender (translucent), but not browned.

- Add the red wine, bring to a gentle boil.

- Lower the heat and simmer until the wine is reduced to a few spoonfuls.

- Add the beef stock and dried mushrooms. Bring the heat back up to a gentle boil and cook for 10 minutes or until reduced by half.

- Strain and return sauce to the skillet. Bring to a simmer and remove from heat.

- Add cold butter and whisk gently to incorporate. Do not place back on heat or butter will separate.

Serves 4; 1 cup sauce

HAMBURGERS WITH HOMEMADE KETCHUP

Ahhh . . . the venerable hamburger. A barbecue staple. This one is different. It features herbed butter *and* stinky blue cheese (or mild if you'd prefer). Plus, you get to make your own homemade ketchup. Here are a few tips to perfect burgers every time:

Secret #1   Don't place the burgers too close together. Make sure there's room between them or the temperature will drop and they won't cook properly.

Secret #2   Don't sear the meat by pressing down with a spatula. All you're doing is squeezing the juices and flavor out of the burgers.

Secret #3   Don't touch the burgers until it's time to flip them. Don't worry about the occasional flare up, they won't last long. Move the burgers over if you get a major flame only.

Secret #4   Let burgers rest under foil for at least 5 minutes after coming off the grill.

2 1/2 lbs medium ground chuck (1.2 kg)

1/4 cup herbed butter (60ml) see note

1/4 cup soft blue cheese (60ml)

Salt and pepper to taste

1 tbsp olive oil (15ml)

6 large sesame or onion buns

Homemade Ketchup

2 cups tomato sauce (500ml)

2 cups canned, chopped tomatoes (500ml)

1 1/2 cups apple cider vinegar (375ml)

1 2/3 cups brown sugar, packed (410ml)

2 tsp granulated garlic (10ml)

2 tsp onion powder (10ml)

2 tsp dry mustard powder (10ml)

2 tsp ground cinnamon (10ml)

2 tsp celery salt (10ml)

1 tsp ground coriander (5ml)

1 tsp cayenne (5ml)

1/2 tsp ground cloves (2.5ml)

1/4 tsp ground nutmeg (1ml)

1 tbsp Worcestershire sauce (15ml)

1 tbsp hot sauce (15ml)

Homemade Ketchup Directions:

- Combine all ingredients in a saucepan.

- Over medium-high heat, bring mixture to a boil and then reduce heat to simmer for 30 minutes. Stir occasionally so the sauce does not stick to the bottom of the saucepot. Remove from heat and pour into a bottle that can be sealed and stored in the refrigerator. This will last for up to a month in the refrigerator.

Yield: 4 cups (1 liter)

Directions:

- In a bowl, combine the ground beef chuck with salt and pepper.

- Form into 6 patties and place them onto a baking sheet.

- Add a knob of chilled herbed butter and 2 tsp blue cheese into the center of each patty. Enclose it completely by overlapping and manipulating the ground beef.

- Place raw burgers into the refrigerator before grilling so they will firm up. Remove from fridge 10 minutes before grilling.

- Prepare the barbecue for direct grilling at high heat. You need to start with the hottest grill possible in order to cook hamburgers without the filling oozing out.

- Season the hamburgers with salt and pepper and drizzle evenly with oil.

- Lift the lid and oil the grill.

- Place the burgers on the grill and listen to the sizzle sound. Turn the heat down to medium high. Don't flip the hamburgers too soon, make sure that they can be easily lifted off the grill using a hamburger flipper.

- Cook for approximately 6 minutes or until dark golden char marks are achieved. Flip and continue to cook a further 6–7 minutes. Remove from grill and tent under foil for 5 minutes before serving.

Yield: 6 burgers

- Note: To make herb butter, combine 2 tbsp of your favorite herb and mix with soft butter. Chill in the refrigerator until firm.

TEXAS BEEF SANDWICHES WITH BARBECUE SAUCE

Better than a burger but a bit more work. The beef is bumped up with a nice spicy Cajun spice rub you make yourself. Try experimenting with different types of wood chips, but mesquite is always good fall back for beef. An ancho chili is a dried poblano and I think it's sweeter than most other chili peppers. Chili flakes will do in a pinch.

8 lbs top sirloin roast (3.62 kg)

1/4 cup olive oil

Salt & pepper to taste

6 12-inch long submarine sandwich buns
  (or for dramatic appeal, one 6-foot-long
  submarine bun)

Wood chips for smoking

Directions:

- In a bowl, mix together cayenne, mustard, coriander, chili powder, thyme, coriander, cumin, ancho chili, salt and pepper.

- Rub all over the beef.

- Make 4 smoke pouches (see page 5).

Cajun Rub

2 tbsp cayenne (30 ml)

1 tbsp mustard (15ml)

2 tsp coriander (10ml)

1 tbsp chili powder (15ml)

2 tsp thyme (10ml)

3 tsp cumin (15ml)

2 tsp ancho chili (10ml)

1 tbsp kosher salt (15ml)

1/2 tbsp pepper (7.5ml)

Sauce

3 tbsp unsalted butter (45ml)

1/2 cup minced yellow onion (125ml)

3 cups chopped tomatoes (750ml)

*1/2 cup firmly packed light brown sugar
    (125ml)*

1/4 cup yellow mustard (60ml)

1/2 cup cider vinegar (125ml)

3 tsp Worcestershire sauce (15ml)

2 tsp Tabasco sauce (10ml)

Salt and pepper to taste

- Prepare the barbecue for indirect grilling. Crank the heat on one side and place the first smoke pouch directly on the burner. Close the lid and wait for smoke. Once barbecue is smoking, reduce the heat to 275F/140C.

- When smoke appears place beef on the indirect side of the grill.

- Close the lid and slow smoke the top sirloin over indirect heat for 4 hours or until instant read thermometer reaches 125F/52C for medium rare. Change the smoke pouch every hour or so.

- Remove top sirloin from grill, place on platter, and loosely cover with foil and rest for about 20 minutes.

- Slice rested beef thinly. Prepare individual sandwiches or slice really big submarine sandwich bun lengthwise. Lay lettuce leaves on the bun to cover. Spoon on beef. Wrap tightly. Cut it into 8-inch piece sandwiches.

Sauce Directions:

- In a small saucepan over medium-high heat, melt the butter, add the onion, and cook, stirring occasionally, until translucent, 4 to 5 minutes.

- Add rest of the sauce ingredients and bring to a boil. Reduce heat and simmer for 10 minutes more.

- Set aside and allow to cool to room temperature.

Serves 10–12

SMOKED BEEF BRISKET

Corned beef, pastrami and smoked meat are all made from the brisket cut of beef which comes from the breast area under the first few ribs. It's a tougher cut but has lots of fat and lends itself well to the low-and-slow cooking process. Order a brisket from your local butcher and make sure he leaves the fat cap on. You're going to smoke this one for 6 or 7 hours so it's definitely a Saturday project while you're doing other stuff around the house. (Get someone else to swap the smoke pouches if you go golfing.)

6-lb fresh beef brisket with a nice fat cap

  (2.72kg)

Rub

1/4 cup brown sugar (60ml)

2 tsp paprika (10ml)

2 tsp chili powder (10ml)

1 tsp garlic powder (5ml)

1 tsp ground cumin (5ml)

2 tsp onion powder (10ml)

2 tsp dry thyme (10ml)

2 tsp cracked black pepper (10ml)

1 tbsp fine espresso powder (15ml)

2 10 oz bottles lager beer

Salt and pepper to taste

Hickory wood chips for smoking

Directions:

- In a bowl, combine rub ingredients.

- Place brisket in a large, shallow baking dish. Massage rub into meat, cover with plastic wrap and put it in the refrigerator to set up overnight.

- Remove brisket from refrigerator at least an hour before cooking.

- Make 5 smoke pouches (see page 5).

- Prepare the barbecue for indirect grilling. Place a drip pan on one side under the grill plate, pour in one bottle of beer and crank the heat on the other side. Place the first smoke pouch directly on the burner. Close the lid and wait for smoke. Once barbecue is smoking, reduce the heat to 220F/110C.

- Season brisket liberally with salt and pepper. Once barbecue is smoking, place the brisket on the side of the barbecue without direct heat.

- Smoke the brisket over indirect heat for 6–7 hours, replacing the smoke pouch every hour or so until you run out of pouches. Continue to add beer to the drip pan during the cooking process.

- Remove the brisket from the grill. Tent with foil and rest for 45 minutes before slicing.

- When slicing the brisket, slice thin against the grain.

Serves 12–15

SMOKED HOT DOGS

Um, I'm putting the hot dogs in the Beef section because I'm assuming you're going to buy some quality all-beef franks and not the ones made with mystery meat. Enjoy.

1 dozen quality all-beef hot dogs

hickory wood chips for smoking

Directions:

- Make a smoke pouch (see page 5).

- Prepare the barbecue for indirect grilling. Crank the heat on one side and place the smoke pouch directly on the burner. Close the lid and wait for smoke. Once barbecue is smoking, reduce the heat to 220F/110C.

- Place the hotdogs on the turned off side of the grill and let them smoke and cook through for 1 hour.

Serves 6

SOUTHWESTERN VEAL SHOULDER

Veal has a much more delicate taste than grown-up beef, so the smoke is really going to stand out in the finished product. As with most things barbecue, this is a pretty simple recipe that requires about 3 hours-and-change to cook. Grilled asparagus and onion wedges make great sides for this dish. Also, the veal is amazing the next day on sandwiches for lunch.

6-lb veal shoulder (2.7 Kg)

Southwestern Rub

2 tsp chili powder (10ml)

1 tsp ground cumin (5ml)

1 tsp ground oregano (5ml)

1/2 tsp garlic powder (3ml)

1/2 tsp onion powder (3ml)

1/2 tsp black pepper, ground (3ml)

1/4 tsp cinnamon, ground (1.5ml)

Mesquite wood chips for smoking

Directions:

- To make Southwestern Rub, place all rub ingredients in small bowl and stir until blended.

- Rub evenly over veal.

- Rest the roast in the fridge for at least 4 hours; overnight would be even better.

- Remove the veal from the fridge a good 30 minutes before smoking.

- Make 3 smoke pouches (see page 5).

- Prepare barbecue for indirect grilling. Crank heat on one side and place the first smoke pouch directly on burner. Close lid and wait for smoke. Once barbecue is smoking, reduce heat to 220F/110C.

- Place the veal on the cool side of grill.

- Close the lid and leave to smoke for 3 1/2 hours and change smoke pouches every hour or so.

- When done, tent with foil for 20 minutes before slicing and serving.

Serves 6-8

TUSCAN GRILLED VEAL CHOPS

I love veal chops. Remember that this is beef so don't overcook – you want it nice and juicy and pink in the middle. It's a delicate, lean cut of meat (even inch-thick chops) and can dry out very easily if you leave it on the grill too long. The combination of apple cider, juniper berries and fennel make for an interesting taste, different from what you're probably used to. Try this once and you'll be doing it all summer. It's a great change from your regular steak. Oh yeah, ask your butcher to "French" the bones for you.

6 large center-cut veal chops, 1-inch thick
   with bone in

2 large garlic cloves

1 cup apple cider (250ml)

1/4 cup olive oil (60ml)

20 juniper berries, crushed

2 tsp fresh rosemary, minced (10ml)

1/2 cup chopped fresh fennel, combination
   bulb and feathery tops (125ml)

Salt and pepper to taste

Directions:

- Cut one clove of garlic into slivers and insert a sliver into each chop, between the meat and the bone.

- Place chops in a large plastic sealable bag.

- Mince remaining garlic and combine it in a bowl with the apple cider, olive oil, juniper, rosemary and fennel. Season with salt and pepper.

- Pour the marinade over the chops and coat well. Place in the refrigerator and marinate for 6 hours. Remove from the fridge 30 minutes before grilling.

- Preheat your barbecue to medium high (and don't forget to oil the grill).

- Grill chops about 7 minutes a side, turning once.

- Tent with foil for about 10 minutes when finished grilling.

Serves 6

SMOKED VEAL LOAF

Sassafras is the plant used to flavor root beer. Pretty cool, huh? If you can't find any sassafras pellets for smoking, then get some sassafras tea at a gourmet or health food store and mix it up with whatever wood chips (preferably apple) you decide to use.

This is kind of like barbecued meat loaf.

Loaf mixture

2 lbs ground veal

1/2 cup dried bread crumbs (125ml)

1 medium onion, finely chopped

2 ribs celery, finely chopped

2 cloves garlic, minced

1/4 cup barbecue sauce (60ml)

1/4 cup ketchup (60ml)

2 tbsp balsamic vinegar (30ml)

2 eggs, lightly beaten

2 tsp coarse salt (10ml)

1 tsp ground pepper (5ml)

Cooking spray

Sassafras wood pellets

Directions:

- Combine all the loaf ingredients and mix well.

- Place the loaf mixture in a lightly sprayed loaf pan and flatten mixture down with a spatula to remove any air holes.

- Make 2 smoke pouches (see page 5).

- Prepare the barbecue for indirect grilling. Crank the heat on one side and place the first smoke pouch directly on the burner. Close the lid and wait for smoke. Once barbecue is smoking, reduce the heat to 220F/110C.

- Add meatloaf to the grill on the unlit side and close lid.

- Cook for an hour, replace smoke pouch and continue cooking for 30 minutes.

- To test for doneness, internal temperature should read 160F/71C on a meat thermometer.

- Remove the loaf and let sit for 10 minutes before slicing.

Serves 8

SEAFOOD STUFFED VEAL TENDERLOIN

Try to chop up the shrimp so the pieces are about the same size as a bay scallop.
Wrapping the veal loin in the prosciutto will keep everything nice and juicy inside.

4-lb veal loin roast (1.8 Kg)

20 sheets of prosciutto, thinly sliced

Rub

1 tbsp garlic powder (15ml)

1/2 tsp all spice (2ml)

1/2 tsp coriander (2ml)

1 tsp onion powder (5ml)

1 tsp cinnamon (5ml)

1 tsp paprika (5ml)

1 tsp thyme (5ml)

1 tsp chilies (5ml)

1 tsp dry mustard (5ml)

2 tbsp brown sugar (30ml)

1 tbsp black pepper (15ml)

Directions:

- Combine rub ingredients in a medium size bowl.

- Slice the veal loin lengthwise. Don't cut all the way through; the veal should fold out like a book.

- Place a sheet of plastic wrap on the counter. Now put the veal on the plastic wrap and place a second sheet on top of the veal.

- Gently pound veal with a mallet just enough to make it flat. You're trying to spread it out and make it thinner without tearing any holes in the meat.

- Massage the rub into the veal, inside and out.

- Place in a sealable plastic bag and let marinate in the refrigerator for 4 hours. Remove from the fridge 30 minutes before cooking.

Stuffing

10 medium shrimp, chopped

20 bay scallops, small

2 1/2 cups chopped leeks, white part only
(625ml)

1 tbsp butter, softened (15ml)

- Line a sheet of plastic wrap (the length of your veal loin) with prosciutto slices, overlapping them slightly.

- Place veal on one end of the prosciutto-lined plastic wrap and evenly distribute the shrimp and scallops in the center of the veal. Top with leeks and dot with softened butter.

- Using the plastic wrap as a guide, roll up the tenderloin so the prosciutto is completely covering the veal loin, tighten plastic wrap around roast and place in the refrigerator for 2 hours to firm up. Remove from the fridge 20 minutes before cooking.

- Preheat the barbecue to 375F/190C with one side turned off.

- Remove wrap from veal. Place meat on the direct-heat side of barbeque and cook for 3 minutes per side, or until prosciutto is golden and crispy.

- Move roast to the other side, close the lid and cook for an hour, or 15 minutes per pound.

- Tent with foil for 15 minutes before slicing.

Serves 8

MUSHROOM AND NUT CRUSTED VEAL CHOPS

Mushrooms and rosemary are classic add-ons to veal as their flavors play nicely against the delicate meat. You really need to get yourself some walnut oil. A great side salad for this dish is a simple arugula salad drizzled with walnut oil and balsamic vinegar and topped with parmesan shavings.

4 veal chops, 1-inch thick, bone in

Marinade

1/2 cup white wine (125ml)

Juice of 1 lemon

2 garlic cloves, chopped

3 springs rosemary, chopped

1/4 cup olive oil

1/4 cup walnut oil

Pepper to taste

Crust

1/4 cup dried wild mushrooms (60ml)

1/4 cup walnuts (60ml)

1 tbsp dried rosemary (15ml)

1 tsp salt (5ml)

1 tsp pepper (5ml)

Directions:

- Whisk marinade ingredients together in a small bowl.

- Place the veal into a sealable plastic bag, pour the marinade over top, make sure the meat is covered entirely and refrigerate for at least 1 1/2 hours.

- For the crust, grind the mushrooms to fine powder in a small food processor or a coffee grinder, and then pour into a mixing bowl.

- Add the remaining ingredients to the grinder. Blitz long enough to make a coarse meal out of the walnuts. Pour into bowl with mushroom powder and mix.

- Remove veal from marinade and pat dry with paper towel.

- Rub dry mixture onto both side of each veal chop.

- Preheat the grill to medium high. Oil the grill liberally.

- Grill the veal for 7 minutes on each side with lid up.

- Tent with foil for at least 5 minutes after grilling

Serves 4

ROTISSERIE VEAL ROAST WITH PESTO CREAM SAUCE

There's lots going on in this recipe. First you marinate, then you baste while slow roasting and then you serve with possibly the simplest side sauce ever made. Your butcher will do all the cutting and tying for you so don't sweat it. The basting ensures a nice golden color and lots of juicy flavor.

3 lbs (1.5 kg) veal center loin, cut, bone in
and tied

Marinade

1/2 cup of olive oil (125ml)

1 small onion, finely chopped

1/2 cup of parsley, chopped (125ml)

4 cloves of garlic, crushed

Juice of 2 lemons

1 tbsp of fresh oregano, torn (15ml)

1 tsp of pepper (5ml)

Basting sauce

1/2 cup of melted butter (125ml)

Juice of 2 lemons

1 tsp of salt (5ml)

Pesto cream sauce

1 cup of store bought basil pesto (250ml)

Juice of 1 lemon

1 cup of whiping cream (250ml)

1/2 tsp of nutmeg (2.5ml)

Drip pan liquid

2 cups of white wine (475ml)

3 rosemary sprigs

Directions:

- Combine all marinade ingredients in a medium sized bowl.

- Put the veal and marinade in a large sealable bag and refrigerate for 5 hours. Don't forget to take it out of the fridge 30 minutes before cooking.

- In a small bowl combine basting sauce ingredients. Mix well and set aside.

- In a medium saucepan, combine sauce ingredients. Heat until warm and flavors have infused. Refrigerate the sauce once it has cooled. Reheat and garnish with fresh mint before serving.

- Place a drip pan in the middle of the barbecue, just below where the roast will be. Turn your side burners on, close the lid and preheat to 300F/150C.

- Wipe excess marinade from roast with paper towel.

- Mount veal firmly and securely on rotisserie rack (follow your manufacturer's instructions). Don't forget to add the balance weight to the rotisserie to counter balance the weight of bone in the meat.

- Pour the white wine into the drip pan and add the rosemary sprigs.

- Baste veal with basting sauce. Close lid and cook for 2 1/2 hours, basting every 30 minutes.

- Remove the veal from the spit and cover with foil. Let rest for 15 minutes.

- Serve with pesto cream sauce.

Serves 8–10

PROSCIUTTO-WRAPPED VEAL

Wrapping the veal in prosciutto is a type of "barding" which means to add fat to lean cuts of meat. The ham will crisp up and keep the veal moist.

3 lbs veal loin, slightly flattened

10 oz of prosciutto, thinly sliced

Black pepper, to taste

Marinade

1 medium onion, roughly chopped

2 sprigs fresh sage

1 cup white wine (250ml)

3 cloves garlic

2 tsp ground pepper (10ml)

2 tbsp olive oil (30ml) plus 1 tbsp (15ml)

Drip pan

2 cups of white wine (475ml)

3 sprigs of rosemary

Directions:

- Combine first five marinade ingredients in blender, start the motor up and pour in the oil. Puree until smooth.

- In a large sealable bag, add marinade and veal. Refrigerate for 12–24 hours. Remove veal from marinade, lay flat and pat dry.

- On a large piece of plastic wrap place slices of prosciutto, making sure the slices overlap slightly.

- Place the veal in the center of the prosciutto, drizzle with oil and season with pepper.

- Roll the veal so it is completely covered in the prosciutto, using the plastic wrap as a guide.

- Wrap again tightly with more plastic and let it set up in the fridge for an hour.

- Remove from the fridge 30 minutes before cooking.

- Remove the plastic wrap (like I needed to tell you this!).

- Place a drip pan under the grill rack on one side and add rosemary and white wine. Prepare the barbecue for indirect cooking by heating only the side without the drip pan.

- Preheat grill to 350F/175C.

- Place veal on the grill side with no direct heat and cook for one hour, until the internal temperature reads 150F/66C on a meat thermometer. Remove from grill and cover with foil. Let rest for 15 minutes before slicing.

Serves 8

JERK MANGO-GLAZED VEAL RIBS

Yes, that's right . . . veal ribs. Not quite as well known as pork or beef ribs, so your dinner guests are going to sit up and take notice. Check out the marinade for this one. There's about a thousand different flavors working together to make sure these are the best ribs you've ever cooked.

2 4-lb racks of veal ribs (2 x 1.8 kg)

Marinade

8 whole green onions

2 tbsp fresh thyme leaves (30ml)

2 tsp ground allspice (10ml)

1 tsp salt (5ml)

2 tsp ground black pepper (10ml)

1 tsp nutmeg (5ml)

1 tsp cinnamon (5ml)

6 cloves garlic, finely minced

2 tbsp finely minced ginger (30ml)

*2 scotch bonnet peppers, seeds removed
    and finely minced*

1 cup mango puree (250ml)

4 tbsp mushroom flavored soy sauce (60ml)

2 tbsp cider vinegar (30ml)

1/2 cup vegetable oil (125ml)

1/2 cup dark rum (125ml)

Juice of 1 lime

Cherry wood chips for smoking

Directions:

- In a food processor combine all the marinade ingredients and blitz until a smooth paste is achieved.

- Set aside 1/2 cup (125ml) of the marinade for basting.

- Place the veal ribs on a large baking tray and pour marinade over the veal. Turn veal to make sure meat is entirely covered.

- Cover with plastic wrap and refrigerate overnight.

- Make 3 smoke pouches (see page 5).

- Prepare the barbecue for indirect grilling. Crank the heat on one side and place the first smoke pouch directly on the burner. Close the lid and wait for smoke. Once barbecue is smoking, reduce the heat to 220F/110C.

- Remove ribs from the marinade and pat dry 30 minutes before cooking.

- Place the ribs on cool side of barbecue opposite the smoke pouch.

- Close the lid, smoke for 3 hours. Change smoke pouch every hour or so.

- Baste with reserved marinade every 30 minutes.

- Place the ribs on a tray and tent loosely with foil and rest for 15 minutes before serving.

Serves 6

SPICY BEEF SKEWERS WITH SOUR CREAM

This is a fun recipe because you form the ground hamburger into sausage-like torpedoes around the skewer. Remember to soak the skewers for a while so they don't burn on the grill.

2 lbs ground beef (1kg)

1 medium onion, grated with box grater

5 garlic cloves, chopped extra fine

2 tsp paprika (10mL)

1 tsp dried oregano (5mL)

1/2 tsp ground cumin (2.5mL)

1 tsp cracked black pepper (5mL)

2 tsp salt (10mL)

2 tbsp vegetable oil (30mL)

Additional salt and pepper to taste
*   if necessary*

2/3 cup sour cream (165mL)

8 bamboo skewers at least 10-inches long

Directions:

- Soak bamboo skewers for 1 hour in cool water.

- Place the ground beef, grated onion, chopped garlic and spices into a large bowl. Add salt and pepper and mix well.

- Divide mixture into 8 equal-sized portions. Using your hands, mold each portion around a skewer, shaping it into a sausage, about 8 inches (20cm) long (oil hands to stop the meat from sticking).

- Preheat the grill to 375F (190C) or medium-high.

- Season the skewers with salt and pepper and drizzle with oil.

- Oil the barbecue grill.

- Place the skewers directly on the oiled grill. To prevent the skewer ends from burning, place a sheet of aluminum foil beneath the uncovered part of the wooden skewers.

- Grill the skewers for 8–10 minutes, turning every 2 minutes. The meat will be golden brown with a slightly crispy exterior. Remove from grill and loosely tent with foil to keep warm before serving.

- Serve with sour cream.

Serves 8

VEAL CHOPS WITH A PORT AND RED WINE GLAZE

This glaze has got the grape going on in four ways: in the port, the wine, the jelly and the vinegar. It has an amazing depth of flavour that will leave your guests swooning.

6 veal chops, 3/4 pound each

1/4 cup of olive oil

2 tbsp of chopped fresh sage (30mL)

Port and Red Wine Glaze

1/2 bottle (375mL) dry red wine

1/2 cup port (125mL)

1/4 cup red wine vinegar (125mL)

1/2 cup of grape jelly (125mL)

1 tsp of salt (5mL)

1 tbsp minced garlic

Directions:

- Place the veal on a tray. Drizzle with the oil and sprinkle fresh sage. Refrigerate for 3 hours.

- Combine the ingredients for the glaze in a saucepan. Bring to a vigorous boil and simmer until it reduces to 1 1/4 cups. This may be done in advance and refrigerated until ready to use.

- Bring the veal chops to room temperature.

- Brush the grill with vegetable oil to help avoid sticking. Lay the chops over high heat to char. Once you have char marks on either side of the chops, lower the heat to 350F and continue to cook. Brush with the glaze every 5 minutes for approximately 12–15 minutes. Grill the veal until it reaches an internal temperature of 150F (66C). It should still be pink inside.

- Place any remaining glaze back over heat, simmer and stir in the butter. Season with salt and pepper and drizzle the sauce over the veal chops. Serve and enjoy!

Serves 6

This Little Piggy

*A cat will look down to a man. A dog will look up to a man.
But a pig will look you straight in the eye and see his equal.*
–WINSTON CHURCHILL

Apple-Smoked Pulled Pork

Baby Pork Back Ribs

Bourbon-Glazed Smoked Spareribs

Country Style Ribs

Dark-Beer-Marinated Pork Tenderloin

Prosciutto-Wrapped Figs Stuffed with Blue
Cheese

Dry Caribbean Baby Back Ribs

Grilled Fresh-Herb-Brined Pork Chops

Pulled Pork Picnic Roast

Root Beer Ribs

Rubbed Smoke Pork Tenderloin Cajun-
Style

Slow-Smoked Thai Ribs

Smokey Canadian Bacon

Stuffed Pork Tenderloin with Golden Raisin
Glaze

Pork Tenderloin with Balsamic and Cherries

"To Live For" Pancetta and Potato Package

Two-Way Pork Ribs with Sweet & Tangy
Barbecue Sauce and Smokey Peach
Barbecue Sauce

Beer Smoked Ribs

Dry Jerk Baby Back Ribs

Rotisserie Baby Back Pork Ribs with
Balsamic Onion Marmalade

Smoked Ribs with Espresso Barbecue
Sauce

Spicy Coconut Ribs

Strawberry & Jalapeno Ribs

Grilled Stuffed Pork Loin

Spicy Jalapeno Stuffed Pork Tenderloin

Pork with Southern Barbecue Sauce

Smokey Canadian Bacon II

Smoked Breakfast Bacon

Maple Mustard Pork Burgers

Slow Roasted Pork Butt

Smoked Pork Belly

Smoked Rotisserie Pig with Root Beer
Barbecue Sauce

Tex Mex Pork Ribs

Hawaiian Piggy on the Cue

Get yourself to the market – pork is lean meat after all. Easy to prepare, pork is a natural for the flame, from the chops to the ribs. And with so many choices, it will blow your house down.

Most Popular Pig

This may be a bit surprising to North Americans: pork is the most consumed meat product in the world. That's right, *the world*. It's economical to produce and purchase and much of the animal can be used in one way or another, making it extremely versatile for all budgets. Pork has suffered a bit of a bad rap, and yes, at one time perhaps there was reason for it. It was high in fat relative to other muscle meats and contained its share of bacteria. However, this little piggy has gone on a diet and cleaned up its pen!

The pork industry went through a dramatic makeover at the end of the 1970s, when North Americans became more health conscious. Responding to public demands for leaner, cleaner cuts of meat and the creation of regulatory Pork Boards, pork producers systematically started to breed and raise pigs to be leaner and healthier – 31% to 50% leaner for most cuts (other than bacon), depending on which source you read. While that is certainly beneficial to our overall health, it unfortunately comes with a price – taste.

The less marbling there is throughout the meat, the less natural flavor and tender, buttery texture. A pork chop, for example, in the 1960s would fry up in a pan to create a veritable feast. Nowadays that pork chop can get really dry really quickly thanks in part to its leanness and also to our fear of undercooking (which I'll get into later).

Chop, Chop

Just like cows, pigs are divided into primal cuts; however, unlike the larger bovines, which are divided into eight cuts, there are only four on the swine:

Shoulder: This area gets a lot of exercise, so it tends to be tough. The low-and-slow method applies to all cuts here. Popular choices from the shoulder: Boston butt, roast or steak; ground pork for sausage; blade steak; and ham hocks. Ham hocks are used mainly for flavoring.

Loin: Located in the middle of the animal, along the top of the spine, this area is extremely lean and can therefore be dry. However, a lot of popular cuts come from here including ribs, tenderloin, pork chops, sirloin and whole loin (butterfly chops).

Leg: The leg is also referred to as ham. We're all familiar with a beautifully prepared ham during the holidays – cooked to perfection with that low-and-slow method.

Belly: Along the underside; this area is the fattiest section of the pig. This is where your succulent bacon comes from along with those cherished spareribs and back ribs.

Stick Out Your Tongue And Say AHH!

All meat products contain bacteria; it's just a fact of life. Pork, however, contains one specific bug (worm, actually) that makes pork-lovers leery. The parasite is called *Trichinella spiralis* and the condition it causes is called trichinosis. Once this worm larva is consumed, the first symptoms are nausea, diarrhea, vomiting, fatigue, fever, and abdominal discomfort. If you're particularly unlucky, headaches, fevers, chills, a cough, eye swelling, aching joints, muscle pains and itchy skin can follow. Thankfully these symptoms are rare. In fact, since 1997, only twelve cases of trichinosis per year on average have been reported in North America. Both breeders and inspectors have made pork a healthier alternative, and although eating pork no longer has any stigma attached to it, it is important to make sure your pork is cooked to at least 160F.

The Good Student

Like beef, pork inspection is quite comprehensive. Every animal for human consumption is inspected for contamination of the intestine, and if passed, given a seal of approval.

The grading system – also much like beef – is voluntary; however, it only has two grades. The first is Acceptable. Acceptable grades are sold to grocery stores and restaurants. Next is Utility. Meats deemed Utility are used in processed foods and are not sold for public consumption.

Will That Be Red or White?

Is it fact or fiction that pork is white meat? Drum roll please . . . the answer is fiction. Pork is red meat. As a matter of fact, all livestock are considered red meat. So why do we think of pork as "the other white meat"? Because of an excellent marketing campaign driven by the U.S. National Pork Board, which goes all the way back to 1987. That slogan capitalized on the fact that pork does indeed turn a whitish color when cooked, comparing it to the perceived "healthier" choices of chicken and turkey.

What makes red meat red? One of the proteins in meat is called myoglobin, which receives oxygen from red blood cells. The amount of myoglobin in an animal's muscles makes up the color of the meat. Beef and pork have more myoglobin then say, chicken and are therefore considered red meat.

To The Market

Okay you're back in the meat section; this time looking for that perfect serving of pork for your meal. It's not complicated at all:

Marbling: Just like with beef, a little bit of even marbling (white fat) throughout is imperative for both taste and texture. Stay away from cuts with more than 1/4 inch of fat on the outside. Ask your butcher to trim it for you, or do it yourself, for that matter.

Firmness: The meat should be firm to the touch, never hard or grisly feeling.

Color: Look for cuts that are a grayish pink color.

Smell: Avoid anything that smells rancid or "off." Fresh pork should have a mild smell.

Fresh not Frozen: Stay away from pork that has been frozen, as it will tend to be dry and stringy. Juices in the bottom of the package will be your warning sign.

Too Hot To Handle

A good rule for cooking pork and all meat products is to bring the internal temperature up to 160F for medium and 170F for well done. This will insure that all parasites and other bacteria are gone.

Now, with all the things to watch out for, I'm not surprised if you're feeling a little sheepish about cooking pork. But really, common sense applies here. Just like all meats, you want to avoid cross-contamination. In other words, never use utensils and vessels on your cooked meat that have touched your raw meat. Disinfect cutting boards, counter and sink surfaces when done. Never partially cook meat to cook at a later date and always store meat, whether cooked or raw, in the fridge. See, that's pretty simple!

If you're brushing a marinade on your pork, which is an excellent choice for ribs, and you want to use the extra marinade for dipping sauce, you must boil it for 5 minutes first. Better yet, set aside some of the marinade when you make it and you'll have no worries.

The Pink Debate

Sometimes freshly cooked pork will have a pink tint in the center. Because of the worry of *trichinosis* we have become guarded about that pink. "Have no fear," I say. As long as the internal temperature has reached 160F it should be safe. The pink could also be the result of using a marinade.

'Twas an evening in November,
As I very well remember,
I was strolling down the street in drunken pride,
But my knees were all a'flutter
So I landed in the gutter,
And a pig came up and lay down by my side.
Yes I lay there in the gutter
Thinking thoughts I could not utter,
When a colleen passing by did softly say,
"Ye can tell a man that boozes
By the company he chooses"
At that, the pig got up and walked away.
    –ANONYMOUS

APPLE-SMOKED PULLED PORK

The "Boston Butt" is a big fatty cut that begs for long, slow cooking. The fat fairly melts away, dripping through the meat and infusing it with lots of taste and tenderness. Remember, fat is taste, fat is your friend. Everything in moderation (sort of) of course. Get yourself some nice sourdough buns and a bunch of condiments and load up the sandwiches with lots of pulled pork.

1 Boston Butt (bone-in pork shoulder roast), 5–6 lb (2.5–3 kg), covered with a layer of fat 1/2–1-inch thick

6 cups apple woodchips

Dry Rub

1/2 cup of brown sugar (125mL)

1/2 cup of kosher salt (125mL)

1/3 cup of paprika (84mL)

3 tbsp of black pepper (45mL)

4 tsp of garlic powder (20mL)

2 tsp of thyme (10mL)

2 tsp of coriander (10mL)

2 tsp of cayenne (10mL)

2 tsp of dry mustard (10mL)

Basting Liquid

Spicy Vinegar-Based BBQ Sauce (page 226)

Directions:

- Combine dry rub ingredients in a bowl.

- Put on a pair of rubber or plastic gloves to protect your hands from discoloring. Apply the rub to the pork with medium to light pressure. Rub the mixture into the pork and ensure that the entire surface is well spiced.

- Place the pork butt into a large plastic bag to rest for 5–8 hours.

- Place 2 cups of the apple woodchips in water and soak for 1 hour.

- Drain half (1 cup) of the wet woodchips and squeeze the excess water out. Spread them evenly on a large piece of tin foil. Place 2 cups of the dry woodchips on top and mix them together. Close the foil around the chips to make a sealed foil package. Use a fork and puncture holes in the top and bottom of the foil package to allow the smoke to flow through and infuse the meat.

- When the pork has finished marinating, let it rest for approximately 30 minutes to bring it to room temperature. This will ensure that it cooks evenly.

- Remove the grill top and place the woodchip package directly over high heat to the far side of the barbecue. Once smoke is visible, turn the heat down to a medium-low heat (220°C).

- Place the pork on the opposite side of the grill from the smoke package. Use indirect heat to smoke the pork by ensuring that there is no direct heat under the meat. The only heat on should be the burner underneath the smoke package.

- Close the lid and allow the pork to cook for 1 hour before opening the lid. After 1 hour, lift the lid and baste the meat quickly. Baste every 20-30 minutes.

- If you would like a more intense smokey flavor on the pork, after 2 hours, build another smoke package using the remaining wet and dry woodchips and swap it for the now finished first package. If not, continue to cook over indirect heat for another 2 hours.

- Continue to cook for the remaining 2 hours, basting every 20–30 minutes. The meat is done when the pork pulls away easily from the skin.

- Perfect in buns and served as sandwiches.

Serves 4

BABY PORK BACK RIBS

The orange zest, mixed with the sesame oil and soy sauce is such a wonderful, silky combination—multilayered yet still uncomplicated.

3 full racks of baby pork back ribs,
*   8 ribs each*
Mildly flavored vegetable oil to brush
*   on the cooking rack*

Barbecue Sauce

1/2 cup Hoisin sauce (125mL)

1/4 cup plum sauce (60mL)

1/2 cup oyster sauce (125mL)

1/4 cup red wine vinegar (60mL)

1/3 cup honey (75mL)

2 tbsp dark soy sauce (30mL)

2 tbsp dry sherry (30mL)

2 tbsp sesame oil (30mL)

1 tbsp Sambel Olek (15mL)

1 tsp of Five Spice Powder (5mL) (Page 74)

1 tbsp of pepper (15mL)

1 tbsp of finely grated orange zest (15mL)

8 cloves of finely minced garlic

1/4 cup of finely minced ginger (60mL)

Directions:

- In a glass bowl combine all the ingredients for the barbecue sauce and mix well. Rub over the ribs making sure to coat the ribs evenly. Cover and refrigerate for 30 minutes or up to 4 hours.

- Remove ribs from the fridge 30 minutes prior to cooking them. Place on a baking sheet and reserve the marinade for basting. Allow the meat to come to room temperature.

- Preheat grill to 300F (150C). Just before use, brush the grilling rack with flavored cooking oil.

- Place ribs meaty side up (bone side down) in the center of the rack. Close the lid of the grill and regulate the heat so that it remains at 300F (150C).

- Grill the ribs until the meat begins to shrink away from the ends of the rib bones, approximately 2 hours.

- After 2 hours, begin basting the ribs every 5 minutes for a total of 25 minutes until ribs are done.

- To serve, cut ribs into individual portions.

Serves 4

BOURBON-GLAZED SMOKED SPARERIBS

Slow smoking the ribs with hickory or mesquite adds a taste note on top of the rub and the basting liquid and the sauce. So much love from one pig.

5 slabs of pork spareribs, trimmed of chine bone and brisket flap – 3 lbs (1.5kg) each

3 cups of woodchips (hickory or mesquite)

Dry Rub

1/3 cup freshly ground black pepper (75mL)

1/3 cup paprika (75mL)

2 tbsp brown sugar (30mL)

1 1/2 tsp chili powder (7.5mL)

2 teaspoons garlic powder (10mL)

2 teaspoons onion powder (10mL)

Basting Liquid

3/4 cup of bourbon (188mL)

3/4 cup of cider vinegar (188mL)

1/2 cup of water (125mL)

Directions:

- Combine the rub ingredients in a large bowl. Rub half of the rub mixture into the ribs and reserve the other half of the rub for use the next day. Place the ribs in a large plastic bag and refrigerate overnight.

- A half hour before you plan to put the ribs on the grill, remove them from the plastic bag and apply the remaining rub from the day before. Let the ribs stand for half an hour to come to room temperature. This will ensure that they cook evenly on the grill.

- Place 1 cup of the woodchips in cold water to soak for half an hour.

- If your grill has several grates, remove one on the far side and set it aside. Preheat the grill to high heat – approximately 400–450F (200–225C).

- Squeeze the excess water from the soaking woodchips and place in the center of a large piece of tin foil. Add the remaining 2 cups of dry woodchips. Fold the aluminum foil around the chips to create a sealed pouch. Using a fork, poke holes in the package on both sides to allow the smoke to filter through.

BBQ Sauce

> 1/3 cup of butter (75mL)
>
> 3 medium onions, minced
>
> 1 1/2 cups bourbon (250mL)
>
> 2 tbsp tomato paste (30mL)
>
> 1/3 cup apple cider (75mL)
>
> 1/3 cup orange juice (75mL)
>
> 1/3 cup of pure maple syrup (75mL)
>
> 1 tbsp of dark molasses (15mL)
>
> 1/2 tsp of black pepper

- Place the smoke package directly over the flame on the far side where the grate has been removed. Close the lid and wait for smoke to start building in the barbecue.

- Once smoking has begun lower the heat under the woodchip pouch and turn the heat off on the other portions of the grill. Wait for the temperature to reach approximately 200F (100C).

- Place the ribs on the grates where the heat is off. Close the lid and allow to smoke with indirect heat for approximately 4 hours, turning and mopping with basting liquid at 1 1/2 hours and 3 hours.

- After the ribs have smoked for approximately 3 hours, brush them with the BBQ sauce. Brush them again 20 minutes later.

- Place the remaining sauce in a small pot on the stovetop and reduce for 15 minutes.

- When the ribs are ready to come off the smoker, cover them in foil and allow them to sit for 10–15 minutes to allow the juices to reconstitute. Serve with hot BBQ sauce.

BBQ Sauce

- To prepare the barbecue sauce, melt butter in a saucepan over medium heat. Add the onions and sauté until golden. Add remaining ingredients and lower the heat to low. Let this mixture reduce and thicken for approximately 40 minutes, stirring every 5 minutes.

Serves 10

COUNTRY STYLE RIBS

Remember that the longer you let the ribs sit with the rub on them, the better the taste. The rub is granular and tears little pockets into the flesh when you rub it in. Letting the ribs sit in the fridge overnight allows the flavor to get into the top layer of the meat. A wet marinade on the other hand will soak right through the meat for a more all round flavor profile.

5 lb slab country style pork ribs (2.5kg)

Rib Rub

1 tbsp Spanish paprika (15mL)

3 tbsp brown sugar (45mL)

1 tsp chili powder (5mL)

Directions:

- Place all rub ingredients into a small bowl and stir until well combined. Rub evenly over ribs. Place ribs on a tray, cover with plastic wrap and refrigerate overnight.

2 tsp garlic powder (10mL)

2 tsp onion powder (10mL)

1 tsp fresh thyme (5mL)

2 tsp dry mustard (10mL)

1 tbsp coarse kosher salt (15mL)

Rib Sauce

1 tbsp olive oil (15mL)

1/4 cup chopped onions (60mL)

1 cup chopped canned tomatoes (250mL)

2 tbsp dark molasses (30mL)

1/2 tsp dry mustard (2.5mL)

1/2 tsp chili flakes (2.5mL)

1 tbsp Worcestershire sauce (15mL)

Salt and pepper to taste

- Melt olive oil in a medium sized skillet at high heat. Add onions and sauté for 2-3 minutes or until translucent. Add the remaining ingredients. Reduce heat to medium low and allow sauce to simmer for 15-20 minutes. Remove from heat.

- Remove ribs from fridge and allow to come to room temperature

- Prepare barbecue for indirect heat. Heat one side of the grill to 220F (110C) or low heat and keep the other side of the grill off. Place drip pan under the cool side of the grill.

- Using basting brush, paint the ribs with rib sauce.

- Place the ribs on cool side of the grill over drip pan.

- Slow cook ribs for 3 hours basting with rib sauce every 30 minutes.

Serves 6

DARK-BEER-MARINATED PORK TENDERLOIN

There's more taste going on in a dark beer so don't even think of substituting some light beer stuff. It's all about the yeasty taste soaking into the meat.

6 pork tenderloin, 1 1/2 lb (750g) each

2 bottles (330mL each) dark beer

2 tbsp Dijon mustard (30mL)

2 1/2 tsp horseradish (15mL)

2 tsp black pepper (10mL)

3 sprigs fresh thyme

3 onions, diced

2 tbsp olive oil

Salt to taste

Directions:

* Place the pork in a large, sealable plastic bag. Combine the dark beer, mustard, horseradish, pepper and thyme in a bowl. Mix together and pour into the plastic bag over the pork. Add the onions and seal the bag – removing as much air as possible. Massage the marinade into the meat and ensure that it is well-coated.

* Refrigerate for 5 hours.

* Remove the pork from the bag and pat dry. Strain the marinade into a saucepan and discard the onion. Reduce the marinade on a stove top for approximately 20 minutes, until the sauce coats the back of a spoon.

* Heat the barbecue to medium high 350F (150C). Rub the tenderloin with olive oil and season with salt.

* Place the meat on the grill and sear until golden brown, rotating to ensure char marks are evident all over the meat. Reduce the heat to 275F (135C) and continue to cook the tenderloin, basting with the thickened marinade every 5 minutes for 15–20 minutes. Serve and enjoy!

Serves 6

DRY CARIBBEAN BABY BACK RIBS

Rum mixed with cinnamon, cloves and allspice. Sounds like a Christmas dish, not a barbecue dish. You'll be pleasantly surprised by this shift away from the ordinary.

4 racks of pork baby back ribs

2 cups mesquite woodchips soaked in
    water for 2 hours

1 cup of dried hickory-flavored woodchips

Marinade

2 cups dark rum (500mL)

1 whole star anise

Dry Caribbean Rub

1 tbsp chili powder (15mL)

1 tbsp dried chives (15mL)

1 tbsp dried onion flakes (15mL)

1 tbsp coarse salt (15mL)

1 tsp fresh ginger, chopped (5mL)

1 tsp freshly ground black pepper (5mL)

1 tsp ground allspice (5mL)

1/2 tsp ground star anise (2.5mL)

1/4 tsp ground nutmeg (1.25mL)

Directions:

- Place rib with dark rum and star anise into large sealable plastic bag(s) and marinade for 3 hours in the refrigerator.

- Prepare Dry Caribbean Rub (see below).

- Drain dark rum marinade from ribs and pat dry with paper towel.

- Work rub over ribs and place back into the fridge to finish marinating for at least 1 hour.

- Preheat grill to high.

- Squeeze the soaking chips dry and combine with the dry chips. Place the chip mixture into a double layer of foil. Close the foil around the chips to make a small package. Poke holes in the foil package on both sides and place directly on top of the coals or gas flame. When the package starts smoking, reduce the heat to medium. Arrange ribs onto hot grate, over the drip pan. Cover and let smoke cook for 2 hours or until meat is very tender and has shrunk back from the ends of the bones.

Dry Caribbean Rub:

- Combine chili powder, chives, onion flakes, salt, ginger, black pepper, allspice, star anise and nutmeg and grind using a spice grinder or mortar and pestle, until you have a fine powder.

Serves 4

PROSCIUTTO-WRAPPED FIGS STUFFED WITH BLUE CHEESE

This is a classic summertime starter. Sit around the patio table and gobble up these figs with a nice glass of wine and some good tunes on the stereo. It's a great way to start an evening with friends and family.

12 figs

1/4 lb prosciutto, thinly sliced (113g)

Blue Cheese Stuffing

4 walnuts, chopped fine

1/4 lb of blue cheese (113g)

1 tbsp cognac (15mL)

1 tsp cracked pepper (5mL)

Raspberry Vinegar

1/2 cup frozen defrosted raspberries (125mL)

1 tsp cracked pepper (5mL)

1 tbsp balsamic vinegar (15mL)

Directions:

- Cut into the figs halfway, being careful not to go all the way through. In a small bowl combine stuffing ingredients.

- Stuff the figs with cheese mixture. Wrap prosciutto evenly around figs. If necessary secure with a tooth pick. Place on well-oiled tray.

- In a small bowl combine raspberry vinegar ingredients and reserve.

- Preheat BBQ to medium-high heat 375F (190C). Oil the grill.

- Brush the figs with raspberry vinegar, place on grill and close lid. Cook for 2 minutes, then rotate figs and cook for a further 2 minutes or until prosciutto is crispy and cheese is melted.

- Remove from grill, serve and enjoy!

Serves 12 appetizer portions

GRILLED FRESH-HERB-BRINED PORK CHOPS

This ain't your Mom's dry pork chop (sorry to all Moms out there!). Brining just means soaking the meat in a liquid with some acidic component (in this case it's apple cider and balsamic) that helps "loosen up" the meat and makes it very tender and juicy.

6 bone-in loin pork chops, each about
  1-inch thick

3 tbsp brown sugar (45mL)

1 tbsp kosher salt (15mL)

1 cup apple cider (250mL)

2 cups cold water (500mL)

2 tbsp olive oil (30 mL) plus olive oil
  for grilling

2 tbsp balsamic vinegar (30 mL)

1 tsp freshly ground black pepper (5 mL)

3 whole sprigs fresh rosemary

2 bay leaves

Directions:

- Combine brown sugar, kosher salt and apple cider in a medium bowl. Stir to dissolve.

- Add water, olive oil, balsamic vinegar, pepper, rosemary and bay leaves.

- Put the pork chops into 2 large sealable plastic bags doubled up. The plastic bags can be standing in a large pot to make it more secure. Pour the brine overtop. Seal the plastic bag and put in the refrigerator to rest for 4 hours.

- Remove the pork chops from the brine and place on a large tray. Pat them dry with paper towel and dispose of the brine. Allow the pork chops to come to room temperature before grilling.

- Preheat the barbecue to 475F (240C).

- Lightly brush both sides of the pork chops with olive oil and season with salt and pepper. Sear the pork chops over direct heat for 2 minutes per side, or until golden brown char marks are achieved.

- Lower the temperature to 300F (150C). Turn off one side of barbecue; continue to cook pork chops over indirect heat (the turned-off side of the BBQ), for a further 15 minutes or until desired doneness.

- Once the juices run clear, take the pork chops off the grill and tent with aluminum foil. Allow meat to rest for 10 minutes before serving.

Serves 6

PULLED PORK PICNIC ROAST

This recipe calls for the big marbled fatty picnic pork shoulder roast. After 5 1/2 hours of slow cooking, you're left with an amazing, melt-in-your-mouth roast that goes great with the peach chutney recipe on page 222.

8 lb picnic pork shoulder

Dry Rub

1 cup brown sugar (250mL)

1 tbsp red pepper flakes (15mL)

1 tbsp dry mustard (15mL)

2 tsp garlic powder (10mL)

2 tsp onion powder (10mL)

2 tsp paprika (10mL)

1 tsp marjoram (5mL)

1 tbsp lemon pepper (15mL)

Drip Pan Ingredients

4 sprigs rosemary

1 cup white wine (250mL)

Directions:

- Combine the rub ingredients together in a medium sized bowl. Rub evenly all over pork shoulder. Place pork in a large sealable plastic bag and refrigerate overnight or up to 24 hours.

- Remove the pork from the bag and set it aside so that it may come to room temperature.

- Prepare grill. Place a drip pan underneath the grill grate on one side of the barbecue, add rosemary and wine to drip pan. Preheat the grill using indirect heat by leaving the heat off under the drip pan and putting the far burner on 220F (104C) or medium heat.

- Place pork on cool side of barbecue over drip pan.

- Close lid and let pork grill slowly for 5 1/2 hours.

Serves 12

ROOT BEER RIBS

Hey, why not? We've done cola before, so why not root beer? It's got the sugar necessary to give the ribs a sweet bite combined with the heat of the chili flakes.

4 sides baby back ribs, approx. 3 lb
   (1.5 kg) each
3 cups cherry woodchips

Marinade

4 cups root beer (1L)
1 cup bourbon (250mL)
1 cup brown sugar (250mL)
2 tbsp dry mustard powder (30mL)
1 1/2 tsp chili flakes (7.5mL)
1 tbsp garlic, finely chopped (15mL)
3 sprigs of fresh rosemary, bruised

Directions:

- Combine marinade ingredients in a medium bowl.

- Place ribs in a non-reactive (glass or ceramic) dish. Pour marinade over ribs and cover with plastic. Refrigerate for 4 hours.

- Place 2 cups of the woodchips in cold water to soak for 1/2 hour.

- If your grill has several grates, remove one on the far side and set it aside. Preheat 350F (176C) or medium heat.

- Squeeze the excess water from the soaking woodchips and place in the center of a large piece of tin foil. Add the remaining 1 cup of dry woodchips. Fold the aluminum foil around the chips to create a sealed pouch. Using a fork, poke holes in the package on both sides to allow the smoke to filter through.

- Place the smoke package directly over the flame on the far side where the grate has been removed. Close the lid and wait for smoke to start building in the barbecue.

- Once smoking has begun, lower the heat under the woodchip pouch and turn the heat off on the other portions of the grill. Wait for the temperature to reach approximately 275F (135C).

- Place ribs over the cool side of the grill. Close lid and smoke for 3 hours or until meat is falling off the bone.

- Remove from barbecue and loosely tent ribs with foil. Let ribs rest for 10 minutes before serving.

Serves 12

RUBBED SMOKED PORK TENDERLOIN CAJUN-STYLE

Dried herbs can be substituted if fresh are unavailable. Note: use about 1/3 less dried herb than the recipe calls for, since the flavor of dried herbs is more intense. To retain that beautiful crust on the outside of your meat, place cooked meat on a wire rack with a dish under it while letting rest (or tent). Use the juices if you'd like. No need to waste them!

2 pork tenderloins, thin sliver skin removed

3 cups cherry woodchips (750mL)

Directions:

- Combine the rub ingredients in a small bowl.

- Rub mixture vigorously over pork, coating the meat. Place pork in a large sealable plastic bag and refrigerate for 3 hours. Remove from fridge a half hour before smoking to bring to room temperature.

Dry Rub

1/2 cup coarse salt (kosher or sea) (60mL)

4 tbsp sweet paprika (60mL)

3 tbsp garlic powder (45mL)

3 tbsp onion powder (45mL)

2 tbsp fresh thyme, chopped (30mL)

2 tbsp fresh oregano, chopped (30mL)

1 tbsp freshly ground black pepper (15mL)

2 tsp fresh sage leaves (10mL)

1 tsp cayenne pepper (5mL)

Watercress and Parmesan Cheese Salad

1 bunch watercress, washed and dried

1 cup parmesan cheese shavings (250mL)

1/2 cup sundried cranberries (125mL)

Dressing

Juice of 2 lemons

Salt and pepper to taste

1/4 cup olive oil (60mL)

- Soak 2 cups (500mL) of cherry woodchips in water for 1 hour.

- Squeeze the excess water from the woodchips and place in the center of a large piece of foil. Add 1 cup (250mL) of dry woodchips and mix. Close the foil around the chips sealing the package. Using a fork, poke holes in both sides of the package.

- Prepare the barbecue for smoking. Preheat one side of the barbecue to 400F (200C) or to high heat. Leave the other side off. Place the smoke pouch underneath the grill directly over high-heat source of the grill. Close the lid and wait for smoke.

- Once barbecue cavity is full of smoke, place tenderloin on the cool side of the grill. Turn the temperature down to 220F (104C) or medium-low.

- Smoke pork for 45 minutes. Remove from grill and loosely tent with foil. Allow meat to rest for 10 minutes before slicing.

- Slice tenderloin against the grain of the meat and serve with the Watercress and Parmesan Cheese salad (recipe follows).

Watercress and Parmesan Cheese Salad

- In a medium sized bowl, whisk together lemon juice and olive oil. Add salt and pepper to taste.

- Spread arugula on a platter and arrange sliced pork tenderloin on top. Sprinkle with parmesan shavings and cranberries.

- Pour dressing over salad. Toss gently to combine.

SLOW-SMOKED THAI RIBS

You can buy fish sauce in pretty much any grocery store these days. On the other hand, it's worth the trip down to your local Chinatown for a big bottle of the stuff at half the price of the "anglosized" version in the Big Box store. Plus Chinatown is a very cool place to hang out.

3 x 1 1/2 lb racks of baby back ribs,
  membrane removed
3 cups apple woodchips (750mL)

Directions:

- In a large bowl whisk together Thai marinade ingredients, set aside.

- Place ribs in a sealable plastic bag. Pour marinade over ribs and place in the refrigerator. Let marinate for 4 hours.

Thai Marinade

2 tbsp peanut oil (30mL)

2 tsp of sesame oil (10mL)

2 tbsp fish sauce (30mL)

2 tbsp garlic, minced (30mL)

1 tbsp fresh ginger, minced (15mL)

1/4 cup chopped fresh cilantro (60mL)

2 stalks lemongrass, outer leaves removed
   and center thinly sliced

2 tbsp sugar (30mL)

1 tbsp of rice wine vinegar (15mL)

Juice of 2 limes

Dipping and Basting Sauce

1 tbsp rice wine vinegar (15mL)

1/2 cup pineapple juice (125mL)

Juice of 2 limes

2 tbsp white sugar (30mL)

1 tbsp garlic, chopped (15mL)

1 tsp chili pure (10mL)

1 stalk lemongrass, finely chopped

- In a small bowl, whisk together dipping and basting sauce and set aside. Cover with plastic wrap and refrigerate until time to baste the ribs.

- Soak only 2 cups (500mL) of the apple woodchips in water for 1 hour.

- Prepare barbecue for grilling with indirect heat by preheating one side of the grill to 400F (200C) or high heat and leaving the other side of the grill off.

- Prepare a smoke pouch by squeezing the excess liquid from the soaked woodchips and place them on the center of a large piece of tin foil. Combine the dry woodchips with the wet and fold the foil around the woodchips creating a pouch. Using a fork, poke several holes in the smoke pouch and place it under the grate on the heated side of the barbecue. Close the lid and wait for smoke.

- Once you have smoke, lower the heat under the smoke pouch to 275F (135C) or medium heat and place the ribs on the opposite side of the grill where the burner remains off.

- Close the lid and smoke ribs for 2 1/2 hours. Baste ribs with dipping and basting sauce in the last half hour. Serve with remaining sauce.

Serves 6

SMOKEY CANADIAN BACON

How did back bacon ever become a Canadian icon? Was it just Bob and Doug? Nah. Anyway, here's a really simple way of smoking your own back bacon, which you can then use in tons of different dishes.

2 lb (1kg) Canadian bacon (back bacon)

4 tbsp vegetable oil (60mL)

4 tbsp brown sugar (60mL)

1 tbsp coarse or kosher salt (15mL)

1 1/2 tsp cayenne pepper (15mL)

2 tbsp ground cinnamon (30mL)

2 tbsp fresh ground black pepper (30mL)

2 cups apple woodchips, soaked and
*   ready for smoking*
2 cups of dry apple woodchips

Directions:

- Rub the Canadian bacon with the vegetable oil.

- Combine all the other ingredients in a bowl and mix them together well. Spread the rub over the bacon, ensuring it is evenly coated. Wrap the meat in plastic and refrigerate for 2 hours.

- Remove the bacon from the fridge and allow it to come to room temperature.

- Prepare the grill for smoking at 200–220F (100C–110C). Squeeze the soaking chips dry and combine with the dry chips. Place the chip mixture into a double layer of foil. Close the foil around the chips to make a small package. Poke holes in the foil package on both sides and place directly on top of the coals or gas flame. It will take approximately 15 minutes for the chips to begin smoking.

- Once the chips begin to smoke, place the bacon on the grill and close the lid. Leave to cook slowly for 90 minutes. Flip the bacon once halfway through the cooking process.

- Let the bacon rest for 20 minutes under some foil to keep the juices in, before slicing and serving.

Serves 8

STUFFED PORK TENDERLOIN WITH GOLDEN RAISIN GLAZE

Pork with something sweet and sour on it is sheer perfection. Much like turkey with cranberry sauce. It's a natural! Tenderloin is a very lean cut of meat so don't overcook, or it'll be tough and dry as shoe leather (not that I've eaten shoe leather!).

3 pork tenderloins, 12 oz (350g) each

10 oz cream cheese (300g)

Zest of 2 limes

2 tbsp fresh sage, roughly chopped (30mL)

Salt and pepper to taste

1 cup spinach leaves washed and dried (250mL)

3 tbsp olive oil (45mL)

3 cups fruitwood chips (apple wood or cherry wood) (750mL)

Glaze

1 cup golden raisins soaked in 1/2 cup port wine

1/2 cup red wine (125mL).

1 tsp cracked black pepper (5mL)

1 tbsp fresh mint leaves (15mL)

1 tbsp lemon juice (15mL)

Directions:

- In a medium bowl mix together cream cheese, lime zest, sage, salt and pepper.

- Using a sharp knife, carefully open the tenderloin like a book by making a slit down the length of the meat without going all the way through the other side. Lay the meat between two sheets of parchment paper and pound with a rolling pin or meat tenderizer to an even thickness of about 1/2 inch (1 cm). Lift off the parchment paper and drizzle the meat with olive oil. Lightly season the pork with pepper. Lay spinach leaves down evenly over pork. Crumble cream cheese mixture over the spinach. Roll the pork up lengthways to form a large sausage-shaped roll and tie with butcher twine. Place on a baking tray and drizzle with oil. Cover with plastic wrap and refrigerate until ready to cook.

- Place 2 cups (500mL) of the woodchips in water to soak for 1 hour.

- To prepare glaze, warm the wine and soaked raisins in a medium saucepan over medium heat, add pepper and let cook for 5 minutes. Remove pan from heat and add the lemon juice and mint. Set aside as basting for pork.

- Prepare barbecue for grilling by preheating one side of the grill to 400F (200C) or high heat and the other side of the grill to 375F (190C) or medium-high heat.

- Drain wet chips from water and squeeze out excess liquid. Place on a large sheet of foil, add dry woodchips and wrap loosely to form a pouch. Using a fork, poke holes on both sides of the pouch. Remove the grill grate from the barbecue and place the smoke pouch directly on the high heat source. Oil the grill.

- Place tenderloin over medium heat side and cook for 3 minutes or until char marks are achieved. Flip the pork and cook for another 3 minutes. Turn the heat source directly under pork off.

- Using a pastry brush, glaze the tenderloins with golden raisin mixture.

- When smoke starts to billow out of the barbecue turn the heat source under smoke pouch to 325F (162C) or medium heat.

- Let pork smoke for 15 minutes and then glaze again. Let cook for 10 more minutes and remove. Place on tray and loosely tent with foil. Let meat rest 10 minutes before slicing.

Serves 6–8

PORK TENDERLOIN WITH BALSAMIC AND CHERRIES

3 pork tenderloins, silver skin removed

2 cup cherries, pitted (500ml)

4 tablespoons balsamic vinegar (60ml)

1 cup red wine (250ml)

1 cup port (250ml)

1 tablespoon brown sugar (15ml)

2 tablespoons olive oil (30ml)

2 tablespoons fresh cilantro, chopped (30ml)

Directions:

- Mix the cherries, vinegar, wine, port, sugar, oil and cilantro together in a non-reactive bowl. Place the pork into a sealable plastic bag and pour the marinade overtop. Place in the refrigerator for 4 hours.

- Preheat bbq to 350 degrees Fahrenheit.

- Remove pork from the fridge for the last 30 minutes of the marinating process. Remove the pork from the marinade and set the marinade aside for later. Pat the pork dry. Season the meat with kosher salt and pepper.

- Place marinade in sauce pan and cook over medium low heat until it thickens and reduces to approximately one cup.

- Place pork on bbq and grill for 5 minutes with lid up.

- Baste pork with marinade once pork is almost cooked.

Serves 6

"TO LIVE FOR" PANCETTA AND POTATO PACKAGE

We call this one "to live for" because once you've tasted it, you'll want to live forever just to keep eating it once every couple of weeks or so.

6 large new potatoes, sliced into disks

2 white leeks, chopped 1/4-inch thick

3 cloves garlic, sliced

10 fresh sage leaves

10 thick slices pancetta, cooked

3 oz gorgonzola cheese

1/2 cup cream (125mL)

Salt and pepper to taste

Directions:

- Preheat barbecue to 325F (162C) or medium heat.

- Tear off a large piece of foil (enough to make an 8 x 8 package), place 1/3 of the potatoes on foil and season with salt and pepper.

- Top with 1/2 of the leeks, pancetta, garlic and sage.

- Place another layer of potatoes on top of the mixture. Top that layer with the remaining leeks, pancetta, garlic and sage and season with pepper. Top with the last of the potatoes.

- Fold up sides of foil package. Sprinkle the layers with gorgonzola and add cream.

- Seal the foil package.

- Place package on grill. Cook for 30 minutes or until potatoes are tender.

Serves 6

TWO-WAY PORK RIBS WITH SWEET & TANGY BARBECUE SAUCE AND SMOKEY PEACH BARBECUE SAUCE

There are two kinds of pork ribs and this recipe uses them both. The back ribs are meatier than the spare ribs, but don't have as much fat which means they won't do for longer, slower smoking. In this case you smoke them both at the same time and serve them up with different sauces: tangy barbecue for the spare ribs and smokey peach for the back ribs. Hmmm, you say. Couldn't I just use one or the other? Well, sure. But this way, you get to try them side by side and decide which you like the best. Please, you can thank me later.

Wine? Definitely a spicy Gewürztraminer or fruity Viognier. Beer? Definitely a cold one.

Baby Back Ribs

3 lbs baby back ribs or one side (1.5 kg)

1 tbsp olive oil (15ml)

Salt and pepper to taste

Spare Ribs

3–4 lbs spare ribs (1.5kg) or one side

1 tbsp olive oil (15ml)

Salt and pepper to taste

6 cups hickory wood chips

Smokey Peach Barbecue Sauce

2 cups canned sliced peaches, drained and
 their liquid reserved (500ml)

1 cup ketchup (homemade (see page 90)
(250ml)

1/4 cup brown sugar, packed (60ml)

3 tbsp fresh lemon juice (45ml)

1 tbsp peach schnapps (15ml)

1 tsp fresh chopped ginger (5ml)

1 tsp salt (5ml)

1 tsp grated lemon zest (5ml)

pinch of freshly grated nutmeg

1 tsp ground cinnamon (5ml)

1/2 tsp ground allspice (2.5ml)

Directions:

- Use a set of pliers (designated for kitchen) to remove the membrane along the back of ribs. Drizzle the ribs with oil, salt and pepper.

- Prepare 2 smoke pouches *(see page 5)*.

- Prepare the barbecue for indirect grilling. Crank the heat up on one side and add the smoke pouch, close the lid. Once you get smoke, reduce heat to 220F/110C.

- Place ribs on side of the barbecue without direct heat. Smoke the ribs over indirect heat for 3 hours, replacing the smoke pouch halfway through.

- When you change the smoke pouch, baste the ribs liberally with the sauces – tangy barbecue on the back ribs; smokey peach on the spare ribs.

- Close the lid and pour yourself a drink. Go watch the game. Seriously, you must be exhausted. Take a load off.

- Cook for a further hour. Baste again with the sauce and cook for another half hour.

- Once ribs are tender and when gently pulled fall off the bone, remove from grill and tent with foil.

- Serve with extra sauce for dipping and lots of paper towels for chin wiping.

Smokey Peach Barbecue Sauce Directions:

- In a blender combine all ingredients, blend well and pour in to a skillet. Simmer mixture for about 30 minutes, stirring occasionally to avoid scorching the sauce at the bottom of the pan. Remove sauce from heat and serve with pork ribs.

Sweet and Tangy Barbecue Sauce

2 tbsp butter (30ml)

1 small onion, minced

2 cups ketchup (homemade, see recipe on
page 90) (500ml)

1/4 cup water (60ml)

1/4 cup apple sauce (60ml)

1/4 cup cider vinegar (60ml)

1/4 cup Worcestershire sauce (60ml)

2 tbsp brown sugar (30ml)

2 tbsp molasses (30ml)

2 tbsp clover honey (30ml)

2 tsp dry mustard powder (10ml)

1 tsp chili seasoning (5ml)

1 tsp garlic powder (5ml)

1 tsp cayenne (5ml)

1 tsp lemon juice (5ml)

 1/4 cup bourbon (60 ml)

Sweet and Tangy Barbecue Sauce Directions:

- In a large skillet melt some butter and sauté the
  onions until they are translucent, about 3 minutes.
  Add remaining ingredients. Stir to blend
  ingredients well, and bring to a boil. Reduce heat
  and simmer for 30 minutes, stirring occasionally to
  avoid scorching the sauce at the bottom of the pan.
  Remove sauce from heat and serve with pork ribs.

Serves 6–8 people

BEER SMOKED RIBS

I think guys like to barbecue because you don't really have to do anything. Dump a bunch of stuff in a baggie and leave it in the fridge overnight. Take the stuff out of the bag and put it on the barbecue and leave it alone some more until it's ready. Easy. Plus, this recipe has beer in it!

6 lbs pork spare ribs, or 2 side ribs (2.7 kg)

Marinade

2 (12oz) bottles lager (680ml)
   (One for drip-pan)
3 tbsp lemon juice (45ml)
2 crumbled bay leaf
3 cloves garlic, minced
2 tsp ground cumin (10ml)
2 tsp onion powder (10ml)
2 tbsp chili powder (30ml)
1/4 cup olive oil (60ml)
2 tsp cracked black pepper (10ml)
2 tsp kosher salt (10ml)

6 cups of mesquite wood chips (1.5 litre)

Directions:

- Pull the membrane off the back of the ribs using pliers dedicated for the kitchen.

- Place ribs in a large sealable plastic bag.

- For marinade, in a medium bowl combine 1 bottle of beer, olive oil, lemon juice, crumble bay leaf, kosher salt, garlic, cumin, onion powder and chili powder.

- Evenly coat the ribs, seal the bag and refrigerate overnight.

- Remove ribs from refrigerator 30 minutes prior to cooking.

- Drain ribs and discard the marinade. Sprinkle ribs with salt and pepper.

- Make 2 smoke pouches (see page 5).

- Prepare the barbecue for indirect smoking by adding the beer-filled drip pan to the unlit side, and oil the grill. Crank heat up on one side and place smoke pouch on the burner. Close the lid and wait for smoke.

- Once barbecue is smoking, place the ribs on the side of the barbecue without direct heat. Smoke the ribs over indirect heat for 2 1/2 hours, replacing the smoke pouch once and refilling the drip pan if necessary. If not, drink the remaining beer.

- Remove ribs from grill. Tent with foil and allow to rest for 15 minutes.

Serves 6–8

DRY JERK BABY BACK RIBS

Don't worry, "Jerk" does not refer to the person making the ribs. Jerk is a Jamaican spice rub that you can make on your own (way more fun than buying a bottle in the store). Adjust the flavors to suit your palate. Make a big batch and keep it in a dry place out of direct sunlight and it will last for a month at least without fading on you.

4 racks of pork baby back ribs

2 cups of dark rum (500ml)

1 cinnamon stick

Dry Jerk Rub

2 tbsp chili powder (30ml)

2 tbsp dried chives (30ml)

2 tbsp dried onion flakes (30ml)

2 tbsp coarse salt (30ml)

2 tsp ground coriander (10ml)

2 tsp ground ginger (10ml)

1 tsp freshly ground black pepper (5ml)

1 tsp ground allspice (5ml)

1/2 tsp ground cinnamon (2.5ml)

1/4 tsp ground cloves (1.25ml)

1/4 tsp ground nutmeg (1.25ml)

3 cups hickory flavored woodchips

Directions:

- Place the ribs, dark rum and cinnamon stick into large sealable plastic bags and let marinate for 3 hours in the refrigerator.

- Combine chili powder, chives, onion flakes, salt, coriander, ginger, black pepper, allspice, cinnamon, cloves and nutmeg and in a spice grinder (or mortar & pestle) and grind away until you have a fine powder.

- Drain ribs from marinade and pat dry with paper towel.

- Rub dry rub over ribs and place back into the fridge to finish marinating for at least 1 hour.

- Preheat the grill to high on one side. Leave the other burner off for indirect smoking with a drip pan underneath.

- Make 2 smoke pouches (see page 5).

- Place one of the pouches on the lit burner and close the lid. When you get smoke, reduce the heat to 220F/110C and place the ribs on the unlit side. Do this quickly so as not to loose any smoke.

- Close the lid and smoke for 2 hours (you'll need to change the smoke pouch after an hour or so) or until meat is very tender and has shrunk back from the ends of the bones.

Serves 4

ROTISSERIE BABY BACK PORK RIBS
WITH BALSAMIC ONION MARMALADE

You can also do this the indirect heat way but what's the point of having a rotisserie attachment on your barbecue if you don't get to use it now and then? The basting sauces ensures you end up with juicy tender ribs smacked full of flavor from the herbs. You can use butcher twine to help hold the ribs on the spit of they get wonky on you.

2 whole racks of baby back ribs

Basting sauce

2 tbsp honey (30ml)

1/4 cup of butter (50ml)

2 tbsp fresh squeezed lemon juice with zest finely chopped (30ml)

1 tbsp chopped basil (15ml)

1/2 tbsp fresh chopped thyme (7.5ml)

1 tbsp fresh chopped rosemary (15ml)

1 tbsp fresh chopped oregano (15ml)

2 tsp ground fennel seed (10ml)

2 tsp cracked black pepper (10ml)

Directions:

- Remove the membrane from the back of the ribs.

- Cut the rack into 3 or 4 rib sections.

- Thread the rib sections on to a spit. Make sure the spit goes through each rib section twice to hold it securely and the ribs are evenly distributed on the spit for smooth rotating.

- In a pot, combine the basting sauce ingredients. Set the pot over low heat and heat until all the butter has melted. Remove from heat. Baste the ribs.

Onion Balsamic Marmalade:

1 1/2 tbsp unsalted butter (22.5ml)

2 cups Spanish onion chopped into medium
  dice (500 ml)

2 tbsp sugar (30ml)

1/2 cup balsamic vinegar (125ml)

1/4 cup dry red wine (60ml)

1/4 cup fresh cranberries (60ml)

2 sprigs fresh oregano

Salt and cracked pepper to taste

- Prepare the barbecue for direct grilling. Preheat the grill to medium low heat. Place a drip pan in the center of the grill. Add the spit to the rotisserie and close the lid to cook at 400F/200C for about an hour and a half or until ribs are tender.

- Baste the ribs every 20 minutes.

- Remove spit from the grill and slide the ribs onto a baking sheet.

- Tent with foil and let rest for approximately 10 minutes.

Onion Balsamic Marmalade Directions:

- Heat the butter in a medium heavy saucepan over moderate heat until hot.

- Add the onion and stir for 5 minutes.

- Sprinkle with 1 tbsp of the sugar, and continue to cook until very soft and browned, about 8–10 minutes more.

- Add vinegar, wine, cranberries and oregano sprigs.

- Reduce heat and simmer until almost all the liquid has evaporated and onion mixture is glistening and syrupy (approximately 5 more minutes).

- Remove from heat.

- Stir in some pepper and salt to taste. If desired, add more sugar.

- Serve with ribs.

- Makes 1 cup of marmalade

Serves 4–6

SMOKED RIBS WITH ESPRESSO BARBECUE SAUCE

We cheat a bit here by starting the Espresso barbecue sauce with some store bought stuff. If you're a real barbecue God (or Goddess) you'll probably have a big bottle of home made stuff in the fridge, so use that. The powdered espresso gives the sauce an unusual kick and the combination of apple cider and Dijon add a tartness that plays nicely off of Mr. Pig.

4 lbs pork ribs, 2 full racks

Rub

2 tbsp hot chili powder (30ml)

1 tbsp paprika (15ml)

1 tbsp ground cumin (15ml)

2 tsp crushed dried chili pepper (10ml)

1/2 tbsp kosher salt (7.5ml)

1/2 tbsp black pepper (7.5ml)

Directions:

- Prepare ribs by removing the membrane from the back of the ribs.

- Mix rub ingredients in small bowl to blend.

- Rub spice mixture all over ribs.

- Place ribs in sealable plastic bag and refrigerate overnight.

- Next day remove the ribs from the refrigerator at least 30 minutes before cooking.

Espresso Barbecue Sauce

1 tbsp olive oil (15ml)

1 tbsp garlic minced (15ml)

1 1/2 cups white onion chopped into small
    dice (375ml)

1 18-ounce bottle good quality barbecue
    sauce (511ml)

2 tbsp golden brown sugar, packed (30ml)

2 tbsp apple cider vinegar (30ml)

1 tbsp Dijon mustard (15ml)

2 splashes hot sauce

1/2 tbsp instant espresso powder (7.5ml)

6 cups of mesquite wood chips (1.5litre)

- Prepare 2 smoke pouches (see page 5).

- Prepare the barbecue for indirect grilling. Crank the heat on one side and place the first smoke pouch directly on the burner. Close the lid and wait for smoke. Once barbecue is smoking, reduce the heat to 220F/110C.

- Place the ribs on the side of the barbecue without direct heat.

- Smoke the ribs over indirect heat for 3 hours, or until tender.

- Meanwhile, in a saucepan over medium heat, heat the olive oil and garlic. Add onion and sauté until tender. Next add the barbecue sauce, brown sugar, apple cider vinegar, Dijon, hot sauce, and espresso powder. Simmer until flavors blend and sauce thickens slightly, stirring occasionally, about 10 minutes.

- Change the pouch after about an hour and brush the ribs with some of the sauce.

- Brush the ribs with some barbecue sauce about 30 minutes from being done.

- Transfer the ribs to a platter. Tent with foil and let rest for 20 minutes.

- Bring the remaining sauce to a simmer.

- Brush the ribs with more barbecue sauce and serve with any remaining sauce.

Serves 6

SPICY COCONUT RIBS

2 sides baby back pork ribs

Marinade

2 cups unsweetened coconut milk (500ml)

3 tbsp brown sugar (15ml)

1 tbsp soy sauce (15ml)

1 tbsp grated fresh ginger (15ml)

1 tsp finely shredded lime peel (5ml)

1 tbsp lime juice (15ml)

1 tsp crushed dried chili peppers (10ml)

2 tsp minced garlic (10ml)

*1/4 cup fresh coriander stems removed
    and roughly chopped (60ml)*

2 stalks bruised lemongrass

Directions:

- In a non-reactive bowl combine the marinade ingredients.

- Prepare ribs for marinade by removing the membrane on the back of the ribs. Place the ribs in a large sealable plastic bag and add half the marinade, reserving the rest for later. Marinate in the fridge overnight.

- Remove the ribs from the marinade at least half an hour before cooking. Discard the marinade.

- Prepare the barbecue for indirect grilling. Crank the heat on one side and oil the grill on the unlit side.

- Place the ribs on the side without heat.

- Close the lid and cook for 3 hours, basting with the reserved marinade every 30 minutes.

- Remove from grill and tent with foil for 10 minutes.

Serves 4-6

STRAWBERRY & JALAPENO RIBS

Trust me. Strawberries and jalapenos make a killer combo. The recipe calls for jams instead of fresh berries to get a thicker consistency in the sauce. Make sure you get unsweetened jam though – no room for sugar in this one. This recipe calls for a double cooking process – once with the rub and again with the sauce.

One more thing, wear plastic gloves when you dice and seed the jalapeno.

1 side baby back ribs

Rub

1 tsp ground cumin (5ml)

2 tsp garlic salt (10ml)

1 tsp celery salt (5ml)

2 tsp dried chili pepper flakes (10ml)

1 tsp dried thyme (5ml)

2 tsp dried oregano (10ml)

2 tsp black pepper (10ml)

1 tsp kosher salt (5ml)

Directions:

- Remove the membrane along the back of ribs with some pliers (preferably clean ones).

- In a small mixing bowl combine rub ingredients.

- Rub the mixture evenly over both sides of ribs.

- Place ribs into a plastic baggie and refrigerate overnight.

- Remove from the fridge at least 30 minutes before cooking.

- Place a skillet over medium high heat, add oil and heat for 30 seconds.

Sauce

1 tbsp vegetable oil (15ml)

1/2 cup diced onion (125ml)

3 cloves garlic, minced

1/2 cup beer (125ml)

1 jalapeno pepper, seeded and finely chopped

3 tbsp bottled barbecue sauce (45ml)

2 tbsp unsweetened strawberry jam (15ml)

Salt and pepper to taste

- Add the onions, garlic and sauté for 2 minutes or until onions are tender but not browned.

- Stir in the beer, diced jalapeno, barbecue sauce and strawberry jam. Reduce heat to low and simmer, uncovered, about 5 minutes – don't let it boil – remove from heat.

- Cool and place into the refrigerator.

- Prepare the barbecue for indirect grilling. Oil one side of the grill and turn the heat on the other side. Crank the heat 'til you get 220F/110C.

- Place the ribs on the side of the barbecue without direct heat.

- Cook for 2 hours.

- Cool to room temperature (you can do this part in advance and stick them in the fridge overnight. Just make sure you bring them back to room temperature before moving on to the next steps).

- Cut down between the ribs.

- Place them onto a big sheet of aluminum foil.

- Pour sauce over ribs and seal the foil pouch.

- Preheat the barbecue to 220F/110C just as before with one side turned off

- Place the foil pouch containing the ribs on the side of the barbecue without direct heat for 20 minutes or until hot.

Serves 4–6

GRILLED STUFFED PORK LOIN

Stuffed pork on the barbecue – will wonders never cease? The sweet peaches play off the heat from the jalapeno. Speaking of which, note that the marinade calls for a jalapeno and the stuffing calls for a Thai red chili. Why two different chili peppers? The Thai chili packs way more heat than the jalapeno and would overpower the other ingredients in the marinade.

1 pork loin roast (about 3 lbs/1.4 kg)

Marinade

3 tbsp rice wine vinegar (45ml)

1/2 cup white wine (125ml)

1 cup canned peaches (250ml)

2 tbsp ginger (30ml)

Directions:

- Puree the marinade ingredients together and dump into a sealable plastic bag

- Add the pork and refrigerate for 5 hours or overnight.

- Remove pork from marinade and wipe clean at least 30 minutes before cooking.

1 jalapeno, chopped and seeded

1 white onion, chopped

1/2 cup mint (125ml)

Stuffing

1 cup fresh peaches, sliced 1/2-inch thick
    (250ml)

3 tbsp cilantro, chopped (45ml)

1 Thai red chili pepper, finely chopped

3/4 cup hazelnuts, chopped (190ml)

Juice and zest of 1 lime

Salt and pepper

Basting Sauce

1/4 cup bourbon (60ml)

1/4 cup honey (60ml)

Butcher twine

- Using a sharp knife (like you would use a dull one), cut pork down the center lengthwise 3/4 of the way through the meat. Do not cut completely through to the other side. It should open like a book. Congratulations. This is what's called "butterflying" a cut of meat.

- Combine the stuffing ingredients in a bowl.

- Spoon onto the center of the pork. Close the pork around the stuffing and truss using butcher twine.

- Preheat the grill to 350F/180C. Leave one side of the barbeque on low.

- Place a drip pan under the low-heat side of grill.

- Drizzle pork with olive oil. Season with salt and pepper.

- Sear the roast on medium-high heat side until brown and golden.

- Move roast over to low-heat side, over drip pan and continue to cook for about an hour or until an internal temperature of 320F/160C is reached.

- Baste with the basting sauce during the last 30 minutes of cooking.

Serves 4–6

SPICY JALAPENO STUFFED PORK TENDERLOIN

Pork tenderloin is very lean and cooks quickly. *Please* do not overcook. You have to remove the silver skin – that translucent connective tissue that looks like, well, like silver skin. If you don't, it will shrink during the cooking and shrivel the tenderloin.

1 1–1 1/4 lb pork tenderloin (500 g)

Stuffing

4 fresh jalapeno chili peppers, seeded,
  and chopped very fine

2 plum tomatoes, chopped and seeded into
  medium dice

2 tbsp minced fresh cilantro (30ml)

2 tsp minced garlic (10ml)

2 tbsp fresh oregano (30ml)

1 shallot chopped fine

2 tbsp lime juice (30ml)

2 tbsp olive oil (30ml)

Salt and pepper to taste

String or butcher twine

Directions:

- Combine jalapeno peppers, tomatoes, cilantro, garlic, oregano and shallot in a bowl with lime juice and olive oil. Season with salt and pepper.

- Prepare the tenderloin by trimming the silver skin.

- Butterfly the tenderloin by slicing through horizontally without going all the way through so it opens up like a book (or a weird pig butterfly).

- Place a sheet of plastic wrap underneath and over the pork.

- Pound with a mallet for an even surface about 1/2-inch thick. Be careful not tear holes in the tenderloin.

- Remove the plastic wrap from the top and spread mixture onto the pork leaving about 1/2 an inch on either end.

- Roll up tightly using the bottom sheet of plastic wrap as guide.

- Tie the tenderloin with several short pieces of string every two inches to secure.

- Cover and place into the refrigerator for at least 2 hours and up to overnight.

- Remove from refrigerator 30 minutes before cooking. Drizzle with oil and season with salt and pepper.

- Preheat the grill to medium high.

- Oil the grill and add the pork loin.

- Cook with the lid up, turning occasionally until golden brown char marks are achieved.

- Reduce the heat to medium low on one side and turn the other side off. Move the pork to the side that's turned off and close the lid.

- Continue to cook for 20 minutes or until a thermometer reaches 160F/71C.

- Remove from grill and tent with foil for 10 minutes.

- Slice in 1/2-inch medallions and serve.

Serves 3–4

PORK WITH SOUTHERN BARBECUE SAUCE

Check out the ingredients in the sauce below: coffee, ketchup, brown sugar, and chipotle peppers. (Chipotles are smoked jalapenos that come in a can or jar smothered in a smokey adobo hot sauce. You can find them pretty much anywhere these days.) Make an extra big batch of this sauce and stick it in the fridge – it will last a week to ten days easy and the flavors get better after sitting for a day or two.

4 10-ounce smoked pork chops

Southern Barbecue Sauce

3/4 cup low-salt chicken broth (175ml)

1/2 cup freshly brewed coffee (125ml)

1/2 cup ketchup (125ml)

1/2 cup (packed) golden brown sugar (125ml)

1/3 cup grated onion (75ml)

1/4 cup rye whiskey (50ml)

1/4 cup cider vinegar (50ml)

2 tbsp Worcestershire sauce (30ml)

1 1/2 tsp minced canned chipotle chilies (7ml)

1–1/2 tsp of adobo sauce from can or jar of
   chipotle peppers (7ml)

3 garlic cloves, minced

1/4 tsp vegetable oil, divided (1ml)

Hickory wood chips

Directions:

- To prepare the sauce, pour chicken broth, cold coffee, ketchup and brown sugar into a skillet. Grate in onion and add mustard, whiskey, vinegar and Worcestershire sauce, chipotle, adobo sauce, garlic and salt.

- Place skillet over medium-high heat and let mixture come to a boil. Turn heat to low.

- Let simmer for 5 minutes or until it thickens up. Set aside.

- Make a smoke pouch with the hickory wood chips (see page 5).

- Prepare the barbecue for indirect grilling. Crank the heat on one side and place the first smoke pouch directly on the burner. Close the lid and wait for smoke. Once barbecue is smoking, reduce the heat to 220F/110C.

- Once barbeque is smoking, place pork on the cool side of the grill, close the lid and smoke for 1 hour.

- Remove the pork from grill and transfer to the skillet with the sauce.

- Simmer in southern barbeque sauce for 10 minutes.

Serves 4

SMOKEY CANADIAN BACON II

For the life of me I have no idea why back bacon is also called Canadian bacon. In fact, it's more like ham than bacon really because you buy it already smoked. There's none of the shrinkage and fat run-off you get with regular bacon. Go figure. Anyway, I love this recipe. Try it once and you'll be hooked forever. Makes for amazing sandwiches or brings a zing to the same old breakfast plate.

1 lb piece Canadian bacon (back bacon)
(500 gr)

2 tbsp canola oil (30ml)

3 tbsp of ground allspice (45ml)

3 tbsp of brown sugar (45ml)

2 tbsp of coarse or kosher salt (30ml)

1 tbsp of dried chili flakes (15ml)

1 tbsp of ground cinnamon (15ml)

1 tbsp of fresh ground black pepper - (15ml)

Apple wood chips

Directions:

- Rub the back bacon with the canola oil.

- Combine all the other ingredients in a bowl and mix them together well.

- Sprinkle the rub over the bacon ensuring that it is evenly coated. Wrap the meat tightly in plastic and place in the fridge for at least 3 hours and preferably overnight.

- Remove the meat from the fridge and let it sit at room temperature for 30 minutes.

- Make 2 smoke pouches (see page 5).

- Prepare the barbecue for indirect grilling. Crank the heat on one side and place the first smoke pouch directly on the burner. Close the lid and wait for smoke. Once barbecue is smoking, reduce the heat to 220F/110C.

- Place the bacon on the unlit side of the grill and cook for 90 minutes. Flip once halfway through the cooking process and change the smoke pouch.

- Let the meat sit at room temperature for 20 minutes under foil before slicing and serving.

Yield: 1 lb (500g)

SMOKED BREAKFAST BACON

Pork belly is the cut from which packaged bacon is sliced. You're going to buy it in one big slab so you can rub it and smoke it and make yourself the most killer kick ass bacon in the entire history of bacon. (Me, over dramatize? Never!)

1 slab pork belly cured with sugar
(3 lbs/1.36 kg)

Rub

3/4 cup brown sugar (180ml)
1 tbsp dried oregano (15ml)
2 tsp chili flakes (10ml)
2 tsp onion powder (10ml)
2 tsp garlic powder (10ml)
2 tsp cracked black pepper (10ml)
1 tbsp cinnamon (15ml)

Apple wood chips for smoking

Directions:

- In a medium bowl, combine rub ingredients.

- Rub onto the pork belly, coating the meat. Massage the rub vigorously into flesh, slightly tearing the micro fibers of the meat.

- Place the pork belly in a large sealable plastic bag and into the refrigerator to marinate overnight. Remove from fridge 30 minutes before smoking.

- Make 3 smoke pouches (see page 5).

- Prepare the barbecue for indirect grilling. Crank heat on one side and place the first smoke pouch directly on burner. Close lid and wait for smoke. Once barbecue is smoking, reduce heat to 220F/110C.

- Remove the pork belly from the plastic bag and place on the cool side of the grill. Smoke for 2 1/2 hours, changing the smoke pouch when smoke dissipates (about every 40 minutes to an hour depending on your barbecue).

- Once pork is smoked and has a beautiful dark color remove from heat.

- Place pork on a tray and tent loosely with foil. Let meat rest 15 minutes before carving into thin slices against the grain of the meat.

Yield: 3 lbs (approx. 1.5kg)

MAPLE MUSTARD PORK BURGERS

The pig never tasted so good. Do not play with your food! Resist the urge to flip the burgers more than once as you want some nice char marks on the outside. The maple syrup and mustards make for an amazing glaze. No ketchup needed for this burger.

Patties

2 lbs ground pork (1kg)

2 large shallots, finely diced

2 cloves garlic, minced

1 tsp salt (5ml)

1 tsp ground black pepper (5ml)

Directions:

- In a medium size bowl combine the ground pork, chopped shallots, minced garlic, salt and pepper.

- Form the mixture into 6 patties of equal size about 1-inch thick (2.5cm).

- Place patties on a tray and cover with plastic wrap. Place in the refrigerator until ready to grill. Remove from the fridge 20 minutes before grilling.

Glaze

3 tbsp pure maple syrup (45ml)

2 tbsp grainy mustard (30ml)

1 tbsp of cider vinegar (15ml)

1 tsp of liquid honey (5ml)

1/2 tsp of dry mustard (2ml)

1 tsp orange zest chopped fine (5ml)

6 large onion buns, sliced

- In a medium bowl whisk together all glaze ingredients.

- Preheat barbeque grill to 375F/190C or medium-high heat. Oil the grill.

- Brush the pork burgers with prepared glaze.

- Place patties on grill for 7–8 minutes basting every 2 minutes or until dark golden brown and slightly crisp on exterior. Flip burgers and continue to cook for another 7 minutes basting every 2 minutes.

- Remove burgers from grill and tent with foil for a few minutes.

- Serve burgers with warm onion buns and desired toppings.

Yield: 6 burgers

SLOW ROASTED PORK BUTT

This is a variation on the back bacon recipe (see page 65). Pork butt is an inexpensive cut of meat with lots of fat that will melt away and infuse the butt with tons of flavor over the long cooking time. Throw a few smoke pouches in there as well if you're so inclined. You can also fill the drip pan with beer, wine or water infused with dried herbs.

6 lbs pork butt

Rub

1/4 cup brown sugar

1 tbsp of chili flakes (15ml)

1/2 cup of parsley (125ml)

3 tbsp of rosemary (45ml)

2 tbsp of oregano (30ml)

1 tbsp of thyme (15ml)

1 tbsp onion salt (15ml)

2 tbsp olive oil (30ml)

1 tsp of pepper (5ml)

Directions:

- In a food processor, grind all the rub ingredients together. Rub this paste mixture all over pork butt.

- Refrigerate the butt overnight. Remove from the fridge 45 minutes to an hour before cooking.

- Score the fat cap down to the meat without cutting into the meat itself.

- Preheat grill to 220F/110C, leaving one side off.

- Place a drip pan under the cool side of the grill to catch any fats.

- Place pork on the cool grill fat-cap-up and close lid. Let the pork cook for 6 hours or 1 1/4 hours per pound.

- Remove roast and loosely tent with aluminum foil and rest for an hour.

Yield: 10 servings

SMOKED PORK BELLY

Mmmmm . . . pork belly. This is definitely a Saturday afternoon project because you're going to slow smoke this one for a good four hours. Maximum flavor impact comes from marinating first, then the smoke (we suggest apple wood but you use whatever you like) and the drip tray gets filled with liquid including some Jack Daniels (or whatever other dark booze you might want to add instead).

2 lbs pork belly cut into 2- x 6-inch squares (1kg)

Marinade

1/4 cup Jack Daniels (60ml)

3 sprigs fresh rosemary roughly chopped

1 tbsp garlic finely chopped (15ml)

1 tbsp grainy mustard (15ml)

3 tbsp olive oil (45ml)

2 tsp chili flakes (10ml)

1 tsp cracked black pepper (10ml)

For Drip Tray

1 medium sized onion sliced into
    1/2-inch slices

2 sprigs fresh sage

1/4 cup Jack Daniels (60ml)

2 cups water (500ml)

Apple wood for smoking

Directions:

- Combine marinade ingredients in a bowl and mix well.

- Place the pork in a large sealable plastic bag and pour the marinade over top. Coat pork evenly and refrigerate overnight.

- Remove pork from refrigerator about 45 minutes before cooking.

- Combine drip tray ingredients and add to pan.

- Make 4 smoke pouches (see page 5).

- Prepare the barbecue for indirect grilling. Crank heat on one side and place the first smoke pouch directly on burner. Put drip pan under side that's turned off. Close lid and wait for smoke. Once barbecue is smoking, reduce heat to 220F/110C.

- Put the pork fat-side up on grill over the drip pan.

- Smoke the pork over indirect heat for approximately 4 hours. Change the smoke pouch when smoke dissipates, about once an hour.

- Remove from grill and let rest covered in foil for 30 minutes. Slice thin.

Serves 6

SMOKED ROTISSERIE PIG WITH ROOT BEER BARBECUE SAUCE

WARNING: This recipe is not for the amateur grill jockey. Do not attempt this without having logged in a few hours smoking a pork butt or some ribs or something. This is the Full Monty. Read the recipe from start to finish at least 3 times before starting. YOU are going to low-and-slow a whole suckling pig! PLUS you get to make a barbecue sauce with root beer! Yes, root beer! Where do you get a suckling pig? From your butcher. Show him the recipe and explain what you want to do. He will order you a fresh pig. What to do if he won't or can't place the order? Get a new butcher.

Seriously, this is an amazing barbecue undertaking. Pull this one off and you are Top Gun. Save this for a long weekend at the cottage or a big backyard party. You want a lot of people around what for the standing ovation you're gonna get.

May the Force be with you.

1 Suckling pig approx. 12–14 lbs
(5.44kg–6.35kg)
Lots of apple wood for smoking
Butcher twine and butcher's needle

Rub

1/2 cup ground black pepper (125ml)

1/2 cup paprika (125ml)

1/2 cup brown sugar (125ml)

1/4 cup kosher salt (60ml)

2 tbsp dry mustard (30ml)

2 tsp cayenne (10ml)

Rub Directions:

- In a large bowl mix together all rub ingredients.

Stuffing

4 gala apples, cored & sliced

3 sprigs rosemary

2 cinnamon sticks

Basting Mop

2 cups apple cider (500ml)

1/4 cup brown sugar (60ml)

2 tsp salt (10ml)

1 tbsp cracked black pepper (15ml)

1 tsp cayenne (5ml)

1 tsp cinnamon (5ml)

Basting Mop Directions:

- In a medium size bowl mix together all basting mop ingredients.

Directions:

- Wash the pig with cold water and pat dry with paper towels.

- Place it on a large tray and massage the rub mixture all over – inside and out.

- Cover with plastic wrap and place the pig in the fridge to rest overnight or up to 24 hours. Remove from the fridge at least an hour before smoking.

- Make 4 smoke pouches (see page 5).

- Carefully place the rotisserie through the mouth of the pig and pass it through the back end. Try not to snigger or say "yuck."

- Stuff the cavity with apple slices, rosemary and cinnamon sticks.

- Using butcher string and a butcher needle, sew the stomach cavity closed.

- Pull the fore legs of the pig forward and secure them in place with butcher twine.

- Bend the hind legs in towards the stomach and secure them with the butcher's twine as well. Wrap butcher twine around pig's head and neck to finalize the tie.

- Lastly, use a paper clip to clip the ears together.

Root Beer Barbecue Sauce

1/2 cup root beer (125ml)

1 cup ketchup (250ml)

1/4 cup fresh lemon juice (60ml)

1/4 cup fresh orange juice (60ml)

3 tbsp Worcestershire sauce (45ml)

1 1/2 tbsp brown sugar (22.5ml)

1 tbsp molasses (15ml)

1 tsp liquid smoke (5ml)

Zest and juice of 1 lemon

1 tbsp fresh grated ginger (15ml)

1 tbsp fresh grated garlic (15ml)

1/2 white onion grated

Root Beer Barbecue Sauce Directions:

- In a medium size bowl mix together all barbecue sauce ingredients.

- Use a large piece of foil to cover the head of the pig before placing the rotisserie on the barbecue. This will prevent the head from burning.

- Remove grates from barbeque and place a drip pan on the middle burner (turned off). Place a smoke pouch on one of the side burners.

- Turn the heat to 400F/200C or high heat under the smoke pouch. Close lid and wait for smoke.

- Mount the rotisserie onto smoking barbeque.

- Reduce heat to 220F/110C.

- Close the barbeque lid and roast the pig for 4 hours or until its internal temperature reaches 155F/68C. To test the pig for doneness, prick the thigh with thermometer in the thickest part of the leg (avoid the bone as the temperature will not be accurate).

- Change the smoke pouch every hour and baste it every 30 minutes with the basting mop. For the final hour baste with Root Beer Barbecue Sauce.

- If skin on pig is not crisp enough, increase heat to 300F/148C for the final 20 minutes.

- If ears and snout have not browned remove the foil at the last 20 minutes.

- Remove from spit, cover loosely with foil and let the meat rest for 45 minutes.

- To carve pig, slice the skin from the base to the tail. Carve into small hams. Slice ribs and finish with the shoulder. Serve with Root Beer Barbecue sauce.

Serves 8

TEX MEX PORK RIBS

2 slabs baby back ribs

Rub

3 tablespoons firmly packed dark brown sugar(45ml)

3 tablespoons chili powder(45ml)

1 tablespoon paprika(15ml)

1 tablespoon garlic salt(15ml)

2 teaspoons ground cumin(10ml)

2 teaspoons black pepper(10ml)

2 teaspoons oregano(10ml)

2 teaspoons cayenne(10ml)

2 teaspoons onion powder(10ml)

salt to taste

6 cups hickory wood chips(1.5 litre)

Directions:

- Remove the membrane on the back of the ribs using a pair of pliers dedicated for kitchen use.

- In a bowl combine brown sugar, chili powder, paprika, garlic salt, ground cumin, black pepper, oregano, cayenne pepper and onion powder. Rub all over both sides of the baby back ribs. Place into a resealable plastic bag and then into the refrigerator overnight.

- Prepare smoke pouch. Place 4 cups(1000ml) of hickory wood chips into a bowl of cold water to soak for 1 hour. Reserve 2 cups(500ml) of dry wood chips.

- To build a smoke pouch, drain 2 cups (500ml) of the wet wood chips and squeeze excess water out.

Spread wet wood chips on a large piece of aluminum foil. Place 1 cup (250ml) of dry wood chips on top along with some oregano and thyme. Mix them together. Close the foil around the chips to make a sealed foil package. Use a fork to puncture holes in the top and bottom of the foil pack to allow the smoke to flow through and infuse the meat. Repeat to make second smoke pouch.

- Prepare the barbecue for indirect grilling. Preheat the barbecue to 220ºF/110ºC. Place one smoke pouch directly over the heat source. Close the lid and wait for smoke. Once BBQ is smoking reduce heat to a temperature of 220F/110C. Place the pork ribs on the side of the BBQ without direct heat. Smoke the pork ribs over indirect heat for 2 hours changing the smoke pouch when the smoke has dissipated.

- Remove ribs from grill and tent with foil. Serve warm.

Serves 4-6

HAWAIIAN PIGGY ON THE CUE

You could probably use aluminum foil instead of corn husks for this recipe but the presentation wouldn't be anywhere near as nice. The husks look great and they keep all the other stuff in while the pork is slow cooking.

Liquid smoke is just that: sort of a smokey hickory flavor in a bottle. You can get it at specialty food stores or barbecue outlets.

1 pork shoulder (5–7 lbs/2.3–3.2kg)

8 corn husks to cover the pork

8 cloves of garlic, halved

4 tbsp kosher salt (60ml)

2 tbsp freshly ground black pepper (30ml)

2 tbsp liquid smoke (30ml)

1 medium sized onion, thinly sliced

1 piece (3–4 inches) fresh ginger, peeled
   and thinly sliced

Lime wedges for serving

Butcher twine

Directions:

- Bring a pot of water to boil and place corn husks in water until bright green or pliable (about 7 minutes).

- Using a sharp knife, make approximately 8 shallow cuts down length of the pork shoulder. Insert a half-clove into each cut. Season liberally with salt, pepper and liquid smoke. Rub this mixture into meat.

- Place 3 pieces of butcher twine 2 inches apart vertically on the counter. Cross these horizontally with another 3 pieces of twine, creating a basket like affect. Lay 4 corn husks on top of the string. Spread half of the onion, ginger and garlic on the corn husks. Lay the pork shoulder on top. Place the remaining onion, ginger and garlic on top of the pork and cover with the remaining corn husks.

- Using the twine, secure the husks around the pork shoulder ensuring that is completely covered. Tie the husks in place and place the pork into the fridge to marinate overnight, up to 24 hours.

- Preheat the grill to 200F/100C with heat only on one side of the barbecue. Place a drip pan under the grate with no direct heat. Place the pork over the drip pan and leave to cook for 5 hours over indirect heat.

Serves 8

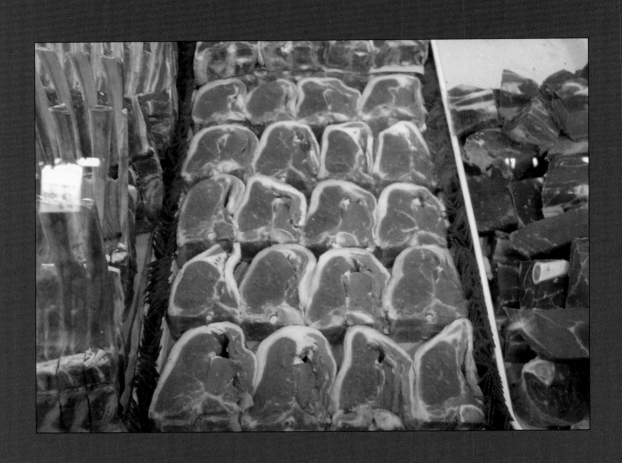

Feeling A Little Sheepish

Mary had a little lamb
Its fleece was white as snow
And everywhere that Mary went
The lamb was sure to go.
–MRS. SARAH JOSEPHA (BUELL) HALE, 1830

Apple Wood-Smoked Lamb Shoulder

Buffalo Burgers

Gin-Smoked Lamb

Grilled Lamb Chops

Grilled Venison Chops

Lamb Burgers

Lamb & Fig Kebabs

Lamb Kebabs

Mint Lamb Steaks with Mango Mint
Chutney

Sweet and Tangy Dijon Lamb Kebabs

Pumpkin Lamb Burgers with Tzatziki
Topping

Asian Spiced Lamb Burgers with Plum
Sauce

Blackberry Peppered Lamb Chops

Onion Water Lamb Chops

Smokin' Stuffed Leg of Lamb

Grilled Leg of Lamb

Port Marinated Racks of Lamb

Lamb Loin with Rosemary

Smoked Lamb Shanks with Hoisin
Barbecue Sauce

Lamb Souvlaki

Grilled Lamb Ribs

Pecan and Honey-Crusted Rack of Lamb

Roasted Leg of Lamb

Spicy Lamb Ribs

Stuffed Leg of Lamb

Lamb and game meats are not just for exotic tastes. They are becoming increasingly popular on restaurant menus and can be ordered from most butcher shops. Adding lamb and game to your grilling repertoire will awaken the taste buds.

Game animals, like lamb, venison and buffalo, are so named because they have been traditionally hunted for sport and these meats are thus described as having a "gamey" flavor and texture. I would describe the taste as stronger than beef, and slightly chewier, too – more so if cooked incorrectly. That mysterious, gamey flavor is a result of the combinations of foods the animal eats in the wild: everything from berries to leaves and grasses (and really, who knows what else?). Since all commercially-raised animals eat what we give them, the industry regulates exactly how the resulting meat will taste.

The recipes in this section are primarily for lamb, with one each for venison (deer meat) and buffalo, as these are becoming increasingly available and more popular than ever.

BAAAHHH!

In North America, lamb has always lagged behind beef, pork and chicken in consumption levels. North Americans eat about 0.7 pounds of lamb per person per year as opposed to New Zealanders who consume approximately 56.5 pounds. That's a huge difference! The two factors contributing to that difference are lack of availability and tradition. The west was won on the back of a horse after all – driving cattle, not sheep. There is a long and deep-rooted association with beef in North America. However, our interest in new cultures – particularly their cuisine – coupled with increasing immigration, the diverse range of ethnic cookbooks now available, and the proliferation of global media has introduced us to new foods and traditions – the enjoyment of lamb being one.

New Zealand, Australia and the Middle East are all major producers and consumers of lamb and mutton. People arriving in North America from these parts of the world bring not only their hopes and dreams, but also their favorite recipes, which are ingrained in their culture. Since these recipes require specialized ingredients, the North American marketplace in turn adapts.

Anatomy 101

Lamb is bred on virtually every continent, including ours. Naturally, I have a few favorite breeds. New Zealand and Australian lamb are great if you're serving to lamb enthusiasts. They tend toward a bold flavor and can be a bit chewy – delicious when properly prepared. Canadian lamb (particularly from Alberta) and Washington State lamb are at the top of my list because they taste less gamey. If you're serving to a diverse group of people, this will surely be a great middle ground. I find that folks new to lamb don't take to it if it's too "wild/gamey" tasting. The Canadian and Washington State lamb have a mild flavor and are forgiving in many different recipes. The texture tends to be silkier and it can be quite tender, much like beef.

A lamb is processed for consumption between the ages of 6–12 months. The smaller, younger animals are usually more tender and mild-flavored than the bigger, older animals. If a lamb is older than 12 months it must be labeled "mutton." The only way to tell the age of the cut is by comparing sizes of the whole legs. Legs 9 pounds and up are older than legs 6 pounds or under. But don't avoid the older cuts altogether. Low-and-slow is a must here. With care, your mutton will be tender and very flavorful!

By now you're familiar with primal cuts of meat. Lamb is similar to beef and pork, however, there are 5 primal cuts for lamb to beef's 8 and pork's 4:

Shoulder: From the neck to the fourth rib. This meat is flavorful, but it contains a lot of connective tissues. Roasts, boneless stewing meat, ground meat and chops come from here. Low-and-slow works best. I love to cook ground lamb with a bit of onion and light seasonings. Put it on a pita with some lettuce, tomato and baba ganoush or tahini and you've got a definite crowd pleaser!

Rib: The rib area sits right behind the shoulder toward the back of the animal. It encompasses the 5th–12th ribs. All eight sections of the ribs together are called the "rack." I like to sprinkle it with salt and pepper and sear it, which caramelizes the exterior. Then I put some Dijon mustard on it, role it in breadcrumbs and spices and cook it bone-side down on indirect heat until it is medium-rare at 125F. The ribs can also be separated and eaten as lamb chops. This meat has a mild flavor and tender texture, is perfect for a marinade, and is quite frankly my favorite. Lamb chops have two types of meat, the strip loin and the tenderloin, which come from the part of the animal that doesn't get a lot of movement, making the meat very tender.

Loin: The loin area starts at the last rib and includes the hip. The loin chop, sometimes called the lamb T-bone, is a popular cut because of its extremely tender and mild – almost sweet – flavor. However, it does tend to be a bit pricy. Sear it, turn the heat down and remove just before it's perfectly cooked – tent for 10 minutes – sheer perfection! Or should I say, "sheep perfection"?

Leg: From the hip to the hoof, the leg is either sold whole or cut up into roasts and shanks, with bones in or out. I personally like to cook leg meat with the bone in, as I feel it imparts more flavor to the meat. I'll also use the leg meat for kebabs, which is a family favorite.

Foreshank and Breast: This area includes the front legs. Each produces a shank and the underbelly, which houses a breast. The foreshank is the leanest cut on the lamb and requires low-and-slow cooking. The breast is often boned, rolled and stuffed and cooked using a moist heat.

Oh Give Me A Home

Where do the buffalo roam these days? Buffalo (also commonly referred to as "bison"), once the main food source for the Plains Indians, used to number in the tens of millions until they were slaughtered indiscriminately. By 1900 there were approximately only 13 American buffalo left, all of them in Yellowstone Park. Today, buffalo farming is a growing industry. There are now 300,000 bison roaming the countryside and out of that, 280,000 are farmed on private ranches.

I'm not going to spend too much time on buffalo meat, however I do want to help spread the word. Buffalo has a rich red meat that is extremely low in fat and high in iron. It's lower in cholesterol than beef, chicken and most fish! A 3-ounce serving of bison contains only 93 calories, 1.8 grams of fat and 43 milligrams of cholesterol. That's music to my doctor's ears!

Farm-raised buffalo are grown without the use of antibiotics or steroids and are allowed to roam (just like in the song). Because the animal eats fresh grass, the meat tends to have a rich, almost beefy taste – not pungent or gamey like some breeds of lamb. Since it is virtually fat-free, cooks should be mindful of the need to keep moisture in the meat. If you're grilling a steak, give it a quick sear, then low indirect heat until medium-rare – it's wonderful. Approximate cooking times:

1-inch thick: Rare 6-8 minutes. Medium 10-12 minutes
11/2-inch thick: Rare 10-12 minutes. Medium14-18 Minutes
2-inch thick: Rare 14-20 minutes. Medium: 20-25 Minutes

For a roast, sear then switch to low-and-slow. Keep a very close eye on the internal temperature:

Doneness:	Internal Temperature:
Rare	130-135 F (54-57C)
Medium-rare	135-140 F (57-60C)
Medium	140-145 F (60-63C)
Medium-well	150-155 F (65.5-68C)
Well-done	155-160 F (68-71C)

Remember, there is very little fat in this meat! Do not overcook it. By the way, tenting is going to work wonders here. Remove from heat just before cooked and cover (tent) for 10 minutes. I've included one buffalo meat recipe in this section for you to try. Once you've mastered that, put your own special touch on it.

Venison is Good Medicine

Venison is much like buffalo meat in composition and nutritional value. It's lean, as low as 0.2% fat for a 4-ounce serving of steak, with 22.9% protein and 0.2% fiber. Because of its leanness, steaks take well to a quick searing to medium rare. Venison can be compared to beef, both in texture and flavor. Roasts do well with the low-and-slow method. The same cooking guidelines for bison meat apply to venison.

It is believed that reindeer were the first domesticated deer. A letter written by Norway's King Ottar in the ninth century describes his fine herd of 600 reindeer. Deer farms have been documented as far back as 2000 BC in China and venison was once a staple food for much of the world. Today deer farming is on the rise as our health-conscious society is beginning to see its benefits.

Let your taste buds do some exploring and discover meats from different cultures and eras. If properly prepared, you won't be disappointed!

Look what venison does to a goofy guitar player from Detroit! I'm going to be 54 this year and if I had any more energy I'd scare you.
–TED NUGENT, ROCK STAR AND HUNTING ACTIVIST

APPLE WOOD-SMOKED LAMB SHOULDER

You're going to cook this one for six hours. That's right, a whole day of barbecueing for the most amazingly tender lamb roast you've ever had. When you're finished cooking, let the lamb sit under tented tin foil for at least half an hour. To juice onion, pulse in blender to a purée, then strain juice through cheese cloth.

6 lb (3kg) lamb shoulder, bone-in

6 cups apple woodchips, soaked in water
*   for 2 hours*
3 cups dry apple woodchips

Marinade

3 tbsp light soya sauce (45mL)

1/2 cup of white onion, juiced (125mL)

2 tbsp ginger (30mL)

1 tbsp garlic (15mL)

2 tbsp red wine vinegar (30mL)

2 tsp Five Spice Powder (10mL) (page 74)

1 tbsp honey (15mL)

1/4 cup olive oil (60mL)

1 cup beer (250mL)

Pita bread and yogurt (optional)

Directions:

- To juice onion, pulse in blender to a puree, then strain juice through cheese cloth

- Prepare marinade by combining all ingredients in a medium-sized bowl.

- Place lamb in a large, sealable plastic bag or non-reactive bowl and pour marinade over top; ensure the entire surface of the lamb is coated.

- Refrigerate for a minimum of 5 hours or overnight. Remove from fridge 1/2 hour before you plan to start barbecuing.

- You will need a total of three smoke pouches. To build a smoke pouch, drain 2 cups (500mL) of the wet woodchips and squeeze excess water out. Spread wet woodchips on a large piece of aluminum foil. Place 1 cup (250mL) of dry wood-chips on top and mix them together. Close foil around chips to make a sealed foil package. Using a fork, puncture holes on the top and bottom of pack.

- Place the smoke pouch under the grate on one side of the grill. Turn heat under the smoke pouch to 400F (200C) or high heat, and close lid. Wait for smoke. Once you see smoke starting to billow out of the barbecue, lower heat under the smoke pouch to 200F (100C) or low heat.

- Place lamb on cool side of the grill. Close the lid and cook for 1 hour per pound of lamb.

- Change smoke pouch every hour and a half.

Serves 6

BUFFALO BURGERS

Remember, buffalo meat is very lean and tasty! In this preparation, you'll be hard pressed to tell it apart from beef. Give it a try. I think you'll be pleasantly surprised!

2 lb lean ground buffalo meat (1kg)

1/2 cup butter, softened (125mL)

1 green onion, finely chopped

2 tbsp cilantro, chopped (30mL)

2 tbsp parsley, chopped (30mL)

1 small, red hot thai chili pepper,
    finely minced

Salt and pepper to taste

Directions:

- In a medium bowl, combine butter, green onion, cilantro, parsley and hot red pepper.

- On a piece of plastic wrap or waxed paper, form the butter mixture into a cylinder, about 1 inch (1.5 cm) in diameter. Wrap and close the ends. Place the butter cylinder in the freezer to solidify.

- Shape ground buffalo into 6 large balls. Cut frozen butter into six 1/4-inch (4mm) discs.

- Freeze remaining butter for use another day.

- Make a depression in the center of each buffalo meatball. Place a frozen butter disc into each meatball and seal inside. Shape meat into patties about 1-inch (1.5 cm) thick, keeping the butter well surrounded by buffalo meat.

- Preheat the barbecue to 375F (190C) or medium-high heat.

- Oil the grill and season the buffalo burgers with salt and pepper.

- Grill the burgers 6 minutes per side.

Serves 6

GIN-SMOKED LAMB

Gin has flavors of juniper berry and berries go really well with lamb. Try pouring a little extra gin into a tall glass with lots of ice and a twist of lemon to sip on while the lamb is cooking.

1 medium-sized onion, chopped

2 cloves garlic

2 lemons, juiced

5 tbsp gin (75mL)

2 tbsp kosher salt (30mL)

1/4 cup olive oil (60mL)

1 x 5 lb leg of lamb (2.5kg)

2 cups cherry woodchips – soaked in
   cold water for 1/2 hour

5 cups dry cherry woodchips

Directions:

- In a food processor combine onion, garlic, lemon, gin and salt and process to combine. Add oil in a thin stream, to form marinade.

- Place leg of lamb into a large sealable plastic bag and add gin marinade. Seal and turn bag to coat the lamb evenly. Refrigerate over night.

- Preheat barbecue to a high heat.

- Drain wet cherry woodchips and combine with dry. Wrap combined woodchips in aluminum foil. Use a fork to puncture holes in the top and bottom of the foil package to allow the smoke to flow through the package. The smoke flavor will infuse the meat.

- Place wood chip package directly over heat until the package begins to smoke. Once smoke is visible, turn to a medium-low heat. (428F /220C).

- Remove marinaded lamb from refrigerator and bring to room temperature.

- Transfer lamb to barbecue and smoke for 35 to 40 minutes per pound or until the internal temperature reads 293F (145C), rare to medium rare.

- Remove the lamb from barbecue and let stand for 10 minutes, slice and serve warm or cold. Enjoy!

Serves 8

GRILLED LAMB CHOPS

There is nothing better on the barbecue than a nice juicy lamb chop; charred on the outside and medium rare on the inside. I like to squeeze a splash of fresh lemon juice on the chops right after they come off the grill.

10 1/2-inch thick lamb chops

Marinade
Juice of 1 ripe beefsteak tomato
1 tbsp garlic, chopped (15mL)
1 tbsp fresh ginger, chopped (15mL)
1/4 cup cilantro, chopped (60mL)
1/4 cup apple cider (60mL)
1 tsp dry mustard (5mL)
3 tbsp brown sugar (30mL)
1/2 cup olive oil (125mL)

Directions:

- Place lamb chops in large, sealable plastic bag.

- Combine marinade ingredients in medium bowl. Mix well and pour over lamb chops. Refrigerate for 6 hours.

- Remove lamb chops from marinade and pat dry. Discard any leftover marinade.

- Preheat barbecue to 325F (190C) or medium heat.

- Drizzle lamb chops with oil and season to taste with salt and pepper.

- Oil barbecue grill and place lamb chops on it. Allow to cook 4 minutes per side (for medium rare) or until desired doneness.

- Remove lamb chops from heat and cover with foil and allow to rest for 5 minutes before slicing.

Serves 10

GRILLED VENISON CHOPS

Venison is very lean and not inexpensive, so please do not overcook. Venison is best served medium rare. Cook it to more than medium and you might as well be grilling soggy old newspaper.

4 racks of venison

Dry Rub

2 tbsp fresh thyme, chopped

2 tbsp fresh rosemary, chopeed

4 tsp of 5 peppercorn mix (10mL)

1 tsp oregano (5mL)

1 tbsp salt (15mL)

Directions:

- Pulse peppercorn in a coffee or spice grinder, add chopped herbs and then rub all over meat. Cover venison and refrigerate for 1–2 hours.

- Preheat one side of barbecue to 375F (190C) or medium-high heat and the other side of barbecue to 250F (120C) or low heat.

- Sear venison 2–3 minutes on each side over the medium-high heat to achieve a crust.

- Move venison over to low side of barbecue and continue to cook for 10–12 minutes for medium rare.

Serves 8

LAMB BURGERS

Any good butcher will have ground lamb on hand. As always, you're encouraged to experiment with ingredients.

1 lb lean ground lamb (500g)

1 tbsp dried mustard powder (15mL)

3 shallots, finely chopped

1 garlic clove, finely chopped

1 tbsp cinnamon (15mL)

1/2 tbsp allspice (7.5mL)

1/2 tbsp coriander (7.5mL)

Salt to taste

1 large egg, beaten

1/4 cup bread crumbs (60mL)

1/3 cup pine nuts, optional (75mL)

Directions:

- Preheat grill to 375F (190C) or medium-high heat.

- Combine all ingredients in a bowl. With cold-water-dampened hands, shape into 4 2-inch thick patties. Place on tray. Cover and refrigerate until ready to grill.

- Lightly oil the grate and grill each burger for 6 minutes per side, or until entirely cooked through. Serve as a sandwich in a pita, or on a burger bun, garnishing if desired with tomato, onion, lettuce and yogurt.

Serves 4

LAMB & FIG KEBABS

Few things go as well together as port, figs and lamb. Please note you need fresh – not dried – figs. And don't cheap out on the red wine you use in the marinade. No, it doesn't have to be a $200 bottle of Chateau Smelly Socks but it should be something you'd like to drink. A good wine with this dish would be a nice zippy Zinfandel or a big Shiraz.

Cippolinis look like little onions but are actually bulbs from the grape hyacinth. Like you needed to know this. No cippolinis? Use shallots instead. Have your butcher debone the lamb leg for you.

2 1/4-lb boneless leg of lamb (1.2kg)

15 cippolini onions

10 black mission figs

1/2 cup port (125ml)

3 tbsp olive oil (45ml)

2 tsp cracked black pepper (10ml)

Directions:

- Place the leg of lamb on a cutting board and cut away the silver skin. Remove excess fat to avoid any nasty flare-ups.

- Cut the lamb into 1/2-inch cubes and place into a sealable plastic baggie.

Marinade

1 cup parsley, roughly chopped (250ml)

1 tbsp oregano, roughly chopped (15ml)

1 tbsp garlic, chopped fine (15ml)

1 shallot, minced fine

1/4 cup olive oil (60ml)

Juice of 1 lemon

Zest of 2 lemons, chopped fine

2 tsp pepper (10ml)

1/2 cup red wine (125ml)

Kosher salt to taste

Cracked pepper to taste

Olive oil for drizzling

14 wooden skewers soaked in water for
at least an hour

- Toss the parsley, oregano, garlic and shallot in with the lamb. Pour in the olive oil, squeeze in some lemon juice, lemon zest and add the pepper and the red wine. Coat evenly and refrigerate overnight.

- Remove lamb from the refrigerator about 30 minutes before cooking.

- Remove lamb from baggie and discard marinade.

- Bring a large pot of water to a boil and add cippolinis. Cook for approximately 2 minutes. Remove and place in an ice bath to cool. Peel the skins off.

- Skewer the lamb cubes alternating with cippolini. Finish with a lamb cube. You should have 3 pieces of lamb and 2 cippolini per skewer. Repeat.

- Place on tray, drizzle with olive oil and season with salt and pepper.

- Slice figs in half and cover with port. Sprinkle with pepper and let stand for 15 minutes. Fit figs securely on to their own bamboo skewers. Drizzle with oil.

- Prepare barbecue for direct grilling. Preheat to medium-high heat. Oil the grill.

- Place the lamb skewers on the grill.

- Place a sheet of aluminum foil under the skewer ends that are exposed.

- Grill for 3 minutes per side for medium-rare or until desired doneness.

- Place the figs on grill for 2 minutes or until lightly charred. Note the high sugar content in the figs can burn easily so watch carefully.

Serves 6

LAMB KEBABS

These are so delicious. No need for a mint sauce with this combo of spices! To ensure evenly cooked meat, cut lamb into 1-inch pieces. Then cut up the center to the middle. Skewer the pieces at the thinner ends and thread.

2-3 lbs (1–1.5kg) boneless leg or shoulder
of lamb, cut into 1-inch cubes
4 Bermuda onions, cut into big chunks
4 red peppers, cut into squares
2 tbsp parsley, chopped (30 mL)
1 tbsp mint, chopped (15mL)
1 1/2 tsp paprika (7.5mL)
2 tbsp fresh sage, chopped
1/2 tsp freshly ground pepper
5 cloves garlic, finely diced
1/2 tsp salt (2.5mL)
2 tbsp olive oil (30mL)
Bamboo skewers soaked in water

Directions:

- Combine all the ingredients except the lamb, red onions and peppers into a large non-reactive (glass or ceramic) bowl. Mix well. Add the cubes of lamb to the bowl and toss until each piece is well coated. Cover bowl with plastic wrap and refrigerate for 4–8 hours.

- Place some bamboo skewers into water to soak for a minimum of 20 minutes.

- Preheat the grill to medium high heat. If you can't hold your hand over the heat for a count of "5 steamboats" the grill is too hot. Lower the heat and let it cool a bit.

- Arrange the lamb on the skewers alternating with a piece of onion and red pepper between each cube of meat.

- Oil the grill to avoid sticking. Arrange the skewers on the grill so that the tips are off the heat. Let cook for approximately 2–3 minutes per side until nicely browned.

Serves 8

MINT LAMB STEAKS WITH MANGO MINT CHUTNEY

6 bone-in leg of lamb steaks (1/2 inch thick)

3/4 cup of olive oil (175 ml)

2 tablespoons of chopped fresh mint (30ml)

1 cup white wine (250ml)

Salt and pepper to taste

Chutney

cup of fresh rinsed and packed roughly chopped cilantro leaves (125ml)

cup of fresh rinsed and packed roughly chopped mint leaves (125ml)

The juice of 1 lemon

2 garlic cloves, chopped fine

1 green chili, chopped and seeds discarded

2 green onions, chopped fine

1 tablespoon of brown sugar

Pinch of salt

4 ripe mangos cut into _ inch cubes

1/4 cup of water (50ml)

The juice of 1 orange

Directions:

- Place the lamb steaks in a sealable plastic bag. Add oil and mint. Toss to coat and refrigerate overnight.

- Combine all of the chutney ingredients in to a bowl and mix.   Place in a dish and refrigerate until time to serve.

- Preheat the grill to 375°F/190°C or medium high heat.

- Remove the lamb from the marinade and wipe clean. Season lamb steaks with salt and pepper. Oil the grill and place the lamb over direct heat. Grill for approximately 4-5 minutes per side until medium rare. Remove and let rest for 5 minutes before serving with chutney.

Serves 6

SWEET AND TANGY DIJON LAMB KEBABS

Sweet molasses and tangy Dijon combined with rosemary (a classic lamb flavor boost) make for a very interesting kebab. This goes great with a pasta salad or grilled spuds.

3-lb leg of lamb, cubed (1.4Kg)

Marinade

2 tbsp Dijon (30ml)

1 tbsp molasses (15ml)

1 tbsp rosemary (15ml)

1 tsp dill (5ml)

1/4 cup olive oil (50ml)

1 tsp pepper (5ml)

1 onion, chopped

Bamboo skewers soaked in water for 1 hour

Directions:

- Place the marinade ingredients into a medium sized bowl and mix together.

- Place the lamb and marinade in a plastic bag and refrigerate for 2 hours. Remove from the fridge 30 minutes before cooking.

- Remove the lamb from the marinade. Skewer 4–5 lamb cubes per skewer.

- Preheat barbeque to medium-high heat.

- Oil grill and season lamb with salt and pepper.

- Place lamb skewers on grill for 6 minutes per side.

- Tent with tin foil for 10 minutes before serving.

Yield: 4–5 Skewers

PUMPKIN LAMB BURGERS WITH TZATZIKI TOPPING

Check this one out. Pumpkin pie spice mix generally consists of allspice, nutmeg, cinnamon and ginger – a combination that works really well with the ground lamb. Don't tell anyone and watch the love when they take the first bite. Tzatziki is the main ingredient in the topping and can be store bought. It's made of yogurt, cucumber, mint and garlic and is perfect on top of this burger. Make an extra big batch as it will keep in the fridge for a week and the flavors get better the longer it mellows.

Patties

1 1/2 lbs ground lamb sausage, squeezed
   from casings
1 cup chopped onions (250ml)
1 1/2 tsp salt (7ml)
1 1/2 tsp pumpkin pie spice (7ml)
1 tsp cayenne (5ml)

Tzatziki Topping

1 cup of diced plum tomatoes (250ml)
1/2 cup chives
1 tbsp balsamic vinegar
1 cup tzatziki

4 6-inch pita breads

Directions:

- Combine patty ingredients, and mix well.

- Using moistened hands, form 4 burgers

- Cover with plastic wrap and let marinate overnight.

- Preheat grill to medium high. Oil the grill

- Grill the burgers for about 7 minutes per side

- Mix the tomatoes with chopped chives and balsamic vinegar, then add to the tzatziki

- Cut 1/4-inch off of each pita. Serve lamb burgers in pita with a dollop of tzatziki topping.

Serves 4

ASIAN SPICED LAMB BURGERS WITH PLUM SAUCE

There are a few great store-bought plum sauces out there but most of them suck. Make your own. It's easy and you can play with the recipe until you get the flavor profile you like the best. Then bottle it, sell it, make a bazillion dollars, retire to your own island off the coast of Greece or something and invite me for dinner.

Patties

2 lbs ground lamb (1 kg)

4 tsp fish sauce (20ml)

1 tbsp fresh minced garlic (15ml)

1 tbsp lime zest (15ml)

2 tbsp cilantro (30ml)

2 tbsp chopped fresh basil (30ml)

Salt and pepper to taste

Plum sauce

5 fresh plums, sliced in wedges for
    approximately 2 cups

1 tbsp ginger chopped fine (15ml)

Juice of 1 orange

2 tbsp sugar (30ml)

1/2 red onion, chopped fine

1 tbsp rice wine vinegar (15ml)

Directions:

- Combine patty ingredients in a bowl and mix well. Refrigerate for at least 3 hours to set up.

- Remove from the refrigerator and make small lamb patties approximately 2-inches across. Place on a baking sheet.

- Combine all plum sauce ingredients in a saucepan.

- Set pot over medium heat and cook for 8 minutes.

- Remove from heat and cool to room temperature

- Prepare barbecue for direct grilling. Preheat the barbecue to medium-high heat. Oil the grill and place the burgers on the grill for approximately 5 minutes per side.

- Remove from grill and tent for 5 minutes with foil.

- Serve with plum sauce.

Serves 6–8

BLACKBERRY PEPPERED LAMB CHOPS

A "double cut" just means you cut the rack every second rib for a thicker chop. You can ask your butcher to do this for you if you'd like. This is one of the most interesting marinades we've ever come up with and believe me, in 104 episodes of *Licence To Grill* we've come up with lots. The combination of berries, port and mint work well with the slightly gamey flavor of the lamb. Please, do not overcook.

10 lamb rack chops, double cut
   (ask your butcher)
2 tbsp olive oil (30ml)
Salt and pepper to taste

Directions:

- In a bowl mash the blackberries with the tines of a fork.

- Add the chopped mint, cracked pink and black peppercorns, port and black pepper.

- Place lamb chops in a sealable plastic bag and cover with the marinade.

Blackberry Pink Peppercorn Marinade

2 pints blackberries

1/4 cup chopped mint (60ml)

1 tbsp pink peppercorns cracked (15ml)

1 cup port (250ml)

2 tsp black peppercorns cracked (10ml)

- Put in the refrigerator to marinate for 3 hours. Remove from the fridge 30 minutes before grilling.

- Prepare the barbecue for direct grilling. Preheat the grill to medium heat. Oil grill.

- Remove lamb from baggie and discard excess marinade. Pat dry with paper towels. Season with salt and drizzle with oil.

- Wrap the exposed bones in foil. This will prevent them from burning, which gives the lamb a bitter flavor.

- Place seasoned lamb on the grill.

- Grill for 3 minutes per side or until nice char marks and deep caramelization is achieved. Watch closely to prevent burning.

- Remove from the grill and tent with tin foil for 10 minutes before serving.

Serves 5

ONION WATER LAMB CHOPS

This is possibly *the best* lamb chop recipe we've come up with. It is absolutely my favorite as I love the way the onion water infuses the lamb meat. Very yummy. Very easy.

8 loin lamb chops (each 4– 5 oz and
   1 1/2-inch thick)
1/3 tsp saffron threads (1.5ml)
1 tbsp hot water (15ml)
2 lbs onions, chopped
2 leeks, chopped, white part only
1 tsp ground turmeric (5ml)
2 tsp celery salt (10ml)
1 tbsp garlic salt (15ml)
1 jalapeno, chopped
Salt and pepper to taste

Directions:

- In a small bowl add the saffron and hot water, let sit for 2 1/2 minutes to steep.

- In a blender, mix half of the onions and half the leeks. Blitz.

- Once they have started to come together add remaining onions and leek and blend. Strain this mixture into a bowl.

- Strain the saffron into the bowl as well.

- Add turmeric, celery salt and garlic salt and stir it all together.

- Place the lamb chops into a sealable plastic bag. Pour marinade over the lamb. Add jalapeno pepper. Refrigerate for 2 1/2 hours. Remove from the fridge a good 30 minutes before grilling.

- Preheat the barbecue to high heat.

- Remove the lamb from marinade and place onto an oiled grill.

- Season the chops with salt and pepper and keep some water handy in case of flare ups on the grill. Barbecue the chops for approximately 3–5 minutes per side.

- Tent with tin foil for 5 minutes before serving.

Serves 4

SMOKIN' STUFFED LEG OF LAMB

I know, I know . . . I keep saying you gotta cook with the bone in whenever you can. But this time, you get to stuff the lamb and then smoke it 'til it's nice and tender and the cheese has melted inside with the pine nuts and spinach. And the aroma . . . oh, your gonna love the smells coming off that barbecue about an hour into the cooking. Get a big stick to beat everyone off as they try and see what's going on under the lid.

5 –5 1/2 lbs boned leg of lamb (2.5Kg)

1 clove garlic, sliced into 4 pieces

Salt and pepper

Marinade

10 garlic cloves

Juice and zest of one lemon

2 tbsp brown sugar (30ml)

1 1/2 tbsp olive oil (22ml)

Directions:

- To prepare the marinade, add first three ingredients to a mini food processor. Start the processor and gradually add oil to the mixture until thick and emulsified.

- Place the lamb in a large sealable bag and pour the marinade overtop. Shake bag so the meat is thoroughly coated. Place meat in the refrigerator and marinate overnight, up to 24 hours. Take the lamb out of the fridge an hour before smoking.

Stuffing

1 tbsp olive oil (15ml)

2 garlic cloves, sliced in half

1/2 medium onion, chopped

1/3 cup pine nuts (75ml)

1 1/2 lbs fresh spinach or packaged
    frozen spinach

1/3 cup chopped fresh parsley (75ml)

8 ounces mild goat cheese

1/4 cup dried cranberries (60ml)

1 tsp Worcestershire sauce (5ml)

Salt and pepper to taste

Drip pan

1 cup white wine (250ml)

3 sprigs rosemary

- To prepare the stuffing, heat oil in a skillet, add chopped garlic and onions and sauté for a few minutes until soft. Add pine nuts and stir. After a few more minutes, scrape the onions, garlic, and pine nuts mixture into a large bowl.

- Clean the spinach. Bring a large pot of salted water to a boil. Add spinach to the water for 30 seconds. Remove the spinach and run under cold water. Pat dry. Chop spinach and add to the pine nut mixture in the large bowl. If using pre-cooked frozen spinach, defrost and squeeze the excess moisture out before placing in the bowl. Add the parsley, goat cheese, dried cranberries, Worcestershire sauce, salt, pepper and mash together.

- Remove the leg of lamb from marinade and pat dry. Slice 4 slits through the leg and stuff one garlic slice into each. Season cavity with salt and pepper.

- Stuff the leg of lamb with the filling and close the meat around the filling. Secure the roast with butcher twine.

- To prepare lamb for grilling, place in a skillet with hot oil and sear meat 1-2 minutes on each side.

- Pour wine in drip pan and add rosemary.

- Remove the grill from one side of the barbeque and insert drip pan. Replace grill.

- Preheat the other side of the grill to 220C/104F.

- Place lamb on grill above the drip pan and cook for 30 minutes per pound.

- Replenish wine in drip pan as necessary.

- Remove lamb from grill, cover with foil and let rest for 20 minutes before serving.

Serves 6

GRILLED LEG OF LAMB

For some reason, I find white wine works better in a lamb marinade than red (although you'd drink red with the lamb – go figure). The recipe calls for 6 garlic cloves but go ahead and add a ton more if you'd like. Remember, barbecue is an art, not a science so messing with recipes is not only allowed, it's encouraged.

1 5-lb leg of lamb, bone-in (2.2kg)

1/3 cup olive oil (80ml)

2/3 cup white wine (150ml)

6 cloves garlic, finely chopped

2 tbsp chopped fresh oregano, plus sprigs
*   for garnish (45ml)*

1 tbsp chopped thyme (15ml)

Salt to taste

Freshly ground coarse pepper to taste

Juice of 2 lemons and the zest, chopped fine

Directions:

- Place the leg of lamb in a glass dish and drizzle with olive oil and wine, add garlic, oregano, thyme, salt and pepper lemon juice and lemon zest. Be sure to coat the lamb all over. Cover with plastic wrap or transfer to a large sealable plastic bag and refrigerate overnight.

- Remove from the refrigerator 1 hour before grilling.

- Prepare grill for direct grilling over medium heat.

- Remove the lamb from the marinade and pat dry with paper towel.

- Grill the meat directly over the heat elements for 1 1/2 hours or until desired doneness, turning halfway through.

- Check for doneness with an instant-read thermometer; it should register 130F /54C while resting. Tent the lamb with aluminum foil and let it rest for 20 minutes.

- Thinly slice, and serve immediately.

Serves 8

PORT MARINATED RACKS OF LAMB

The rack is probably the easiest and fastest cut of lamb to prepare on the barbecue. It has flavor from the bone, nice fat marbling and a pronounced lamb taste. Delicious. Less than 15 minutes on the grill and you're done which is just enough time to whip up a salad and some cocktails before your guests arrive. Perfect chichi weeknight dinner. Three racks easily serve 6 people. This marinade calls for a big boozy port to bump up the flavor even more. Get your butcher to remove the chine bone and French the rack for you.

3 racks of lamb, chine bones removed,

   racks Frenched

Marinade

1/4 cup plus 1 tbsp olive oil (60ml plus 15ml)

1/2 cup ruby port (125ml)

1/4 cup red wine vinegar (60ml)

1/4 cup fresh lemon juice (60ml)

1/4 cup whole grain Dijon mustard (60ml)

3 tbsp rosemary, finely chopped (45ml)

1 tbsp coarsely cracked black pepper (15ml)

1 tbsp fresh garlic (15ml)

2 tbsp shallots, minced (30ml)

1 tbsp of brown sugar (15ml)

Salt and pepper to taste

Directions:

- Place the racks of lamb into a sealable plastic bag.

- In a large glass or ceramic (non-reactive) bowl, combine 1/4 cup olive oil with rest of the marinade ingredients. Mix together and pour into the bag over the lamb.

- Seal the bag and place it in the fridge to marinate for 2 hours. Take the racks out of the fridge 30 minutes before grilling.

- Preheat the grill to 375F/187C.

- Remove the lamb from the marinade and scrape off as much of the liquid as possible, then pat dry with paper towel.

- Rub the lamb with the remaining 1 tbsp of olive oil and season with salt and pepper.

- Wrap the Frenched bones of the lamb in tin foil.

- Oil the grill and place the lamb meat-side down for 6 minutes with the lid up. Move meat away from any flare ups that may occur.

- Flip and continue to grill for another 6 minutes or until internal temperature reaches 130F/65C (medium rare).

- Let the lamb rest for 5 minutes under a foil tent and remove the foil from the bones before serving.

Serves 6

LAMB LOIN WITH ROSEMARY

A lamb loin is the same cut as a rack but without the bones. It's juicy and easy to prepare. Absolutely positively tent with foil for at least 5 minutes before serving and slice into medallions.

5 tbsp extra-virgin olive oil (75ml)

1/4 cup dry red wine (60ml)

1 1/2 tbsp chopped fresh rosemary (22.5ml)
     or 2 tsp dried (10ml)

2 large garlic cloves, pressed

2 small shallots, diced

1/2 tsp salt (2.5ml)

1/2 tsp ground black pepper (2.5ml)

2 lamb loins

Fresh rosemary sprigs

Directions:

- Whisk oil, wine, diced shallots, rosemary, garlic, salt and pepper in a bowl.

- Place the lamb loins in a large plastic sealable bag, pour marinade over the meat and coat.

- Let stand at room temperature for 1 hour or refrigerate for 4-6 hours. Remove from the fridge at least 30 minutes before grilling.

- Preheat grill to medium-high heat. Don't forget to oil the grill.

- Remove the lamb from marinade, shaking off excess and pat dry with paper towel.

- Season the lamb with salt and pepper. Grill lamb to desired doneness, about 4 minutes per side (depending on thickness) for medium-rare.

- Transfer to a platter and tent with tin foil for 5 minutes.

- Slice into medallions, garnish with rosemary springs and serve.

Serves 4

SMOKED LAMB SHANKS WITH HOISIN BARBECUE SAUCE

The superb lamb shank is a tougher cut of meat that requires long slow cooking with lots of liquid until it's practically falling off the bone and every mouthful is a sublime taste experience that makes the eyes roll back in your head and you go, "Oh man, gimme more of that!" Chinese five-spice is a combination of cinnamon, cloves, fennel, star anise and peppercorns. You can find it in any good grocery store or make your own.

Hoisin is a sweet and spicy Chinese condiment made from soybeans, garlic, chili peppers and a bunch of spices. It's also called "Peking" sauce in some places and is a killer accompaniment to the lamb when combined with barbecue sauce (your own concoction or store bought if you'd like) and applesauce. Enjoy.

6 lamb shanks

1/4 cup sesame oil (60ml)

Rub

1 tbsp salt (15ml)

1 tbsp sugar (15ml)

1 tsp black pepper (5ml)

1 tsp Chinese five-spice (5ml)

Hoisin Barbecue Sauce

1/2 cup barbeque sauce (125ml)

1/2 cup Hoisin sauce (125ml)

2 tbsp rice wine vinegar (30ml)

1 tbsp hot sauce (15ml)

2 tbsp of applesauce (30ml)

Hickory wood chips for smoking

Directions:

- Rub the shanks with the sesame oil.

- In a small bowl, mix together salt, sugar, pepper and Chinese five-spice.

- Rub mixture over lamb shanks evenly. Let sit at room temperature under plastic wrap for 1 hour or in the fridge for 4 hours. Remove from the fridge at least 30 minutes before cooking.

- Make a smoke pouch (see page 5).

- Prepare barbecue for indirect grilling. Crank heat on one side and place the smoke pouch directly on burner. Close lid and wait for smoke, then reduce the heat to 220F/110C

- Once temperature is reached, place lamb shanks over the unlit side of grill. Close lid of barbeque.

- Smoke the lamb for one hour.

- Meanwhile, mix together the Hoisin Barbecue Sauce ingredients in a medium size bowl.

- After 1 hour remove the lamb, and place on a baking tray with high sides.

- Brush each lamb shank with the Hoisin Barbecue Sauce.

- Cover the shanks loosely in tin foil. Seal package well and return to the unlit side of the barbecue

- Close the lid and cook for 1 hour.

- Remove the lamb from grill. Let it cool slightly and remove foil. The lamb should almost fall off the bone. Transfer the lamb (carefully – use tongs and a spatula) to a platter and tent with foil for 10 minutes

- Serve with additional Hoisin Barbecue Sauce.

Serves 6

LAMB SOUVLAKI

"Souvlaki" is the name of an ancient Greek general who convinced the invading hordes to lay down their arms in return for lamb barbecued on the end of their spears. Kidding. Actually, the word originally meant the skewer and not that which is skewered there upon. It is a classic Greek dish (See? I told you *everyone* barbecues!) with a simple marinade that features yogurt, mint, garlic, lemon and lime (optional) juice. Note the recipe calls for the lean lamb loin so cooking time is short.

2 lbs trimmed lamb loin, cut into
    1-inch cubes (0.9Kg)
1 tbsp olive oil for brushing
Salt and pepper to taste

Marinade

1 cup yogurt (250ml)
4 tbsp chopped mint (60ml)
2 tbsp garlic, minced (30ml)
Zest of 1 lemon
Juice of 1 lime
3 tbsp olive oil (45ml)
1 tsp cracked pepper (5ml)

6 wooden skewers soaked in cool water
    1 hour prior to grilling

Directions:

- Combine marinade ingredients in a bowl and mix well.

- Place cubed lamb in a sealable plastic bag. Pour marinade over lamb.

- Seal the bag and refrigerate for at least 6 hours and overnight is even better.

- Remove the lamb from the fridge a good 30 minutes before cooking.

- Wipe off the marinade and pat the lamb dry with paper towel.

- Thread the lamb cubes evenly onto 6 soaked bamboo skewers. Season lamb with salt and pepper and brush with olive oil. Wrap foil around the bit of the skewer that remains uncovered.

- Preheat barbeque to medium high and oil the grill

- For medium-rare lamb grill for 3 minutes per side for a total of 6 minutes cooking time, or until desired doneness.

- Remove lamb from the grill and loosely cover with foil. Let meat rest for 10 minutes before serving.

Yield: 6 skewers

GRILLED LAMB RIBS

No one ever thinks of lamb ribs. They're small and have a decent amount of fat (which is a good thing). There's not a lot of meat but what's there is perfect for the barbecue. Plus, think of the look on your guests' faces when you tell them what they're hoovering back.

3 1/2 lbs lamb ribs (1.59kg) with lots

   of fat (ask your butcher)

2 onions, chopped fine

2 tsp minced garlic (10ml)

1 tbsp chopped fresh oregano (15ml)

2 tsp chopped thyme (10ml)

1 tbsp liquid honey (15ml)

1/4 cup olive oil (60ml)

1 cup dry white wine (250ml)

1 tsp ground black pepper (5ml)

1 tsp ground cinnamon (5ml)

1 tbsp finely chopped lemon zest (15ml)

1/4 cup fresh lemon juice (60ml)

Cracked pepper and kosher salt to taste

Directions:

- To make the marinade mix in a small bowl the onion, garlic, oregano, thyme, honey, olive oil, white wine, pepper, cinnamon, lemon zest and lemon juice.

- Pour into baggie with ribs, reserving 1/3 cup (80ml) for basting later.

- Refrigerate overnight. Remove from the fridge at least 30 minutes before cooking. Discard excess marinade and season liberally with salt and pepper.

- Preheat the barbecue to 220F/110C with one side turned off for indirect cooking.

- Place the ribs on the side of the barbecue without direct heat.

- Cook with the barbecue lid closed for 1 1/2–2 hours or until tender.

- With 15 minutes of cooking time remaining, lift barbecue lid and drizzle ribs with reserved marinade.

- Tent the ribs with tin foil for 10 minutes before serving.

Serves 6

PECAN AND HONEY-CRUSTED RACK OF LAMB

The longer you let the lamb sit in the fridge with the crust on, the better. In the restaurant business, this is known as letting the meat "set up", so that the crust can properly adhere to the lamb. This makes for a better crust when it hits the grill. Be sure to trim the rack of any silver skin or excess fat beforehand. Silver skin is a tough membrane that sometimes is found running across tenderloin meats. If you don't trim it off, it will shrink while cooking and tighten the meat up.

4 racks of lamb, 5 bones each

1 1/2 cups pecans, chopped (375mL)

1/2 cup honey (125mL)

2 tbsp olive oil (30mL)

Zest of 2 limes

1 tbsp cracked black pepper (15mL)

Salt to taste

Directions:

- Season lamb racks with salt and pepper.

- Blend nuts, lime zest, olive oil and honey to form crust.

- Pat crust evenly on racks, pressing down lightly.

- Wrap in plastic wrap and refrigerate for 6 hours or overnight.

- Preheat one side of the barbecue to 375F (190C). Oil barbecue grill rack.

- Place the lamb over the cool side of the grill and cook with the lid down for 15 minutes (for medium rare).

- Remove lamb and loosely cover with foil. Let lamb rest for 10 minutes before carving.

Serves 6

ROASTED LEG OF LAMB

Mint and garlic were made for lamb. This recipe is a simple classic that really takes no time to prepare—with amazing results.

5 lb leg of lamb, butterflyed (2.5 kg)

Stuffing

1/2 bunch of flat leaf parsley, about 20 stems

1/2 bunch mint, about 20 stems

4 garlic cloves

2 tbsp balsamic vinegar (15mL)

Salt and pepper to taste

Directions:

- Blend parsley, mint, garlic and balsamic vinegar in a food processor or blender, pulse to a smooth paste.

- Place leg of lamb skin side down. With a sharp knife cut 1/2 inch (8mm) deep slits across the lamb about 2 inches (5cm) apart.

- Using your fingers push the paste deep into the slits.

- Place on a tray and season with pepper to taste. You may season with a small amount of salt if desired.

- Preheat barbecue to 325° F/162°C or medium heat. Oil the grill.

- Place lamb on grill and cook for 12-15 minutes per side or until crispy dark char-marks are achieved.

- Flip the roast over and continue to cook for another 10–12 minutes. Remove roast from grill, place on tray and loosely cover with foil. Let meat rest 15 minutes before slicing.

Serves 6

SPICY LAMB RIBS

Lamb ribs are tiny compared to what you're normally used to. The meat is tender and they work well with this spicy dipping sauce. Plus, there's no cutlery to wash after dinner.

4–5 pounds lamb ribs (1.8–2.2 kg)

2 dried chipotle peppers, stems removed

2 tsp red chili flakes (10mL)

2 tbsp cumin seed (30mL)

2 tbsp black peppercorns (30mL)

Salt to taste

3 tbsp sugar (45mL)

Olive oil for drizzling

4 cups cherry woodchips (1 litre)

Directions:

- Soak 2 cups of woodchips (500mL) in water for 1 hour. Drain chips and mix with 1 cup of the dry chips (250mL). On a large piece of aluminum foil place the chips and wrap up to form a secure but loose package. Using a fork poke holes through the aluminum foil, this will allow smoke to escape.

- Remove the skin from outer backside of ribs using kitchen pliers.

Barbecue Sauce

2 tbsp minced garlic (30mL)

1 jalapeno pepper seeded and diced

2 chipotle peppers, diced

1 Spanish onion, peeled and chopped

1 cup of canned, chopped plum tomatoes
    (250mL)

3 tbsp brown sugar (45mL)

1/4 cup red wine vinegar (60mL)

1/4 cup fresh chopped cilantro (60mL)

2 tbsp olive oil (30mL)

Salt and pepper to taste

Additional chili flakes to taste

- In a spice grinder, grind the chipotle pepper, chili flakes, cumin seeds and peppercorns. Transfer to a medium bowl and add the salt and sugar. Using rubber gloves to keep the hot peppers off your skin, rub the ingredients into the flesh of the lamb tearing the micro fibers of the flesh as you rub.

- Prepare barbecue sauce. In a large sauté pan add olive oil, garlic, onions and peppers and cook until slightly translucent. Add the brown sugar, red wine vinegar and tomatoes. Simmer for 15 minutes. Remove from heat add the cilantro, salt and pepper to taste and chilies, if desired.

- Prepare barbecue for smoking with indirect heat. Remove the grill rack from one side of the barbecue. Place smoke pouch in and turn the heat to high. Close the lid of the barbecue. Once the cavity of the BBQ is full of smoke, place your ribs on the grill rack without direct heat. Reduce heat to 220F (104C) or low temperature and close lid. Smoke ribs for 45 minutes.

- After 45 minutes remove smoke pouch.

- Wrap ribs in foil and return to barbecue. Continue to cook for 2 hours or until meat is almost falling off the bone.

- When ribs are tender remove from heat and baste with sauce. Cover with foil and let rest 10 minutes before carving.

Serves 8

STUFFED LEG OF LAMB

You absolutely have to marinate this leg for 24 hours to get maximum flavor infused into the lamb meat from the white wine and rosemary. And check out the ingredients in the stuffing. Try this once and it will become part of your regular repertoire.

5 to 5 1/2 pounds boned leg of lamb (2.5kg)

1 cup white wine (250mL)

3 sprigs rosemary

Marinade

10 garlic cloves

Juice and zest of one lime

2 tbsp honey (30mL)

1 1/2 tbsp olive oil (22mL)

2 tsp dried rosemary

Stuffing

1 tbsp olive oil (15mL)

2 garlic cloves, sliced in half

1/2 medium onion, chopped

*2 cooked chicken breasts, minced in
    food processor*

*1 1/2 lb spinach, cooked, drained and
    chopped (750g)*

8 oz mild goat cheese (250g)

1/3 cup chopped chives (75mL)

1/4 cup dried cherries (60mL)

1 tsp Worcestershire sauce (5mL)

Salt and pepper to taste

Directions:

- To prepare the marinade, add garlic, honey and the lime zest and juice to a mini food processor. Start the processor and gradually add oil to the mixture until thick and emulsified.

- Place the lamb in a large sealable bag and pour the marinade over top. Shake bag so the meat is thoroughly coated. Place the meat in the refrigerator and marinate overnight, or up to 24 hours.

- Remove the leg of lamb from the marinade and pat dry. Slice 4 slits through the leg and stuff one garlic slice into each. Season the cavity with salt and pepper.

- Stuff the leg of lamb with the stuffing (preparation directions below) and close the meat around the filling. Secure the roast with butcher's twine.

- To prepare lamb for grilling, place in a skillet with hot oil and sear the meat 1–2 minutes on each side.

- Pour wine in drip pan and add rosemary.

- Remove the grill from one side of the barbecue and insert drip pan. Replace grill. Preheat the other side of the grill to 220F (104C).

- Place lamb on grill above the drip pan and cook for 30 minutes per pound. Replenish wine in drip pan as necessary.

Serves 6

Two If By Sea

One fish, Two fish, Red fish, Blue fish
–DR. SEUSS

Blackened Scallops with Guacamole on Tortilla Chips

Cedar Planked Arctic Char

Cedar-Planked Salmon

Corn Husk Grilled Red Snapper

Crab Legs with Lemon Lime Butter

"Fun Time" Shrimp Quesadillas with Pineapple and Red & Yellow Peppers

Fennel Crusted Tuna

Whole Trout with Breadcrumbs and Anchovies

Trout with Prosciutto and Sage

Trout with Blackberry Glaze

Salmon with Strawberry Salsa

Grilled Haddock with a white Wine Garlic Sauce

Grilled Swordfish with Caribbean Salsa

Grilled Sea Bass with Mango and Red Onion Salsa

Grilled Grouper with Almond Butter

Gin-Marinated Grilled Shrimp

Grilled Chipotle-Lime Shrimp

Grilled Clams with Lemon Butter Sauce

Grilled Fresh Sardines

Grilled Lobster with Saffron-Lime Mayonnaise

Grilled Marlin with Coconut Chili Crust

Grilled Tuna with Peach and Onion Relish

Honey White Wine Marinated Smoked Lobster Tail

Iced Oysters Off the Grill

Bucket of Clams with Lemon Grass Butter

Barbecued Peppered Mussels

Oriental Grilled Catfish

Scallop and Salmon Skewers

Skewered Scallops with Prosciutto

Snow Bass in Parchment

Smoked Prosciutto-Wrapped Cheesy Shrimp

West Indian Rum Shrimp

Grilled Shrimp in Peanut Sauce

Asian Grilled Shrimp

Grilled Oysters on the Shell

Grilled Octopus

Crab Burgers

Grilled Lobster Tail with Curried Butter

Grilled Scallops with Apple Cider Accent

Scallops with Parmesan Crust

Wild Salmon with Raspberry Glaze

Seafood, mysterious to many, irresistible to others, can be finicky to prepare, intimidating to purchase, and it can put your wallet on the line. But with a little know-how and confidence, you'll soon be hooked.

Carpe Diem - Fish Of The Day?

Nope, Carpe Diem does not mean "seize the carp" or "catch of the day." It's Latin for "seize the day." And while we're at it, the word "seafood" is not necessarily limited to "fish from the sea." Seafood actually has two meanings according to my online dictionary:

– Edible fish or shellfish from the sea.

– Edible fish (broadly including freshwater fish), shellfish or roe, etc.

The Good Fat

Yes it's true. Not all fat is created equal! I'm not talking about that big old bulge above our belts after a good meal; I'm talking about the fat that we consume. Fish oil has recently garnered increased attention for its health properties. This, of course, is something our grandmothers have always known, but thankfully today's gel tabs are much easier to swallow than a spoonful of cod liver oil! Fish oils are polyunsaturated and are called omega-3 fatty acids. Omega-3 and omega-6 are the two essential fatty acids needed by the body, yet the body can produce neither of them on its own. Omega 6 is readily available in cooking oils, which people in western cultures get in abundance. Omega-3, on the other hand, is lacking in most western diets.

And Then There Were Three

I know I'm spending a bit of time here, but I want you to be armed with information about why fish is so healthy. Next time your teen turns up his nose, you can tell him that research has shown that eating fish such as tuna, salmon and mackerel will help his brain function so he can study more; improve heart efficiency so he can do more exercise; and boost his immune system so he won't miss school. I'm sure he'll be very appreciative and will thank you endlessly!

There are actually three types of omega-3 essential fatty acids: EPA and DHA, found in fish, some meat products and eggs; and ALA found in assorted nuts, seeds, dark green leafy vegetables, and some vegetable oils. By the way, you're onto something if you like sushi rolls; fresh seaweed is a good source of both EPA and DHA.

A Pound Of Fish

Even though there are reams of articles and evidence pointing to the benefits of eating fish, it is estimated that North Americans prepare on average only 15 pounds per person per year at home. However, we eat almost twice that amount in restaurants. This leads me to believe that people just need more information and then they can buy and prepare seafood with confidence. Buying fish need not be an ordeal. Search out a fishmonger who comes with good recommendations. When buying fish look for the following:

Smell: Fish should smell like you're standing beside the ocean, not like you've been in it for a few days.

Appearance: If you're buying a whole fish, it should look like it was just pulled out of the water. The eyes should still be bright; the skin should be firm – not dry and scaling off. If it's a fillet or steak you're after, they should be evenly colored with no brown, mushy spots.

Storage: Fish is an extremely perishable food. Once it's brought home from the store, refrigerate it immediately and cook within two days. If you've bought it frozen, keep it frozen. To thaw, it's best to put the fish in the fridge the night before you're going to cook it, or in a pinch, hold fish under cold running water. Don't use hot water as the heat will start to cook your lighter fish varieties and it will be unevenly thawed.

Tip – If your fish has been in the freezer a bit too long and you want to revive it, try soaking it in milk as it thaws. This will remove some of the freezer taste and help it smell freshly caught again. Discard milk before cooking.

Them Bones

O.K., everybody sing along: "Your toe bone's connected to your foot bone. Your foot bone's connected to your anklebone. Your anklebone's connected to your . . ." All right already, I'll stop! What is it about fish bones? There aren't a lot of them relatively speaking. Not an anklebone in sight. Fish bones are elusive little things. You can get one stuck in your cheek really easily, as they are hard to see. To detect fish bones, run your hand along the uncooked fillet or steak, or even better, drape the fillet over an inverted bowl. That will make the bones protrude upwards. Use a pair of tweezers or needle nose pliers to remove.

Tip – For you forward-thinkers: save the bones from your white fish and make a stock. A fish stock is a wonderful addition to all kinds of soups and sauces. Avoid using fish bones from darker fish like salmon; the stock won't be clear and the broth will be fattier as a result as they are fattier fish to start with.

Just A Tiny Bit Of Science (I promise)

Remember in the pork section we discussed myoglobin, the molecule that transports oxygen throughout the body? The more the animal uses its muscles, the more oxygen is needed to fuel them and the more myoblobin is needed, therefore making the muscle appear red or darker in color. Fish lead a charmed life – no gravity to fight; no legs for walking – so they produce very little myoglobin, making the muscles light in color and translucent in nature.

We've also talked about coagulation in cooked meat, and the same applies to fish. As the fish cooks, water is removed from the molecules and they shrink closer together. This will turn the once-translucent fibers into opaque molecules. See, I kept my promise, that wasn't so bad.

Can't Stand The Heat

Fish has almost no connective tissue, and because of that it is a very delicate meat to cook. A reliable guide for cooking is 10 minutes per inch at its thickest part. Some people like to test its doneness by "flaking" the fish. That will indeed work, however I caution you: by the time it flakes, it's also a bit dry. Instead, you might want to check its coagulation. If the meat looks opaque, then it's generally ready. I like to undercook it slightly, then tent it or let it rest for about 5 minutes. The residual heat in the fish will take care of the rest and tenting will bring the moisture back to the whole fish rather than just its center.

Will You Marinate Me?

Fish takes to a marinade like it takes to water. Start with an acidic property like lemon, add some oil to even it out, throw in some fresh or dried herbs, a bit of salt and pepper and you've got a feast in the making. Sounds almost too good to be true? There's a catch (no pun intended). Because seafood tends to be delicate and lacking in dense connective tissue, it absorbs acids much faster then other meats. So a marinade that contains lemon or vinegar will go to work breaking down fibers at an alarming rate, leaving your fish on the mushy side. And I can speak with absolute authority when I say, *you don't want mushy fish!*

Thirty minutes is all you need to marinade your delicate catch of the day and up to 60 minutes for a denser fish like a salmon or swordfish steak. And please, don't stick to the usual seasonings like dill and onion. Branch out a bit. Try a jalapeño, or chopped tomatoes. Be brave, it won't hurt you, I promise. Unless, of course, you add too much jalapeño. Then you'll have very clear sinuses.

Avoiding Sticky Situations

I'm a huge fan of fish, particularly when cooked on the barbecue. It's not as tricky as it would seem. The key to grilling fish, especially a fragile white fish, is to oil up the grill and make sure it's hot. There's nothing worse than having your fish stick to the grill and then having to scrape it off to eat it. If that happens, try putting a chutney or salsa on top to hide it. As long as it's not grossly overcooked, it should still be salvageable.

I like to cook my fish directly over the flame, but I'll sometimes use a fish basket. It makes turning it over a snap. Again, I caution you: if the fish basket isn't well oiled, the fish will stick to it as well. Some people like to cook fish on a wet cedar plank, which is also great or there are some folks who prefer to make a foil "boat" and cook the fish in this. This method will guarantee that it doesn't stick, but you won't get a nice crust on the fish and you'll lose some of the barbecue taste.

So many fish in the sea, so little time. The varieties and choices of fish are endless. I have to say I have a few favorites. Snapper is one of my favorites; it's light and delicate, yet very versatile. I like snapper done whole, with a jerk marinade, either straight on the grill or with a grill basket. Before cooking, give the fish a few slashes along the thicker part of the back to help the heat penetrate evenly.

Tuna – it's not just for cans! It's perfect for the grill because it's extremely dense. I prefer tuna cooked medium rare. Be careful grilling tuna though; it's extremely lean, so it can dry out very quickly.

I love shrimp, lobster, scallops and crayfish (also known as crawfish or crawdad). Crayfish are great because they're bigger than shrimp, and have the consistency of lobster (they're relatives). You can cook shellfish in its shell, which sort of acts like a little steamer oven; and for us tactile types, it's fun to get in there with your fingers and remove the shells after it's cooked.

Before you dive into the recipes in this section, I want to give you a few tips

about cooking shrimp and lobster: They are both incredibly easy to cook, however, the secret is: DO NOT overcook. For perfect shrimp, cook them about 1 1/2 –2 minutes, turning half way through. You'll notice that they will turn pink when done. When using a marinade make sure it isn't left on for more than 30 minutes or the acidic properties (citrus, vinegar, wine, etc.) will cook them and they'll get tough and rubbery.

Shrimp are sold according to how many typically fit in a pound: 8–10 per pound, 16–20 per pound and 21–25 per pound. Your fishmonger will guide you through this process.

I could eat lobster every day. My favorite is the 1 1/2–2 pounder. They tend to be sweet and tender at that size. Leave the lobster in the shell over the barbecue. It will help protect it from the fire and the meat is easy to eat right out of the shell. Some people think that lobster meat is done when it's a bright pink, but I beg to differ. By then it's like shoe leather. Look for a delicate light-pink color. Dip into a butter-based or mayonnaise sauce and you've got yourself a piece of paradise.

Listen my children and you shall hear
Of the midnight ride of Paul Revere,
On the eighteenth of April, in Seventy-five;
Hardly a man is now alive
Who remembers that famous day and year.

He said to his friend, "If the British march
By land or sea from the town to-night,
Hang a lantern aloft in the belfry arch
Of the North Church tower as a signal light, –
One if by land, and two if by sea;
And I on the opposite shore will be, . . ."
– FROM "THE LANDLORD'S TALE; PAUL REVERE'S RIDE"
     BY HENRY WADSWORTH LONGFELLOW

BLACKENED SCALLOPS WITH GUACAMOLE ON TORTILLA CHIPS

Nothing worse than an overcooked scallop. Don't leave these wonderful little taste nuggets on the grill for more than 90 seconds a side. You want them just warmed through in the middle and nice and crusty with the blackened spices on the outside.

12 large sea scallops

1 tbsp Blackening Spice (15mL) (recipe below)

12 large tortilla chips

Guacamole

2 large ripe avocados

Juice of 1 lime

1 medium red onion, finely chopped (30mL)

1 tsp jalapeno pepper, finely chopped (5mL)

1/2 tsp ground cumin (2.5mL)

Salt and pepper to taste (5mL)

1/2 red bell pepper, chopped

1 tbsp chopped cilantro (15mL)

Blackening Spice

1/2 cup paprika (125mL)

1/4 cup salt (60mL)

1/4 cup onion powder (60mL)

1/4 cup garlic powder (60mL)

1/4 cup plus 1 tsp cayenne (65mL)

1/4 cup white pepper (60mL)

2 tbsp black pepper (30mL)

1 1/2 tbsp dried thyme leaves (22mL)

1 1/2 tbsp oregano leaves (22mL)

Directions:

- In a medium bowl, mash avocado flesh with a fork. Add lime juice, onion, jalapeno, cumin, and salt. Mix to combine. Gently fold in bell pepper and cilantro.

- Rinse and dry scallops using a paper towel. Sprinkle liberally with blackening spice on both sides.

- Preheat barbecue to 400F (204C). Oil grill.

- Place scallops directly on grill and cook for approximately 1 1/2 minutes per side. Remove scallops. To serve, place a dollop of guacamole on each tortilla chip and top with a scallop.

Blackening Spice

- In a medium bowl mix all spices together well.

- Store in an air tight jar.

Serves 12 appetizer portions

CEDAR PLANKED ARCTIC CHAR

4 (about 2 pounds each) whole Arctic char,
cleaned

1 branch oregano

1 bunch fresh chives

1 bunch fresh dill

1 bunch fresh tarragon

8 sprigs thyme

2 tablespoons olive oil (30ml)

12 lemon slices

2 tablespoons olive oil (30ml)

salt and pepper to taste

Directions:

- Soak two 8 x 16-inch untreated cedar planks soaked in water for at least one hour.

- Season the fish cavity with olive oil, salt and pepper. Equally divide herbs to the cavities of the fish and close securely.

- Prepare barbecue for direct grilling. Preheat the grill to high heat.

- Place the soaked cedar planks on top of the grate to the far side of the grill and close the lid. Wait for small billows of smoke and then lift the lid and place the fish on the smoking wood.

- Turn off the heat underneath the char and cook for about an hour at 220F/110C leaving one side of the BBQ on.

- The char should take approximately 40 minutes to 1 hour to cook. Test doneness by opening the cavity and flaking fish.

- The fish should be slightly opaque and pink. Remove from planks.

- Note: Make sure your cedar planks are smoldering through the whole cooking process to ensure good smoke flavour.

Serves 6- 8

CEDAR-PLANKED SALMON

Cedar-planked salmon has become something of a Canadian culinary staple. Every high-end restaurant in the country was doing this dish for a while. Make sure you soak the planks for a good long time so they hold on the grill and infuse the salmon with not only a nice cedar flavor, but also a nice super pink color.

3 cedar planks broken into 8 x 6-inch pieces
1 side of Atlantic salmon cut into 8 portions,
   approx. 6 oz each

Marinade

1/4 cup vodka (60mL)
1/4 cup fresh lemon juice (60mL)
1 tbsp prepared horseradish (15mL)
1 clove garlic, chopped fine
2 tbsp juniper berries (30mL)
2 sprigs fresh thyme

Directions:

- Soak cedar in cold water for 1 hour.

- Mix marinade ingredients and place in sealable plastic bag, add salmon and marinate in refrigerate for 1 hour.

- Preheat barbecue to 400°F.

- Place soaked cedar planks on grill rack until they start to smoke.

- Reduce heat to 300°F and place salmon pieces on to cedar. Close lid on barbecue and cook for approximately 15 minutes. Salmon should have a golden color and flake with ease with clear juices running through. Serve with tarragon mayonnaise (page 226) and enjoy!

Serves 8

CORN HUSK GRILLED RED SNAPPER

I love to do a snapper whole on the barbecue and have tried it many different ways.
The way this mild fish absorbs the garlic in this unique recipe adds a new dimension
to a staple fish dish.

2–5 lb red snapper, gutted but scales,
  head and tail left on (1–2.5kg)

1 scotch bonnet pepper, seeds and veins
  removed

4 cloves of garlic

2 teaspoons of salt, or to taste (10mL)

1/3 to 1/2 cup of red wine vinegar
  (75 to 125mL)

1/2 cup of chopped fresh parsley (125mL)

3 tablespoons of vegetable oil (45mL)

4 corn husks, silk removed

Directions:

- Combine pepper, garlic, salt, red wine vinegar and
  cilantro in blender and blend until the mixture is
  smooth.

- Place red snapper in a nonreactive container and
  pour paste over fish, coating it well on both sides.
  Cover and refrigerate for 2 hours.

- While fish is marinating, prepare corn husks.
  Remove corn from husk, leaving enough of the cob
  to hold the husk in place. Soak husks in cold water.

- Preheat grill to a medium heat.

- Once fish has marinated, wrap fish with damp corn
  husks and place on barbecue rack. Cook fish with
  barbecue lid closed for approximately 10 minutes.

- When the fish is cooked, juices will be bubbling
  and you will be able to lift out the central bone
  easily. Serve and enjoy!

Serves 4

CRAB LEGS WITH LEMON-LIME BUTTER

There's not a whole lot you need to do to king crab legs. O.K. we have white wine, garlic, butter and hot pepper flakes. Now that's heaven!

2 lb (1kg) frozen king crab legs, thawed

Lemon-Lime Butter

1 cup butter, melted (250mL)

3 cloves garlic, chopped

Zest of 4 lemons

Juice of 1 large lime

3 tbsp white wine (45mL)

1/2 tsp hot chili flakes (5mL)

1 stalk lemon grass, peeled and chopped

1 tbsp olive oil (15mL)

Directions:

- Preheat grill to 375F (190C) or medium-high heat.

- Rinse crab legs well and place on grill to cook for 4–6 minutes.

- Remove crab legs from grill and serve with lemon-lime butter for dipping.

Lemon-Lime Butter Directions:

- Combine all ingredients in large saucepan. Let simmer over medium high heat until flavors are infused.

Serves 6

"FUN TIME" SHRIMP QUESADILLAS WITH PINEAPPLE AND RED & YELLOW PEPPERS

When fishmongers refer to shrimp as being "16/20", it means that's roughly how many you get per pound. The honey glaze gets pumped with a little orange juice and is a really nice contrast to the cheese filling.

2 lb tiger prawns (16–20/lb), peeled and deveined (1kg)

2 tbsp olive oil (30mL)

Salt and pepper to taste

2 red bell peppers

2 yellow bell peppers

1 tbsp vegetable oil (15mL), plus 1 tbsp(15mL)

10 slices pineapple, 1/4-inch thick (6mm)

8 large flour tortillas (8inch/51cm)

1/4 cup vegetable oil for brushing and grilling (60mL)

Honey Glaze

1 tsp lemon zest (5mL)

1/3 cup Dijon mustard (125mL)

2 tbsp honey (30mL)

3 tbsp orange juice (45mL)

1 tbsp Worcestershire sauce (15mL)

Cheese Mix

1 jalapeno pepper, finely diced

3 green onions, finely diced

4 cilantro sprigs, leaves only, chopped

5 cups cheddar cheese, grated (1.25L)

Pepper to taste

Directions:

- Place shrimp in a medium bowl. Toss with olive oil and season with salt and pepper.

- In a separate bowl whisk together Honey Glaze ingredients.

- Slice each bell pepper into 6 pieces and remove seeds. Brush each piece with vegetable oil.

- Peel, core and slice fresh pineapple into 1/4-inch (6mm) thick slices and brush with vegetable oil.

- Preheat barbecue to 425F (210C) or high heat.

- Combine Cheese Mix ingredients in a bowl and place in the refrigerator until needed.

- Oil barbecue grate and place shrimp on the grill, cook for 1 minute per side (or until bright pink in color), basting constantly. Remove from grill and let cool. Remove tails from shrimp, slice in half, lengthwise and set aside.

- Reduce barbecue temperature to 350F (175C) or medium heat.

- Oil barbecue grate and place pineapple and peppers on direct heat. Grill pineapple for 1 minute per side or until nice, golden char marks are achieved. Grill the peppers for 1–2 minutes per side. Baste pineapple and peppers constantly with Honey Glaze while grilling.

- Remove from the grill and slice red peppers into small bite size pieces. Slice pineapple into quarters.

- Lightly brush tortillas with vegetable oil. Divide cheese mixture over 4 tortillas and top with shrimp, pineapple and peppers. Cover with another oiled tortilla.

- Reduce barbecue temperature to 250F (120C) or medium-low heat.

- Oil grill grate and place quesadillas down on grill and cook for 4 minutes or until golden brown. Flip quesadilla over and grill for another 4 minutes.

- Remove from grill and slice into wedges.

Yields 16 pieces

FENNEL CRUSTED TUNA

I'm begging you, please don't overcook the tuna. It should be served medium rare just like a nice lean cut of beef. Medium at best, okay? Otherwise it's just going to be dry and a waste of your time, money and taste buds. The classic coating for a tuna steak is crushed peppercorns. Using fennel seeds gives this dish a nice mellow licorice kick.

2 1-inch-thick tuna steaks (1 lb/450g each)

1 tbsp plus 1 tsp of crushed fennel seeds (20ml)

1 tbsp plus 2 tsp of minced lemon zest (25ml)

1 tsp kosher salt (5ml)

Olive oil spray

Lemon wedges

Directions:

- In a bowl, combine fennel seeds, lemon zest and salt and rub coarsely into flesh of the tuna. Cover tuna with plastic wrap and refrigerate for 2 hours.

- Remove the tuna from the fridge and let come to room temperature 30 minutes before grilling.

- Preheat the barbecue to high heat and oil the grill.

- Drizzle oil over tuna, season with salt and pepper.

- Place tuna on grill and cook for 2 minutes per side.

- Serve with fennel tops and lemon wedges as garnish

Serves 4

WHOLE TROUT WITH BREADCRUMBS AND ANCHOVIES

I love cooking whole trout. You get the added flavor bonus of cooking on the bone. For you fish-bone-adverse people out there, these bones peel away from the flesh quite easily. This is our play on a classic trout dish with breadcrumbs. The anchovies and rosemary make for an interesting taste combination. Serve this with couscous salad and some grilled carrots

4 whole fresh trout, 3/4 lb each (340g)
  scaled and cleaned

5 tbsp extra virgin olive oil (75ml)

1 medium Spanish onion, minced

1 egg

3 tbsp chopped fresh parsley (45ml)

1 tbsp anchovy paste (15ml)

1 tsp fresh rosemary, minced (5ml)

2 tsp fresh thyme, (10ml)

1 1/2 cups coarse fresh white breadcrumbs
  (375ml)

Salt and pepper to taste

Toothpicks in water for one hour

Directions:

- Heat 3 tbsp (45ml) of oil in skillet over medium heat. Add onions and sauté until soft. Transfer to large bowl and cool.

- Add the egg and 2 tbsp (30ml) parsley, the anchovy paste, rosemary and thyme. Mix in breadcrumbs until well combined.

- Season the stuffing with pepper to taste.

- Season the fish cavities with salt and pepper

- Spoon stuffing into cavity (do not pack tightly). Use toothpicks to close cavity.

- Preheat barbecue to 375F/190C.

- Brush the grill with oil.

- Brush the trout all over with 1 tbsp (30ml) oil. Season the skin with salt.

- Place whole trout on the grill and cook for 5–7 minutes per side with the lid down.

- Using metal spatula, transfer fish to platter. Remove toothpicks and sprinkle fish with remaining parsley.

Serves 4

TROUT WITH PROSCIUTTO AND SAGE

Check out how easy this recipe is. The sage and prosciutto combo are perfect with the sweet juicy trout meat.

6 trout, 10 oz (315 g) each, cleaned, boned
    and scaled, with heads intact
Salt and pepper to taste
2 tsp freshly ground pepper (10ml)
24 fresh sage leaves
12 large thin slices of prosciutto
1/2 cup olive oil (125ml)

Directions:

- Prepare grill to medium heat

- Cut shallow diagonal slits in the meatiest part of both sides of the fish.

- Season both the inside and outside of the fish with salt and pepper.

- Place 4 sage leaves in the cavity of each fish.

- Place two slices of prosciutto down vertically so that they overlap slightly.

- Starting at end closest, place a fish perpendicular to the prosciutto and roll to cover fish.

- Brush both sides of the fish generously with olive oil and place gently on the grill.

- Turn only once during the cooking process when the prosciutto is nice and golden brown, about 4–5 minutes a side.

Serves 6

TROUT WITH BLACKBERRY GLAZE

You can have your friendly local fishmonger skin the trout for you if you'd like. While we make lots of noise about using fresh ingredients, frozen berries are actually better for the glaze because of their consistency. As always, the chipotle adds a smokey heat to the dish. Serve a big red wine with lots of berry flavors like a Zinfandel or a Shiraz.

6 6oz trout fillets, skin removed (6 x 170 g)

2 tbsp olive oil (30ml)

Salt and pepper to taste

Blackberry Glaze

2 cups previously frozen blackberries,
    defrosted (500ml)

Juice of 1 lime

1 chipotle chili, seeded and diced

1 tbsp chopped fresh ginger (15ml)

1 tbsp sugar (15ml) or to taste

Salt and pepper to taste

Cilantro sprigs to garnish

Directions:

- Place defrosted blackberries in a colander set over a bowl. Allow the juice to drain through by pressing down with a spatula. You should have 1 cup (250ml) of juice in a bowl. Discard any seeds.

- In a small saucepan combine the limejuice, chipotle, ginger, sugar, salt and pepper. Add the reserved blackberry juice.

- Set over medium-high heat to simmer for 5 minutes. Strain into a bowl and set aside.

- Preheat barbecue to 375F/190C or medium-high heat.

- Drizzle trout fillets with oil and season with salt and pepper.

- Oil barbecue grill.

- Grill trout for 2 minutes or until golden char marks are achieved. Flip the trout and continue to cook for 3 minutes. Baste the trout continuously with the blackberry glaze. Remove trout from grill when desired doneness is achieved. Serve hot with remaining blackberry sauce and cilantro sprigs.

Serves 6

SALMON WITH STRAWBERRY SALSA

There's salmon and then there's *salmon*. Fresh before frozen. Wild before farmed.
Salmon is a great fish that doesn't need a lot of messing around when you cook it.
The strawberry salsa works really well if you serve a nice Viognier or fruity
Chardonnay.

1 center cut side of salmon, skin on

1 tbsp freshly ground pepper (15ml)

Juice of 1 lemon

Juice of 2 limes

2 tbsp chopped fresh thyme (30ml)

2 tbsp chopped oregano (30ml)

2 tbsp olive oil (15ml)

Salt and pepper to taste

Aluminum foil

1 tsp vegetable oil for brushing foil (5ml)

Strawberry Salsa

1 cup chopped strawberries (250ml)

1 tsp lime juice (5ml)

1 tsp balsamic vinegar (5ml)

1 tsp sugar (5ml)

1 tsp cracked black pepper (5ml)

1 tbsp chopped mint (15ml)

Directions:

- Cut the salmon into 6 pieces.

- Place the salmon in a non-reactive dish. Squeeze lemon and lime juice over the fish. Sprinkle with chopped herbs and drizzle with oil. Let sit for 30 minutes.

- Preheat the barbecue for indirect cooking at 325F/160C with one side turned off.

- Place the salmon on a sheet of aluminum foil that has been brushed with vegetable oil.

- Place the salmon on the side that's turned off, close the lid and cook for 20–25 minutes or until desired doneness.

- Remove from grill, place on platter and serve with strawberry salsa.

Serves 6

Strawberry Salsa Directions:

- Clean and hull the core from strawberries, chop into 1/4-inch dice and place in a medium bowl.

- In a separate small bowl whisk together lime juice, balsamic vinegar, sugar and black pepper until well combined.

- Pour over strawberries, sprinkle with freshly chopped mint and gently mix.

- Serve immediately. Don't let it sit too long or the berries will get mooshy.

Yield: 1 cup (250ml)

GRILLED HADDOCK WITH A WHITE WINE GARLIC SAUCE

Haddock is a fish most people don't think of right away. It's a saltwater fish related to cod and has a sweet mild taste. It's perfect for people who don't like fish that taste fishy. (Huh?) This simple sauce doesn't overpower the fish. Grilled asparagus goes really well with this one.

3 haddock fillets, cut in half

2 tbsp olive oil (30ml)

Salt and pepper to taste

White wine garlic sauce

1/4 cup diced shallots (62ml)

2 1/2 cups white wine (375ml)

2 cloves roasted garlic

3 tbsp cold butter, cut into cubes (45ml)

Directions:

- Preheat the barbecue to medium-high heat and oil the grill.

- Drizzle the fillets with oil and season with salt and pepper.

- Place the fish delicately on the grill and cook for 2 minutes per side.

- For the sauce, put the wine and shallots in a saucepan and reduce by half. Add roasted garlic and using a hand blender mix thoroughly.

- Bring the sauce to a gentle boil. Remove from heat; add the butter gradually and whisk to incorporate.

- Strain sauce and keep on low heat until ready to serve. Drizzle over haddock.

Serves 6

GRILLED SWORDFISH WITH CARIBBEAN SALSA

Swordfish is meaty and holds up well on the grill. Make sure the coconut is unsweetened and adjust the hot sauce to suit your tastes. Serve the swordfish with grilled sweet potato and a nice Riesling. Make extra and invite me over. I'll bring dessert.

Caribbean Salsa

1/3 cup red onion, minced (75ml)

3 oranges, peeled with pith removed,
    seeded, sectioned and halved

1 1/2 cups vine ripened tomatoes, chopped
    and seeded (350ml)

Directions:

- Prepare salsa by combining all ingredients; toss.

- Cover and refrigerate to set up for an hour before serving.

- In a bowl, combine oil, wine, thyme, garlic, and shallots.

1/3 cup fresh parsley, chopped (75ml)

1/3 cup fresh cilantro, chopped (75ml)

1/4 cup shredded fresh coconut
   (unsweetened) (60ml)

Juice of one lemon

Juice of one lime

Juice of one orange

3 tbsp balsamic vinegar (45ml)

Splash of hot sauce

6 swordfish steaks 6 oz. each, cut 1-inch thick

1/3 cup of extra virgin olive oil (75ml)

2/3 cup of white wine (150ml)

Thyme sprigs

3 cloves garlic, minced

3 shallots, minced

- Put the swordfish steaks in a large sealable plastic bag.

- Pour the marinade over the swordfish steaks and marinate for 20 minutes.

- Preheat grill to high heat.

- Remove the steaks from the marinade and pat dry with paper towels.

- Place the steaks on the grill and cook for approximately 4 minutes per side until opaque at the center.

- Serve with salsa on top.

Serves 6

GRILLED SEA BASS WITH MANGO
AND RED ONION SALSA

There's been a lot of talk about sea bass being an endangered species. Chilean sea bass
in particular has been almost fished out. Bass is sort of a generic catch-all name for
lots of fresh and saltwater white fish that aren't even related. The best way to assuage
extinction concerns is to find yourself a good fishmonger.

4 1/2 lb sea bass fillets (approx 2 kg)

4 tbsp olive oil (60ml)

Salsa

1 mango, chopped small

1 red bell pepper, chopped small

1 red onion, chopped small

1 fresh jalapeno pepper, chopped fine

1/4 cup cilantro, chopped (62ml)

1 tsp ground garlic (5ml)

1/4 cup pineapple juice (62ml)

6 tbsp fresh lime juice (90ml)

Salt and pepper, to taste

Spice Rub

1 tbsp dried basil (15ml)

1 tbsp dried thyme (15ml)

1 tbsp salt (15ml)

1 tbsp fresh cracked black pepper (15ml)

Directions:

- Mix all salsa ingredients together and set aside. Refrigerate until ready to use.

- Mix all spice rub ingredients together in a small bowl.

- Brush the fish fillets with olive oil and rub 1 tbsp of the spice rub into each fillet and let sit for 5 minutes.

- Preheat the barbecue to medium high.

- Grill the fish for 4 minutes per side.

- Serve with salsa.

Serves 4

GRILLED GROUPER WITH ALMOND BUTTER

Make sure your fishmonger removes the skin from your fillets. This is a nice juicy fish with a sort of delicate taste that works nicely with the almond extract in the butter. Go for a lighter wine like a pino gris or a sauvignon blanc with this dish.

4 grouper fillets

4 tbsp olive oil

Salt and pepper to taste

Almond Butter

1/2 cup (1 stick) unsalted butter, softened
   (125ml)

4 oz almonds, crushed

2 tsp parsley, diced (10ml)

Splash of almond extract

Directions:

* Mix the butter, almonds, parsley and almond extract together in a bowl. Roll up into a log in plastic wrap and rest in the fridge for at least 1 hour.

* Preheat the grill to high heat. Season grouper with oil, salt and pepper and place onto oiled grill for 3 1/2 minutes per side.

* Remove from grill and serve warm with almond butter discs melting on top.

Serves 4

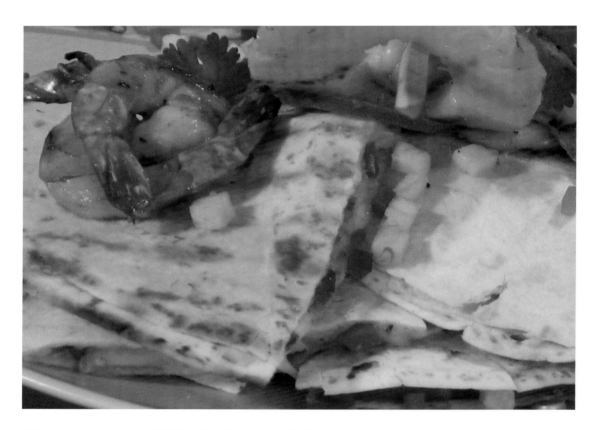

GIN-MARINATED GRILLED SHRIMP

Remember to set a timer when marinating the shrimp. You don't want to leave them much more than 30 minutes or they will go rubbery on you.

20 medium-sized shrimp, peeled and
  deveined

1/2 cup vegetable oil (125mL)

1/2 cup gin (125mL)

1/2 cup cilantro, chopped (125mL)

1/3 cup chopped onion (66mL)

1 tbsp garlic, minced (15mL)

Directions:

- Place the shrimp in a large sealable plastic bag. Mix together the remaining ingredients in a bowl and pour into the bag over the shrimp. Toss to coat well and refrigerate for no more than 30 minutes.

- Preheat the grill to high – 400F (205C)

- Remove the shrimp from the marinade. Season with salt to taste. Place the shrimp on the grill and cook until they are no longer translucent on one side, approximately 1–2 minutes. Turn and continue to cook for another minute or two until slightly golden brown and cooked through.

Serves 4

GRILLED CHIPOTLE LIME SHRIMP

A chipotle pepper is a smoked jalapeno in a spicy tomato sauce. They come in cans and can be found in most grocery stores these days. You can easily go up to six cloves of garlic in this recipe if you'd like.

30 tiger prawn shrimps in shell (21–25/lb),
*   cleaned, deveined*

1 chipotle pepper, chopped

3 cloves garlic, chopped

1 tbsp sugar (15mL)

Juice of two limes

1 cup pineapple juice (250mL)

Salt to taste

Directions:

- Place shrimp in large sealable plastic bag.

- In a medium-sized bowl, mix together the chipotle, garlic, sugar and salt. Add lime and pineapple juice.

- Pour mixture over shrimp and seal baggie.

- Refrigerate for 30 minutes.

- Preheat the grill to 400F (204C) or high heat.

- Oil the grill. Remove the shrimp from the marinade and season with salt and pepper. Place the shrimp on the grill and cook for 2 1/2 minutes, flipping halfway through or until shrimp is pink.

Serves 6

GRILLED CLAMS WITH BUTTER SAUCE

If you can't find clams, then mussels work in a pinch. Don't forget that when buying clams, the smaller the better. Bigger ones tend to be chewier.

4 lb of clams (2kg) (you can substitute mussels for this recipe)

1/2 cup of butter (125mL)

1/4 cup of white wine (60mL)

2 cloves garlic, chopped

1/2 tsp of freshly ground black pepper (2.5mL)

Directions:

- Preheat barbecue to a high heat.

- Clean and de-beard clams.

- Melt butter in a medium saucepan and add white wine, garlic and pepper and set aside.

- When barbecue is hot, place clams and/or mussels directly on rack and grill until they open, remove and place into a bowl. Discard any shells that do not open.

- Pour warm broth over clams and cover to keep warm.

- Serve hot and with lots of bread to sop up delicious broth.

Serves 8

GRILLED FRESH SARDINES

Sardine is a generic fish that refers to any number of small oily fish. Fresh sardines are an amazing treat when you can find them (depending on where you live). The difference between a fresh and canned sardine is the same as the difference between fresh and canned tuna. It's not even in the same ballpark.

12 fresh sardines, cleaned, head and
    tails left on
1/4 cup coarse sea salt (62mL)
2 tbsp freshly ground black pepper (30mL)
3 tbsp extra virgin olive oil (45mL)
12 lemon wedges

Directions:

- Rinse the sardines under cold water. Drain and blot dry with a clean towel. Pour the olive oil over the sardines and toss them gently to coat. Sprinkle generously with salt and pepper on both sides.

- Preheat the grill to medium high heat. If you can't hold your hand over the heat for "5 steamboats" the grill is too hot. Lower the heat and let it cool a little.

- Cook the sardines for approximately two minutes per side. Serve hot with lemon wedges.

Serves 6

GRILLED LOBSTER WITH SAFFRON-LIME MAYONNAISE

The mayonnaise with the Dijon and basil are incredible on the buttery textured lobster. One of my favorites! This recipe serves a crowd but can easily be cut in half.

10 live lobsters

Pinch of saffron threads (a little goes a long way)

1 cup real mayonnaise (250mL)

2 tsp Dijon mustard (10mL)

4 tsp lime juice (20mL)

Salt and white pepper to taste

1/3 cup olive oil

Directions:

- Place saffron threads in a bowl and pour boiling water over to cover. After 1 minute, once the threads have turned yellow, drain.

- Combine mayonnaise with saffron threads, Dijon mustard, lime juice and salt and pepper. Cover well and chill until needed.

- Preheat grill to 350F (125C).

- If you have to kill the lobster yourself, freeze the lobster for 2 hours, and then plunge them into a pot of salted boiling water for only 2 minutes. Remove the lobster and plunge them into cold water to refresh. Cut them in half. Remove the stomach sac from behind the eyes.

- Brush olive oil over the cut side of each lobster half. Place cut-side-down on grill, cover and grill for 8 minutes or until they are cooked through.

- Serve grilled lobster with saffron-lime mayonnaise.

Serves 20

GRILLED MARLIN WITH COCONUT CHILI CRUST

Make sure the coconut you use is unsweetened. Thai green curry sauce is available in most grocery stores these days.

6 1-inch-thick marlin steaks

Juice of 1 lime

Salt and pepper to taste

2 tbsp olive oil

Coconut Crust

1 cup unsweetened coconut (250 mL)

1 tsp Thai green curry (5 mL)

2 tsp Red Thai finger chili (10 mL)

1 tsp liquid honey (5 mL)

1 tsp chopped ginger (5 mL)

Directions:

- In a medium bowl, combine all ingredients for the crust and mix until well combined.

- Preheat barbecue to medium-high heat 375°F/185°C.

- Drizzle fish with lime juice and season with salt to taste.

- Place the fish on the grill and cook 2-3 minutes, until nice char marks are achieved. Flip and top with Coconut Crust.

- Close BBQ lid and continue to cook a further 4 minutes, until the crust is golden and fish is cooked to medium.

- Serve with Mango Cucumber Salsa (page 219).

Serves 6

GRILLED TUNA WITH PEACH & ONION RELISH

3 tablespoons canned peach juice (45ml)

3 tablespoons lime juice (45ml)

2 cloves garlic, minced

3 tablespoons fresh mint leaves, chopped (45ml)

1 medium red onion, finely chopped

1 can peaches, chopped

red bell pepper, seeded and finely chopped

Salt and freshly cracked black pepper to taste

4 Tuna steaks

Directions:

- In a medium size bowl mix peaches, mint and lime. Add garlic, red onion, bell peppers and mix. Add peach juice, salt, pepper and mix

- Chill until ready to serve.

- Pre-heat the grill to high heat.

- Season the tuna with oil, salt and pepper. Place tuna onto oiled grill. Cook the steaks for approximately 3 to 5 minutes per side.

- Remove tuna from the grill and serve with onion relish.

- The char should take approximately 40 minutes to 1 hour to cook. Test doneness by opening the cavity and flaking fish.

- The fish should be slightly opaque and pink. Remove from planks.

- Note: Make sure your cedar planks are smoldering through the whole cooking process to ensure good smoke flavour.

Serves 4

HONEY WHITE WINE MARINATED SMOKED LOBSTER TAIL

2 cups of seafood stock (475ml)

1 cup of dry white wine (250ml)

1/2 cup of honey (125ml)

1/4 cup of extra virgin olive oil (60ml)

2 tablespoons of kosher salt (30ml)

2 bay leaves

2 teaspoons dried thyme (10ml)

4-7 ounce Maine lobster tails, uncooked

3 handfuls of wood chips

Directions:

- 1 hour before grilling time, combine all the ingredients with the exception of the lobster, into a saucepan. Bring to a boil over high heat and stir until honey and salt have fully dissolved.

- Let the marinade cool to room temperature.

- Place the lobster tails into a shallow glass dish. Pour the cooled marinade overtop of the tails, cover with saran wrap and place in the fridge to marinate for 1 hour.

- Soak the wood chunks for a hour.

- Preheat grill to 500ºF on one side and leave the other side off. If you are working with a charcoal grill, push the coals to one side and leave the other side clear.

- Squeeze the excess water from the chunks and combine with the dry wood chips. Place in tin foil and make sealed pouch. Using a fork, poke holes in both sides of the pouch and place directly on top of the heat source. If using charcoal, wait until coals have turned to white ash and sprinkle wet wood chips directly onto coals.

- Close the lid and wait for smoke. Reduce the heat to 200ºF-100ºC.

- Remove the lobster from the marinade. Place the marinade in a saucepan over medium high heat and boil for 5-10 minutes. Keep warm over low heat.

- Place the lobster tails shell side down on the far side of the grill as far from the smoke and heat possible. Smoke for 40 minutes until cooked through. Baste after 20 minutes.

Serves 4

ICED OYSTERS OFF THE GRILL

2 dozen oysters, shucked with bottom
   shells and oyster liquor reserved

1 cup bottled clam juice (250mL)

7 tbsp fresh lemon juice (105mL)

4 tbsp extra-virgin olive oil (60mL)

2 tbsp freshly ground black pepper (30mL)

5 cloves garlic, chopped fine

2 tbsp cilantro (30mL)

12 ice cubes

3 cups apple woodchips (750mL)

Directions:

- Place 1 cup of the apple woodchips into a bowl of cold water to soak.

- In a large glass bowl, combine the clam juice, lemon juice, oil, pepper, garlic, and oyster liquor. Place oysters in a large plastic sealable bag and pour marinade over top. Seal the bag and place in the refrigerator for approximately 30–45 minutes.

- Prepare the smoke package. Squeeze the wet woodchips dry and spread them onto a large sheet of aluminum foil. Place the remaining 2 cups of dry woodchips on top and mix them together. Fold the foil around the chips sealing them inside. Using a fork, poke holes in the package on both sides.

- Remove the grill top on the far left of the barbecue and place the woodchip package directly on top of heat source. Turn the burner to the far left of the barbecue to high. Leave the remaining burners off.

- Place the empty oyster shells on a wire rack. Remove the oysters from the marinade and place each one back into a shell. Add a healthy teaspoon of the marinade to each shell. Reserve the remaining marinade to baste the oysters.

- Place the ice in a drip pan. Place the wire rack with the oysters on top of the ice in the drip pan. Place the pan on the right side of the barbecue away from the heat. Let the smoke infuse the oysters for approximately 40 minutes with the lid down.

- Dampen the finished oysters with a touch of marinade and serve warm with lemon wedges and more pepper.

Serves 4

BUCKET OF CLAMS WITH LEMON GRASS BUTTER

The name of this dish pretty much says it all. Like most things in life, size does matter when it comes to clams, only here you want smaller instead of bigger. Serve with lots of really good crusty bread.

1 lb fresh clams (450g)

Lemon Grass Butter

1/2 cup butter, melted (125ml)

2 cloves garlic, chopped

1 cup tomatoes, chopped (250ml)

Juice of 1 lemon

3 tbsp white wine (45ml)

1 tsp hot pepper flakes (5ml)

1 stalk lemon grass, peeled and chopped

Directions:

- Put all of the Lemon Grass Butter ingredients into a pot and let simmer over medium high heat until flavors are infused.

- Preheat grill to medium high.

- Scrub and rinse clams well.

- Place the clams on the grill with tongs, cook for 4 minutes or until all clams have opened. (Discard any that do not open.)

- Remove clams from grill, place in large bowl or bucket. Pour lemon grass butter mixture over top of clams. Serve immediately.

Serves 6

BARBECUED PEPPERED MUSSELS

If you've been reading through this book, you know how much I hate overcooking. It's a natural instinct to leave something on the heat for a minute or two or more when you're unsure. Mussels are sweet and juicy and dry out easily – they are ready to eat as soon as they open. Discard ones that don't.

2 1/4 lbs mussels, cleaned, sorted and debearded (1 kg)

1 cup of vermouth (250 ml)

Cold water to cover

2 bay leaves

Herbed Butter

1/2 cup room temperature butter 125 g

1 tbsp brined green peppercorns, drained, coarsely chopped (15ml)

1 tsp the brine from the peppercorns (5ml)

2 tbsp chopped fresh parsley (30ml)

1 tbsp chopped fresh tarragon (15ml)

1 tbsp chopped fresh thyme (15ml)

1 tbsp chopped fresh chives (15ml)

2 tsp freshly grated lemon zest (10ml)

Directions:

- Place cleaned mussels in a large stock pot and cover with the vermouth and water. Add bay leaves and bring to a boil. Steam for 4 minutes or until they are all open. Remove from the liquid.

- Meanwhile, prepare butter. Combine all of the butter ingredients and mix well.

- Remove and discard the top shell from each mussel.

- Spread herbed butter onto each mussel (overtop of meat) and place face-up on a perforated grill tray.

- Preheat the grill to medium high. Place the tray of mussels on the grill until heated through and the butter melts.

- Serve with lots of good bread, cheese and salad.

Serves 6

ORIENTAL GRILLED CATFISH

If you can't get your hands on some catfish then you can substitute any meaty whitefish, like a nice piece of tilapia or snapper. The recipe also works with salmon so go ahead and experiment. Remember to oil the grill really well before adding the fish so it won't stick.

6 catfish fillets, 6-8 ounce each (170 –227g)

2 tbsp vegetable oil (30mL)

Marinade

1 cup of light soy sauce (250mL)

2 tbsp peeled and minced ginger (30mL)

2 tsp dried chili flakes (10mL)

2 tbsp white granulated sugar (30mL)

5 cloves garlic, minced

1 tbsp sesame oil (15mL)

2 tsp cracked Szechwan peppercorns (10mL)

Directions:

- Rinse fish under cold water and pat dry. Place the fish in a sealable plastic bag.

- Combine marinade ingredients in a small non-reactive bowl and whisk together. Reserve 1 cup (250mL) of marinade for basting later. Pour the remainder over fish and seal the bag. Place both the fish and the reserved marinade into the refrigerator for 30 minutes.

- Preheat barbecue grill to 375°F (190C) or medium high heat.

- Oil grill grate.

- Remove fish from marinade and discard excess liquid. Pat the fish dry and season lightly with salt and pepper.

- Place the fish on the preheated oiled grill and cook, lid up, for 5–6 minutes per side. Baste with the reserved marinade after flipping. The fish should flake easily. Remove fish from grill.

Serves 6

SCALLOP AND SALMON SKEWERS

The scallops and salmon take the same amount of time to cook so they work well together on a skewer. You can also substitute vermouth for the white wine and lime juice for the lemon.

1 lb sea scallops (500g)

1 lb salmon, cut into 1 1/4" cubes (500g)

12 bamboo skewers, soaked in water

Vegetable oil for grill

Marinade

3/4 cup dry white wine (175mL)

1/3 cup light vegetable oil (75mL)

2 tbsp shallots, minced (30mL)

2 cloves garlic, pressed

Juice from 1/2 a lemon

1/4 tsp salt (1.25mL)

1 tbsp fresh thyme, chopped (15mL)

Directions:

- Combine all marinade ingredients in a ceramic or glass dish and mix well.

- Rinse scallops and cubed salmon with cold water and blot them dry with paper towel. Submerge seafood into marinade and let stand for no longer than 30 minutes.

- Preheat grill to medium-high heat

- Remove seafood from marinade and pat dry. Drain bamboo skewers and thread the scallops and salmon alternately onto skewers.

- Gently oil your grill and place the brochettes onto preheated grill. Cook evenly for approximately 2 minutes per side or until desired doneness. Serve and enjoy!

Serves 4

SKEWERED SCALLOPS WITH PROSCIUTTO

Two favorite things that grill so well with sweet salty prosciutto are scallops and figs, just not at the same time. This simple recipe works really well with a nice balsamic glaze drizzled on the plate. To make the glaze, get yourself a bottle of cheap balsamic (the ten dollar stuff) and boil it down to a thick syrup on the stove top. That's it, easy to make with tons of flavor.

1 1/2 lb sea scallops (750grams)
20 prosciutto slices, paper thin
Coarse salt and pepper
12 bamboo skewers, soaked in water

Directions:

- Preheat grill to medium-high heat.

- Rinse scallops with cold water and blot them dry with paper towel.

- Season scallops with salt and pepper. Place each scallop on a slice of prosciutto and wrap scallop until covered completely.

- Repeat until all scallops are wrapped.

- Thread wrapped scallops onto drained skewers.

- Place on grill and cook for approximately 5 minutes or until prosciutto is golden brown. Serve warm and enjoy!

Serves 4

SNOW BASS IN PARCHMENT

If you're concerned about the over fishing of Chilean sea bass, then ask your fishmonger for another variety like this snow bass. There are hundreds of different species of bass out there, so what do you say we give those little Chilean guys a break?

4 whole 1 lb snow bass, scaled, bones
  and fins removed

2 tbsp extra-virgin oil (30mL)

1 stalk of celery, sliced

4 small garlic cloves, sliced paper-thin

1 leek, white part cleaned and thinly sliced

1/4 jalapeno pepper, seeded, minced

1/2 red and yellow pepper, julienned

2 tbsp white wine (30mL)

2 limes, juiced

1/4 cup cilantro leaves (60mL)

Salt and pepper to taste

4 x 8-inch (10cm square) pieces
  parchment paper

Aluminum foil

Directions:

- Prepare barbecue for grilling with indirect heat by preheating one side of the grill to 350F (176C) and leaving the other side of the grill off. Place aluminum foil on grill.

- Heat 2 tbsp (30mL) of olive oil on medium heat in a small sauté pan. Add the garlic, shaking the pan constantly to avoid burning. When garlic begins to turn a golden color, remove from the heat. Pour the garlic and oil into another container and set aside.

- Place an 8-inch (10cm) square piece of parchment paper on a flat surface, with one corner facing you. Season the bass with salt and pepper and place in the lower third of the paper.

- Top the fish with 1/2 teaspoon (2.5mL) of garlic and oil, 1/4 of the leeks, celery, bell peppers and jalapeno. Add 1/2 teaspoon (2.5mL) of wine, 1 teaspoon (5mL) lime juice, and 1 teaspoon (5mL) cilantro.

- Fold the paper over the fish and fold the edges over, forming an envelope. Making sure there are no openings. Repeat with the rest of the ingredients to create 4 packages.

- Place fish on cool side of barbecue and grill with indirect heat at 350F (176C) for 25 minutes. Serve the fish in the packages. A delicious gift!

Serves 4

SMOKED PROSCIUTTO-WRAPPED CHEESY SHRIMP

This recipe calls for the biggest shrimp you can find this side of a lobster tail. The combination of goat cheese and cream cheese give the dish a rich, smooth texture balanced with sweet roasted garlic and the salty ham.

12 jumbo shrimp, (6–8/lb) peeled
and deveined

1/2 cup cream cheese (125mL)

1/2 cup goat cheese (125mL)

1 tsp pure honey

2 tbsp chives, chopped (30mL)

2 tbsp roasted garlic (30mL)

Salt and pepper to taste

12 sheets prosciutto, thinly sliced

Directions:

- In a medium bowl, mix cheeses, chives, honey, roasted garlic and salt and pepper. Combine well.

- Butterfly the shrimp using a sharp knife (cut shrimp lengthwise 3/4 of the way through, so shrimp opens up like a book).

- Place 1 tablespoon stuffing inside each shrimp, spread evenly.

- Wrap a slice of prosciutto around each shrimp, ensuring the stuffing is not exposed.

- Drizzle shrimp with oil.

- Preheat barbecue to medium heat.

- Place shrimp on well oiled grill.

- Cook for 2-3 minutes per side or until prosciutto is crispy and shrimp is no longer opaque.

- Remove from heat and serve immediately.

Serves 6

WEST INDIAN RUM SHRIMP

First you get to marinate the shrimp in rum and all sorts of spices. Then you get to smoke them with cherry wood. Your guests are going to die from pleasure, and they don't have know how easy it is to make. Just sit back and enjoy the applause.

4 lb large raw shrimp (2kg)

Marinade

2 cups dark rum (500mL)

1/2 cup melted butter (125mL)

3 tbsp honey (15mL)

2 tbsp pure vanilla extract (30mL)

2 tsp ground allspice (10mL)

2 tsp ground cinnamon (10mL)

5 tbsp very finely chopped ginger (75mL)

10 cloves garlic, finely minced

Finely minced zest from 1 lime

1 tbsp Tabasco sauce (15mL)

1 cup cherry woodchips soaked in cold
*   water for 30 minutes*

2 cups dry cherry woodchips

Directions:

- Preheat barbecue to 220°F (110°C).

- Shell and devein shrimp.

- In a small bowl combine marinade ingredients and mix well. Toss in shrimp and coat evenly. Place in the fridge to marinate for as little as 20 minutes to no more than 1 hour.

- Remove the shrimp from the marinade and place in a bowl. Let them come to room temperature; stand for 10 minutes, covered. Shrimp must be at room temperature when smoking.

- Squeeze the water from the wet chips and place them in the center of a large piece of tin foil. Add the dry chips and mix. Fold the foil into a sealed pouch. With a fork, poke holes in both sides of the pouch from which the smoke will escape. The more holes – the more smoke!

- Keep the burner under the woodchip pouch on medium- to high- heat and turn the other burners off. Once the grill is smoking, quickly place the shrimp directly over the grills that are off. Smoke shrimp with indirect heat for 10–15 minutes or until shrimp are evenly pink and slightly caramelized on the outside. Transfer shrimp to a warm serving platter and enjoy!

Serves 4

GRILLED SHRIMP IN PEANUT SAUCE

Shrimp has a pretty unique taste – it's not like you're going to mistake it for anything else. But it also absorbs whatever flavors you throw at it. Nice shrimp.

1 1/2 lbs of 6/8 shrimp, shelled and deveined

3/4 cup coconut milk (188 ml)

1/3 cup lime juice, freshly squeezed (84ml)

3 cloves garlic, minced

1 tsp salt (5ml)

1 tsp ground pepper (5ml)

Directions:

- Rinse the shrimp and pat dry with paper towel.

- Place in a large sealable plastic bag.

- In a bowl, combine the coconut milk, lime juice, garlic, and salt and pepper.

- Pour over the shrimp and marinate for 30 minutes at room temperature.

Sauce

3 tbsp extra virgin olive oil (45ml)

5 cloves garlic, minced

1 bunch scallions, green and white parts
   minced

2 tbsp fresh ginger, minced (30ml)

1/2 medium green pepper, stemmed,
   seeded and finely chopped

1/2 medium red pepper, stemmed, seeded
   and finely chopped

2 fresh tomatoes, peeled, seeded and
   finely chopped

1 1/4 cup coconut milk

1/2 cup creamy peanut butter

5 tbsp freshly squeezed lime juice

1/4 tsp cayenne pepper

1/2 cup cilantro, freshly chopped (125ml)

Salt and pepper

- Meanwhile, in a saucepan over medium heat, sweat off the garlic, scallions and ginger in oil.

- Add the green and red pepper and continue to cook for 5 minutes.

- Add the tomatoes and cook for another 2 minutes until some of the liquid has evaporated.

- Stir in coconut milk, peanut butter, lime juice, cayenne and half of the cilantro.

- Reduce the heat to low and continue to cook uncovered for approximately 10 minutes until the sauce beings to thicken.

- Adjust the seasoning and set aside until it is time to serve.

- Preheat the grill to high.

- Remove the shrimp and discard the marinade.

- Pat the shrimp dry with paper towel.

- Oil the grill and cook the shrimp for 2 minutes per side until pink.

- Brush them with some of the peanut sauce after the first flip.

- Sprinkle the remaining cilantro into the sauce just prior to serving.

Serves 8

ASIAN GRILLED SHRIMP

Chinese five-spice powder is a combination of cinnamon, cloves, fennel, star anise and peppercorns. Any decent grocery store will stock it or even better, experiment and make your own.

1 lb 6/8 shrimp, shelled and deveined (450g)

1 tsp sesame oil (5ml)

1 tbsp rice wine (15ml)

1 tbsp soy sauce (15ml)

1 tbsp honey (15ml)

1 tbsp sesame seeds (15ml)

2 tsp five-spice powder (10ml)

3 garlic cloves, whole, smashed

4 slices fresh ginger

Directions:

- Combine all of the ingredients in a sealable bag and mix well. Leave to marinate for 30 minutes.

- Preheat the grill to high heat.

- Oil the grill. Remove the shrimp from the marinade and place directly on the grill. Reserve the marinade.

- Cook for 2 minutes per side until pink.

- Put the remaining marinade in a saucepan and bring to a simmer. Reduce by half and drizzle over cooked shrimp.

GRILLED OYSTERS ON THE SHELL

As a rule I think oysters should be eaten raw but this is a nice change now and then.

Crushed iced for serving

12 oysters

1 lemon, sliced into wedges for squeezing

Directions:

- Preheat the barbecue to medium high.

- Spread out crushed ice on a platter and keep it chilled while preparing the oysters.

- Make sure all oysters are tightly closed, and discard any that are not.

- Place the oysters directly on the grill, with the deep side down, so that when they open the juices will remain in the lower shell. Close the lid. The oyster will begin to open after 3–5 minutes.

- With oven mitts and a sharp knife or shucker, open oysters fully. Remove the oyster from the flat side of the shell and place them with the juices on the deep side of the oyster shell. Place on the ice bed.

- Discard any oyster shells that do not open. Sever with lemon wedges and enjoy!

Serves 2

GRILLED OCTOPUS

You are truly blessed if you live somewhere you can get fresh octopus. Frozen will have to do otherwise. This ain't no rubbery roadhouse calamari. Grilled octopus is a real treat.

2 lbs cleaned, trimmed octopus (900g)

2 tbsp fresh lemon juice (30ml)

3 tbsp red wine vinegar (45ml)

8 tbsp extra virgin olive oil (120ml)

1 tbsp dried oregano (15ml)

1 tsp coarse salt (5ml)

1 tsp cracked black pepper (5ml)

1/4 cup finely chopped parsley (62ml)

Directions:

- Preheat the barbecue to medium-high heat and oil the grill.

- Scrape any reddish skin off of the octopus.

- Leave the legs whole and cut the body into quarters.

- Rinse the octopus under cold water and blot dry.

- You can thread the legs onto long metal skewers or place them directly onto the grill.

- Arrange the octopus on the grill and turn every minute or so until they are nicely charred on all sides (about 3 minutes per side – 8–12 minutes in all).

- Cut the grilled octopus into bite sized pieces and place in a bowl.

- Mix remaining ingredients together. Pour over the octopus and toss. Leave the octopus to marinate for 30 minutes.

- Adjust seasoning and serve with lemon wedges.

Serves 4–6

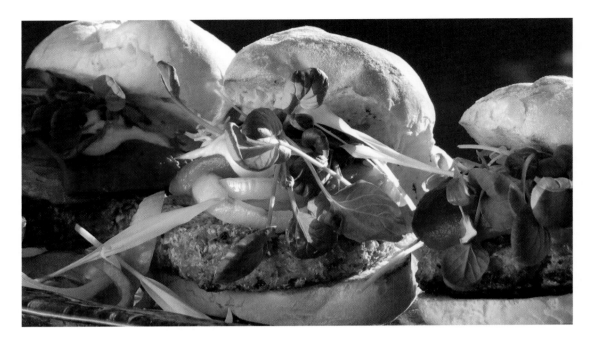

CRAB BURGERS

Make sure you pick through the crab meat with your fingers to find any bits of shell that might be in there. This is a variation on the venerable crab cake. The breadcrumbs will brown up nicely on the grill and the jalapeno adds a bite to the mild crab.

6oz fresh crab meat (180g)

1 1/2 cups breadcrumbs (375ml)

1 cup finely chopped green onion (125ml)

1 tsp finely chopped jalapeño

2 1/2 tbsp mayo (37ml)

1/2 tsp celery salt (2.5ml)

1/2 tsp ground black pepper (2.5ml)

1 tbsp lemon zest

Juice of 1 lemon

1 egg

1 1/2 tbsp Dijon mustard (22ml)

Directions:

- Combine all of the ingredients – except 1/2 cup (125ml) of breadcrumbs – into a bowl and mix.

- Form into patties.

- Dip each patty into remaining breadcrumbs.

- Cover and refrigerate until time to grill. Remove from the fridge 15 minutes before grilling.

- Heat the barbecue to medium high and oil the grill.

- Grill the burgers for 5 minutes per side until golden brown.

- Serve on grilled onion buns with garlic aioli and sprouts

Serves 4

GRILLED LOBSTER TAIL WITH CURRIED BUTTER

It's pretty impossible to find fresh lobster tails, so go for frozen. The thing to do is find a decent fishmonger who turns over his or her inventory on a regular basis. You don't want to pay big bucks for a lobster tail that's been sitting in the freezer forever.

6 lobster tails (6–8oz each), previously
*   frozen, thawed and cleaned*
Juice of 3 limes

Curried Butter

8 tbsp (1 stick) of unsalted butter at
*   room temperature (125ml)*
1 tsp curry powder (15ml)
1/2 tsp dried thyme (2ml)
1/2 tsp cayenne powder (2ml)
1/2 tsp cumin (2ml)
1/2 tsp ground cardamom (2ml)
1/4 tsp salt (1ml)

Directions:

- In a large bowl mix all of the spices with the softened butter.

- Turn the lobsters upside down with the shell on the counter, and using kitchen shears cut along the inner shell to expose the meat.

- Pull the shell open to about an inch wide.

- Squeeze about 1/2 tbsp (7.5ml) of lime juice on each tail. Spread a tbsp of the curry butter over each tail.

- Preheat the grill to medium-low heat

- Place the lobster tails shell-side down on the grill and cook for approximately 10 minutes or until the meat is opaque.

Serves 6

GRILLED SCALLOPS WITH APPLE CIDER ACCENT

Scallops are meaty yet delicate in flavor. They dry out very quickly so please don't overcook. Make sure you pat them dry with paper towel before skewering.

24 large sea scallops

3 tbsp olive oil (45ml)

2 tsp salt (10ml)

1 1/2 tsp ground black pepper (7.5ml)

Juice of 2 lemons

1 cup apple cider (250ml)

8 wooden skewers soaked in cool water
    for 1 hour.

Directions:

- Place 3 scallops on each skewer and drizzle with olive oil, salt and pepper.

- In a small bowl, combine lemon juice and apple cider.

- Preheat barbecue to medium high and oil the grill with a lightly oiled cloth.

- Place scallops on grill (1–2 minutes per side) and baste continuously with lemon cider mixture.

Serves 8

SCALLOPS WITH PARMESAN CRUST

Crusty scallops on the barbecue? You bet. These guys are great on a little mixed green salad or as a side with a steak or a lobster tail.

1 1/2 lbs sea scallops (675g)

3 tbsp melted butter (45ml)

8 wooden skewers, soaked in water
   for an hour

Coating

1/2 cup finely crushed melba toast crumbs
   (125ml)

5 tbsp parmesan cheese, grated (45ml)

1 tbsp parsley, chopped (15ml)

Paprika to taste

Directions:

- In a sealable bag, combine all coating ingredients and shake well. Brush the scallops with melted butter and toss into baggie. Shake to coat well.

- Preheat the barbecue to medium high and oil the grill.

- Skewer the scallops through center of meat and place on the grill to cook for 2 minutes per side.

- Remove and serve immediately.

Serves 8

WILD SALMON WITH RASPBERRY GLAZE

If you can't find wild salmon, then the farmed version will have to do. It's nowhere near as good but it's better than nothing. Of course, fresh is better than pre-frozen salmon. Not true of the raspberries however. While barbecue season offers up tons of fresh berries, the frozen variety with seeds removed actually are easier to work with in making this glaze. Just throw a couple of fresh ones on the plate for garnish.

8 x 6-oz salmon fillet (6 x 170g)

4 tbsp olive oil (60mL)

Salt and pepper to taste

Raspberry Glaze

3 cups frozen raspberries, defrosted (750mL)

2 tsp chopped fresh ginger (10mL)

1/2 tsp smoked paprika

Juice of 1 lemon

1 tbsp sugar (15mL) or to taste

Salt and pepper to taste

Directions:

- Place frozen, defrosted raspberries in a colander set over a bowl. Allow the juice to drain through by pressing down with a spatula. You should have 1 cup (250mL) of juice in a bowl. Discard fruit.

- In a small saucepan combine lemon juice, paprika, ginger, sugar, salt and pepper. Add the reserved raspberry juice and simmer over medium-high heat for 5 minutes. Strain into a bowl and set aside.

- Preheat barbecue to 375F (190C) or medium-high heat. Oil grill.

- Drizzle fillets with oil and season with salt and pepper.

- Place fillets and cook for 2 minutes or until golden char marks are achieved. Baste the trout continuously with the glaze. Flip the fillets and continue to cook and baste for 3 minutes. Remove fish from grill when desired doneness is achieved. Serve and enjoy!

Serves 8

Chicken or Dare

The greasy doorknob, the constant licking of the fingers. He's hooked on this chicken, isn't he?

– JERRY SEINFELD (ABOUT KRAMER) IN "THE CHICKEN ROASTER"

Asian Chicken Thighs with Black BeanSauce

Brown Ale and Maple-Glazed Chicken Wings

Caribbean Style Chicken with a Peanut Brown Sugar Spiced Rub

Brick Chicken

Chicken Drumsticks Wrapped in Bacon

Chicken Teriyaki

Chicken with Wild West Sauce

Cinnamon Chicken with Nutty Relish

Coffee & Pepper Rubbed Chicken

Smoked Spicy Turkey

Curried Chicken Kebobs

Garlic Rotisserie Chicken

Brined Smoked Turkey

Port Marinated Smoked Chicken

Grilled Chicken Breast with Balsamic & Herbs

Grilled Chicken in a White Wine Tarragon Sauce

Grilled Lemonade Chicken

Grilled Stuffed Chicken Breasts

Spicy Barbecued Chicken Legs

Grilled Chicken Burritos

Grilled Chicken Skewers

Hickory Smoked Turkey Legs

Lemon Grass Smoked Duck

Marmalade Duck

Peking Style Spit-Roasted Duck

Rotisserie Game Hens

Smoked Raspberry Cornish Hens

Grilled Miso Chicken

Lemon Ginger Drumsticks with Mango Mustard Seed Glaze

Lemon Pepper Cornish Hens

Muffin Tin BBQ Eggs

Orange Tequila Chicken Breasts

Peanut Chicken Burgers

Pecan and Dijon-Crusted Chicken

Quail Stuffed with Couscous

Tea-Smoked Chicken

White Wine and Dijon Mustard Whole Chicken

North Americans are hooked on chicken. According to statistics, in 1960 we consumed an average of 28 pounds of chicken per person per year. In 2005, North Americans ate approximately 85 pounds of chicken per person per year. Interestingly, in 1960 total red meat consumption was 131.6 pounds per person and in 2005 it was 112.8 pounds per person. Fish and shellfish went from 10.3 pounds in 1960 to 15.6 pounds in 2005. Notice anything? Despite the fact that red meats are now available in leaner varieties, North American tastes continue to shift away from them.

Chicken Little, Henny Penny, Goosey Poosey and Cocky Locky

Folks, I have to tell you: when it comes to poultry there is so much more than chicken. Some of my favorites are quail, Cornish game hen, turkey and squab. These birds are all terrific on the grill. You can butterfly most of them by taking the bone out of the center to cook flat, or put them on a rotisserie. Marinades, rubs and brines all are excellent methods for barbecuing poultry.

Fowl Play

The chickens we eat in North America today are largely descended from the Southeast Asian red jungle fowl, first bred in India around 2000 B.C. – now Cornish- (British) and White Rock- (American) bred. Cornish hens, capons, hens, roasters and broil-fryers are all chickens with relatively short life spans; from 7 weeks for capons to 1 1/2 years for tougher stewing hens:

Cornish Game Hen: Weight: 1–2 pounds. Great roasted; whole or stuffed.

Capons: Male chickens, the youngest in this list – usually about 7 weeks old. They are surgically unsexed and weigh 4–7 pounds. Tender meat; great roasted.

Roaster: These are the chickens we're most familiar with, and as per the name, they're excellent for roasting whole. Weight: 5-7 pounds. By the way, legs and thighs are underutilized on the barbecue. Too bad, too, because they tend to be fattier, and therefore quite moist when cooked properly

Broil-fryers: Weight: 2 1/2-4 1/2 pounds Young, tender meat. Delicious, using just about any method.

Stewing/baking hen, cock or rooster: Best for low-and-slow cooking or stewing. These are older chickens and therefore not as tender.

A Squab, A Turkey and A Quail Go Into A Grill

Let's not forget the other fowl. Here are a few wonderful varieties I enjoy:

Squab: Also known as game birds, squabs are young pigeons bred for meat. They are usually processed at about 4 weeks of age. (Aren't you glad you're not a squab?) Young, fresh squab meat will look rosy pink in color and have a flexible neck. It should look plump and juicy – definitely not dry. Squab is ideal for high-heat fast grilling – 5 minutes maximum. I like this bird done medium-rare, as it can get way too dry cooked any longer. By the way, an older squab will have darker skin, a smaller neck and be firmer to the touch. They are still edible but require a slower technique with closer attention to basting than the quick-cook younger bird.

Turkey: Thanksgiving turkey done on the barbecue? You bet! The pilgrims did it. It's easy and a very tasty change from the ordinary. You can smoke a turkey, or sear and then cook it slowly, or you can brine it. I personally like the results I get with brine. It tends to plump up the meat and help to retain moisture for slow cooking. A very simple brine includes water, brown sugar, a cinnamon stick and whole star anise. I like to let the bird soak in the brine for at least 24 hours then cook it slowly with a bit of smoke.

Quail: Native to North America, this small game bird eats mostly nuts and seeds. Some say that it is its diet that makes quail so mild flavored and tasty without much manipulation in the kitchen. As a matter of fact, with just a little olive oil, salt and pepper, quick, high-heat grilling for 2–3 minutes per side; it's incredible! If you'd like to use a marinade, an easy one for quail is red wine with just a touch of vinegar, olive oil and/or a dash of sesame seed oil, salt and pepper. Marinate for 30 minutes and mmm, mmm good!

Doctor, Doctor Give Me The News

Unfortunately, poultry – chicken in particular – can be home to some pretty nasty little bugs. The two most prevalent are *salmonella* and *campylobacter*:

Salmonella: Not just one germ but rather a group of bacteria that can be the cause of diarrheal illness in humans. The salmonella bacterium has been identified for over 100 years and is one of the most common forms of food poisoning. The infection usually will cure itself within 5–7 days; however the afflicted person needs to keep a careful eye on avoiding dehydration.

Campylobacter: A group of spiral-shaped bacteria that can afflict both animals and humans. Symptoms include: cramping, diarrhea, fever and abdominal pain, usually noticeable within 2–5 days after exposure to the organism. The bacterium lives at the body temperature of fowl and is thus adapted to birds, who are carriers. The bacterium is delicate and will not tolerate oxygen or drying. Freezing will reduce the number of bacteria on raw meat.

Scrub, Scrub, Scrub

Doesn't all this talk about bacteria in chicken make you want to rush out and get some? Maybe not, you say? Fear not; there is a way to lessen your exposure to these microscopic critters:

Washing: Many people think you should wash chicken before you cook it. You certainly can if you wish. However, washing chicken can potentially spread the bacterium over everything that it touches in the process. A far more effective way to kill off any bacteria present is to ensure that the internal temperature of cooked chicken reach at least 165 F.

Plastic Or Wood?: Much has been written about the plastic vs. wood cutting-board debate. I personally don't want to add volumes to it, however suffice it to say they are both conductors of bacteria. It's a matter of common sense. After using your board for cutting your poultry pieces (not paltry pieces), scrub it down with hot water and soap – white vinegar works really well, too. Every so often, really give your board a serious scrubbing with household bleach and let it air dry.

Not All Chickens Are Created Equal

Just like beef and pork, chickens are subject to the same form of inspection and grading. Inspection of the internal organs for signs of disease is mandatory. Chickens that pass inspection are given a seal of "wholesomeness." To further help the consumer, chickens are also graded on a voluntary basis. **Grade A** chickens are plump, clean, with no broken bones or bruises and no skin discolorations. **Grades B** and **C** have some sort of visible damage, but are still considered healthy and edible. These chickens are often cut for packaging or used for commercial purposes.

Safe Keeping

Most of us are already familiar with buying chicken. But what do you look for when you're at the grocer? Do you simply pick up the Styrofoam package, give it a poke and a shake and put it in your cart? Here are a few tips that might help you:

When chickens are processed, the blood is drained before packaging, and only a very small amount of blood will remain in the muscle tissue. Watch out for an improperly bled chicken, which will tend to have a cherry-red hue to the skin. Usually these chickens are detected at the plant and not passed through.

A small amount of pink-colored fluid in the bottom of the package is normal. This is water that has been absorbed during the chilling process.

Keeping chicken cold will help reduce the spread of bacteria and increase shelf life. Chicken should feel cold to the touch when purchased and can be stored in the fridge for up to 2 days or frozen, ideally no longer than 1 month.

Defrosting is best done slowly either in the refrigerator, in cold water or in the microwave. I'm not keen on microwave defrosting, as it tends to thaw chicken unevenly and you can get cooked bits that will be dry and chewy.

If thawing in the refrigerator, plan ahead. Boneless cuts will thaw overnight, while whole birds will require 2 days or longer. If you choose not to use the chicken that you've defrosted in your fridge, you can safely put it back in the freezer for future use.

For more spontaneous defrosting, put your chicken in an airtight bag and submerge it in a container of cold water, changing the water every 30 minutes to make sure it stays cold. A whole bird will take 2–3 hours and chicken parts will defrost in about an hour. If using this method, definitely cook the chicken before freezing again.

When defrosting in the microwave, care is needed. First set the microwave's heat intensity to its lowest setting. This will still produce heat, so there is a chance the chicken will begin to cook, especially around the edges. Cook chicken immediately to at least 165F.

Never partially cook chicken for later use. If the heating process has been started, cook immediately.

When using a marinade on raw chicken, do not use any leftover marinade on cooked product. If you must, boil it for at least 5 minutes.

Last But Certainly Not Least

Remember to tent your meat after it's been cooked. Go ahead and take it off the grill at around 155F. (For chicken parts, that should take about 15–20 minutes; for a whole bird, about 1–11/2 hours in a barbecue that is at 400–500F.) Leave the thermometer in the meat, cover and let the temperature rise to 165F. Your reward for this last step will be a juicy, succulent meal.

Tip – Backyard barbecues and family reunion cookouts are breeding grounds for food poisoning. When I was a kid, nobody gave much thought to leaving a half-eaten chicken out all day, then saving it for leftovers. For safety's sake, refrigerate cooked chicken after 4 hours. This is especially true for meat that has been stuffed.

Do not be afraid of simplicity. If you have a cold chicken for supper, why cover it with a tasteless white sauce which makes it look like a pretentious dish on the buffet table at some fancy dress ball?
–FROM SIMPLE FRENCH COOKING FOR ENGLISH HOMES (1923) BY
 X. MARCEL BOULESTIN, CHEF AND FOOD WRITER (1878-1943)

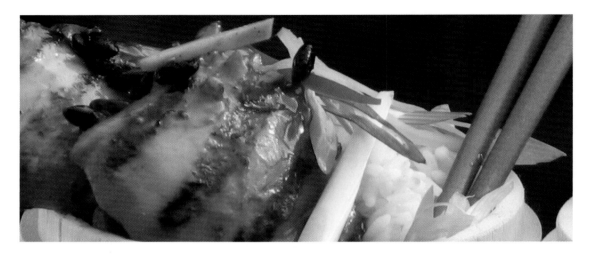

ASIAN CHICKEN THIGHS WITH BLACK BEAN SAUCE

Chicken thighs are probably the most underused cut of the bird. Thighs have nice flavorful dark meat and you get to cook on the bone for extra chicken taste. Any pale ale will do instead of Chinese beer for the dipping sauce.

12 boneless, skinless chicken thighs

Marinade

3 tbsp dry sherry (45ml)

2 tsp soy sauce (10ml)

1 tsp white sugar (5ml)

Black Bean Dipping Sauce

1/2 cup black bean sauce (125ml)

1 tsp grated fresh ginger (5ml)

2 green onions sliced thin

1/4 cup Chinese beer (60ml)

1 tbsp white sugar (15ml)

Directions:

- Mix the marinade ingredients until well combined and pour into a plastic baggie. Add the chicken and refrigerate for 30 minutes.

- Remove from the fridge 15 minutes before grilling.

- Preheat the barbeque to medium high.

- Remove the chicken from marinade and pat dry. Discard the leftover marinade.

- Place the chicken on a well oiled grill.

- Grill the chicken for 4 minutes per side or until cooked through and golden brown.

- Remove from grill and cover with foil for 5 minutes before serving.

- Serve with Black Bean Dipping Sauce.

- To prepare Black Bean Dipping Sauce, mix all sauce ingredients in a small bowl.

Serves 6

BROWN ALE AND MAPLE-GLAZED CHICKEN WINGS

Brown ale has a bit more depth of flavor than the pale kind but not as "thick" as the dark lager. Orange, lime, ginger and cilantro in the marinade give the chicken wings a kick you ain't gonna get in your neighborhood pub.

1 1/2 lbs of chicken wings (675g)

Marinade

1 orange, halved and sliced

1 lime, halved and sliced

3 cloves of garlic, chopped

1/2 knob ginger, chopped

1/2 red onion, halved and sliced

1/2 bunch cilantro, chopped

1/2 bottle brown ale

6 tbsp of vegetable oil (90ml)

1 tbsp hot sauce (15ml)

Directions:

- Make the marinade by combining orange and lime slices, garlic, ginger, onion, cilantro, brown ale, vegetable oil and hot sauce in large non-reactive bowl.

- Pour yourself a beer if you'd like. Hey, it's hot outside.

- Place the chicken wings in a large sealable plastic bag, pour marinade over top and marinate in refrigerator for 6 hours, or up to 24 hours. Remove from fridge 30 minutes before grilling.

Brown Ale Maple Glaze

1/2 bottle brown ale

2 cups orange juice (500ml)

3/4 cup maple syrup (175ml)

3 tbsp hot sauce (45ml)

1 tbsp ginger, chopped (5ml)

2 tbsp lemon juice (30ml)

Celery salt to taste

2 tbsp garlic salt (30ml)

- Make the glaze sauce by combining all ingredients in a non-reactive bowl.

- Preheat the barbecue to high and oil the grill

- Place the chicken wings on the grill and cook for about 5 minutes per side.

- Brush the wings with maple glaze sauce and cook an additional minute on each side. Don't do this too early in the cooking process or you'll get flare ups that will ruin the wings

- Serve with the same beer as in the glaze.

Yield: 1 1/2 lbs of chicken wings (675g)

CARIBBEAN STYLE CHICKEN WITH A PEANUT BROWN SUGAR SPICED RUB

The reason we're using thighs for this recipe instead of the more popular chicken breasts is all about the fat. There isn't enough fat on a breast to keep it moist and juicy through a 50 minute cooking process. Remember fat is good, fat is taste, fat is your friend (in moderation of course).

Spice Rub

1/2 cup finely ground roasted peanuts (125ml)

1/4 cup packed light brown sugar (60ml)

1 tbsp kosher salt (15ml)

2 1/4 tsp cayenne (10.1ml)

1 tsp crumbled bay leaf

1/2 tsp plus a pinch ground cloves (2.5ml)

1/2 tsp plus a pinch ground nutmeg (2.5ml)

1/2 tsp ground cinnamon (2.5ml)

1 tsp dried chilies (5ml)

Salt and pepper to taste

10 chicken thighs, skins on, bone in

1 12-oz bottle dark beer

Directions:

- To make the spice rub, combine the peanuts, brown sugar, salt, cayenne, bay leaf, cloves, nutmeg, cinnamon and chilies in a bowl.

- With a small, sharp knife, score each thigh twice on each side, 1/2-inch deep.

- Place the chicken in a large bowl and add the spice rub and toss to coat evenly.

- Prepare the barbecue for indirect grilling. Preheat the barbecue to 250F/110C.

- Place a drip pan over heat source and pour in beer.

- Place the chicken thighs on the side of the barbecue without direct heat.

- Cook chicken thighs over indirect heat with the lid down for 40 to 50 minutes or until juices run clear and skin is crispy.

- Remove from the grill, tent with foil for 5 minutes, plate and serve.

Serves 5

BRICK CHICKEN

The weight of the brick on top of the bird reduces the cooking time (the brick also transfers heat…sort of) and the combination of the cilantro and lime juice gives this recipe a *zing* when you pop it in your mouth. Make an extra breast and cut it up for lunch the next day on good bread with garlic mayo and your favorite hot sauce.

Rub

2 tsp ground cumin (10ml)

1 tsp ground coriander (5ml)

1/2 tsp salt (2.5ml)

1/2 tsp freshly ground black pepper (2.5ml)

1/2 tsp cinnamon (2.5ml)

1/4 tsp celery salt (1.25ml)

2 tbsp red chili pepper (30ml) - optional

Directions:

- Combine all of the rub ingredients in a small bowl and mix.

- If using whole chicken breasts, cut in half and trim off excess fat.

- Rinse the chicken under cold water and pat dry (this help makes the skin crispy and cleans off any gunk).

- Pat the rub mixture into both sides of each breast and place them in a glass or ceramic dish. Drizzle with 2 tbsp of olive oil and rub again on both sides.

2 whole skinless, boneless chicken breasts

   (12–16 oz each)

(or 4 half breasts, 6–8 ounces each)

1/4 cup extra virgin olive oil (60ml)

4 cloves garlic, finely chopped

1/2 cup fresh cilantro, chopped (125ml)

1/3 cup fresh lime juice (75ml)

2 bricks wrapped in aluminum foil

- Sprinkle with chopped garlic and cilantro.
- Pour the lime juice and remaining olive oil over top and flip the chicken to ensure even coating.
- Place the chicken in a large plastic sealable bag and leave to marinate in the fridge for 1 to 2 hours.
- Preheat the grill to medium/high heat 400F/200C
- Oil the grill. Have a drink.
- Place the chicken on the grill. Place one foil-wrapped brick on top of each 2 breast halves. Leave the lid up.
- After two minutes, lift the brick and rotate the chicken a quarter turn, but do not flip. Replace the brick and continue to cook for another 2 minutes.
- Flip the chicken, place on an angle, replace the brick on top and continue to cook for another 5 minutes, again rotating the breasts a quarter turn after a few minutes.
- Remove the bird from the grill and tent with foil for 5 minutes before serving.
- NOTE: Don't try to eat the brick!

Serves 4

CHICKEN DRUMSTICKS WRAPPED IN BACON

This is *so* easy and *so* good. Look how few instructions there are! Serve these little guys up with a mustard dipping sauce, potato salad and a tall cool drink.

24 chicken drumsticks, washed and dried

2 tsp ground pepper (10ml)

1 lb bacon

1/2 cup olive oil (125ml)

24 toothpicks

Directions:

- Soak toothpicks in cool water for 15 minutes.

- Wrap bacon around the thick part of the chicken, leaving 1-inch at top. Secure bacon with soaked toothpick, season with pepper and drizzle with olive oil.

- Preheat grill to 375F/190C

- Place chicken on grill and cook until bacon is golden brown (7 minutes per side).

Serves 8

CHICKEN TERIYAKI

Woo hoo! You get to make your own teriyaki sauce! Once you've done the recipe you can adjust this sauce (and all others in this book) to suit your own personal tastes. For instance, the recipe calls for 1 measly tablespoon of chopped garlic but you can (and should) load up with way more – assuming you don't have a date tonight. Way better than store bought sauce any day plus no shelf stabilizers or artificial preservatives.

1/2 cup soy (125ml)

1/2 cup sherry (125ml)

1/2 cup brown sugar (125ml)

1/4 cup rice wine vinegar (62ml)

1 tbsp garlic, chopped (15ml)

1 1/2 tbsp ginger, grated (22.5ml)

1 tbsp oil (15ml)

8 chicken breasts

bamboo skewers

Directions:

- Add all ingredients (except chicken) to a saucepan and bring to a boil. Reduce heat and simmer for 5 minutes until it thickens and the flavors mingle.

- Let the sauce cool to room temperature.

- Cut the chicken breasts into strips and place in a sealable plastic bag. Pour cooled marinade over top and place in fridge for a minimum of 2 and up to 4 hours.

- Remove the chicken from the fridge 30 minutes before grilling.

- Place the bamboo skewers in water and leave to soak for 30 minutes.

- Thread the chicken strips on the soaked bamboo skewers and place on a tray.

- Preheat the grill to medium high.

- Oil the grill and place the chicken skewers down on the grate on an angle. Rotate halfway after 1 minute to get cross hatch marks.

- Cook for approximately 3 minutes per side or until golden and chicken is cooked through.

Serves 8

CHICKEN WITH WILD WEST SAUCE

Ask your butcher to halve the birds for you. Free range is better than penned, grain fed is better than not. Also, ask for a capon from the butcher instead of a regular chicken for an extra taste treat. Capons are roosters and are bigger than your regular chicken, so they serve more people. If you can, get your hands on smoked paprika for an extra taste dimension.

2 x 3 lb whole chickens, halved

Wild West Paste:

4 tbsp of room temperature butter (60mL)

4 tbsp of Worcestershire sauce (60mL)

2 tbsp of paprika (30mL)

*2 tbsp of finely diced canned chipotle
    chili peppers in adobo sauce*

1 tsp of dry mustard (5mL)

1 tsp of garlic salt (5mL)

1 tsp of lemon pepper (5mL)

Wild West Basting Sauce:

6 tbsp of Worcestershire sauce (90mL)

3 tbsp of water (45mL)

1 tsp of dry mustard (5mL)

Directions:

- Combine Wild West Paste ingredients and massage the chicken halves thoroughly. Rub the paste inside and out working it as far as possible under the skin without tearing it. Place the chicken halves into plastic bags and refrigerate.

- Remove chicken from fridge and let stand covered at room temperature for about 30 minutes.

- Bring grill to a medium heat (4–5 seconds with hand test).

- Mix Wild West Basting Sauce ingredients and place in a spray bottle or in a dish with a basting brush and set aside.

- Transfer chicken to grill and cook skin-side-up and covered for 20 minutes. Do not flip the chicken during this period. Continue to cook the chicken for an additional 30–40 minutes, turning every 10 minutes and ending with the chicken skin-side-down for a final crisping.

- Brush the chicken with Wild West Basting Sauce about halfway through the cooking process.

Serves 4

CINNAMON CHICKEN WITH NUTTY RELISH

Remember to always barbecue your meats bone-in for extra flavor.

6 large skinless chicken breasts, bone-in, pounded to 3/4-inch thick.

Dry Rub

1 tbsp ground cinnamon (15mL)

1 tsp nutmeg (2.5mL)

1 tsp mustard seed powder (5mL)

1/2 tsp coriander (2.5mL)

1 tsp ground cardamom (5mL)

2 tsp garlic powder (10mL)

1 tsp of kosher salt (5mL)

1 tsp of freshly ground pepper (5mL)

1 1/2 tsp brown sugar (7.5mL)

Directions:

- Combine the Dry Rub ingredients together in a small bowl. Rinse and pat the chicken breasts dry. Dust equal amounts of the rub mixture on each piece of chicken and rub it into the meat. Be sure to rub the mixture into both sides of the chicken breasts. Place chicken breasts on a tray or platter, cover and refrigerate for a minimum of 2 hours up to overnight.

- Combine Nutty Relish ingredients in a small bowl and set aside.

- Preheat the grill to 325F (190C) or medium heat.

- Remove the chicken from the fridge and allow it to come to room temperature while the grill heats.

Nutty Relish

1/4 cup chopped onion, soaked in hot
    water for 20 minutes and drained (60mL)

1 red bell pepper, diced (30mL)

1 yellow bell pepper, diced (30mL)

3 tsp raspberry vinegar (10mL)

2 tsp honey (5mL)

1 cup of roasted and peeled hazelnuts,
    coarsely chopped (250mL)

1 tbsp minced dried mint (15mL)

- Oil the grill liberally. Place the chicken on the grill, skin-side-down. Keep the lid open and a spray bottle with water close by to douse any jumping flames. Grill chicken breasts on each side until opaque and juicy (approximately 6–8 minutes).

- Remove the chicken from the grill and tent with aluminum foil. Let rest for 5 minutes before serving. Serve with Nutty Relish and enjoy!

Serves 6

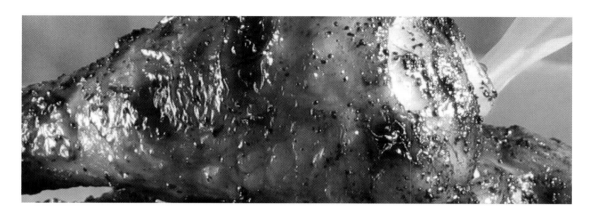

COFFEE & PEPPER RUBBED CHICKEN

Coffee and cinnamon give this rub a kick that will have your guests sit up and notice. The apple slaw is a nice counter-punch to the smokey hot chipotles and lime juice. This one's a keeper. Use thighs and drumsticks for maximum flavor.

6 chicken thighs with skin and bone in

6 chicken drumsticks

Rub

2 tbsp ground French roast coffee (30ml)

2 tsp freshly ground black pepper (10ml)

1 clove garlic, minced

2 tsp cinnamon (10ml)

1 tsp olive oil (5ml)

2 tbsp brown sugar (30ml)

Salt to taste

Apple Slaw

2 Granny Smith apples, peeled, cored
   and sliced thin

1 chipotle, diced

1 tsp chipotle sauce (5ml)

Juice of 2 limes

1/4 cup red onion, julienned (60ml)

1/4 cup cilantro, chopped (60ml)

Directions:

- In a small bowl, combine rub ingredients. Rub all over chicken.

- Place the chicken in a plastic bag and into the refrigerator overnight.

- Preheat the grill to 350F/180C.

- Place chicken on grill and cook with lid down for 7–8 minutes per side.

- Tent with foil for 5 minutes before serving.

- Serve with Apple Slaw

Apple Slaw Directions:

- Combine all ingredients in a small bowl, cover and refrigerate 1 hour before serving.

Serves 6

4 chicken breasts, bone in, skin on

Salt and pepper

3 handfuls cherry wood chips

- Prepare the barbecue for indirect cooking by oiling the side the chicken will go on. Crank the other side up to high heat and leave the oiled side turned off.

- Build smoke pouch (see page 5). Place directly over heat source of the grill, close the lid and wait for smoke.

- Drain the chicken from the marinade and scrape off the excess liquid. Rub the chicken with the remaining 1 tbsp of olive oil and season with salt and pepper.

- When smoke starts to billow out, reduce the heat to 200F/100C.

- Quickly lift the lid and place the chicken on the cool side of the barbecue. Close the lid and leave to smoke for 1 hour.

Serves 4

SMOKED SPICY TURKEY

Why do we overlook turkey except at Christmas and Thanksgiving? It's a rich and delicious meat that holds up really well on the barbecue. Any decent butcher would be pleased to sell you the breast alone. In this recipe we get a little mad scientist and inject the meat with flavor. Pickle juice, by the way, is just that: the juice from the jar of pickles in your fridge. You can buy a kitchen syringe at any good kitchen supply or gourmet store. I've even seen them at hardware stores come barbecue season.

Injection liquid

1/3 cup olive oil (83ml)

1/3 cup pickle juice (83ml)

1 tsp yellow mustard (5ml)

2 tsp Worcestershire sauce (10ml)

Directions:

- In a small bowl, mix olive oil, pickle juice, mustard, Worcestershire sauce, and salt and pepper. With a kitchen syringe, pull this mixture up into the syringe and inject it deep into the thickest part of the turkey breast. Repeat this process into different areas and angles of the turkey breast until all of the injection liquid has been used.

5–7 lb turkey breast

Salt and pepper

3 handfuls hickory wood chips

3 handfuls apple wood chips

Hot Times Rub

2 tbsp celery salt (30ml)

2 tbsp brown sugar (30ml)

2 tsp ground cinnamon (10ml)

1 tsp ground clove (5ml)

1/2 tsp dry mustard (2.5ml)

- In a new bowl (like I had to tell you this), combine all of the dry rub ingredients. Massage the rub all over the turkey breast, rubbing it over and under the skin. Place the breast in a sealable plastic bag and refrigerate for 24 hours.

- Remove the turkey from the fridge a half hour before cooking.

- Prepare a smoke pouch (see page 5).

- Prepare the barbecue for smoking over indirect heat by oiling the grill, then firing it up on high heat on one side and no heat on the other.

- Place the smoke pouch directly over high heat source of the grill, close the lid and wait for smoke.

- When smoke begins to billow out of the barbecue, reduce the heat under the smoke pouch to achieve a steady heat of 200F–220F/93C–104C.

- Place the turkey on cool side of the grill and smoke with lid down for 3 1/2 hours. You'll probably have to replace the smoke pouch halfway through.

- Tent with foil for 20 minutes before carving.

Serves 6

CURRIED CHICKEN KEBOBS

1 pound skinless boneless chicken thighs, cut into 1" cubes (2.5cm) (700gr).

1 red onion, cut into 1" cubes (2.5cm)

2 red bell peppers cut into 1" cubes (2.5cm)

2 tablespoons extra-virgin olive oil (30ml)

salt and pepper to taste

Marinade:

1/4 cup olive oil (60ml)

1/4 cup cilantro chopped (60ml)

1/4 cup mint chopped (60ml)

1/4 cup shallots chopped fine (60ml)

2 teaspoons curry powder (10ml)

Salt and pepper to taste

Olive oil for drizzling

wooden skewers that have been soaking in water for at least an hour

Place the chicken in a resealble plastic bag.

Directions:

- In a bowl combine olive oil, cilantro, mint, shallots, curry powder and mix.

- Pour into bag with chicken. Coat well and then into the refrigerator overnight.

- Remove chicken from the refrigerator.

- Remove the chicken from the bag, discard.

- Marinade and season chicken with salt and pepper.

- Thread chicken & vegetables onto the skewers alternating between the onion, peppers and chicken.

- Place the skewers on a baking sheet.

- Drizzle with olive oil.

- Prepare barbecue for direct grilling.

- Preheat the grill to a medium-high heat.

- Oil and add the skewers so they overhang the edge of the grill.

- Cook for about 8 minutes, turning once every 2 minutes to get nice char marks on all sides .

- Remove the skewers from the barbecue and tent with foil.

Serves 6

GARLIC ROTISSERIE CHICKEN

When chefs have a night off, there's nothing they like better to make at home than a simple roast chicken. This recipe is so simple, yet it yields such wonderful results. Save the bones to make stock the next day.

1 lb (500g) whole chicken

4 cloves garlic, peeled

3 tbsp fresh basil, snipped (45mL)

3/4 tsp salt (3.75mL)

1 tbsp olive oil (15mL)

1 tbsp lemon juice (15mL)

Directions:

- In a bowl combine basil, salt, olive oil and lemon juice and set aside.

- Starting at the neck on one side of the breast, slip your fingers between skin and meat, loosening the skin as you go work towards the tail end. Once your entire hand is under the skin, free the skin around the thigh and leg area up to but not around, the tip of the drumstick. Repeat on the other side of the breast.

- Rub basil mixture under skin directly on to meat. Slip garlic cloves under skin, evenly spaced. Cover and refrigerate for 4 hours.

- Using butcher's twine, truss the chicken so that it holds together. It will also cook the meat evenly.

- Place a drip pan in the center under the grill, turn the front and the rear burners on high and leave the middle burner off and preheat to 325F (180°).

- Place the chicken on to the spit according to the rotisserie manufacturer's directions.

- Cook until the skin of the chicken is generously brown and the flesh is cooked through. Every 20 minutes or so, baste the chicken with juices that accumulate on the drip pan.

- When cooked, the chicken's internal temperature should be 180F (90C). Remove chicken from rotisserie, cover with foil and let stand for 10 minutes before carving. Serve and enjoy!

Serves 5

BRINED SMOKED TURKEY

Turkeys are big and don't have a whole lot of fat on them, especially the breast meat. So, how do you keep it moist and juicy for an extended cooking time? You brine the bird, baby. Brining means plumping up the meat by soaking it in flavored water. This works well with meats that are lean (no fat means it'll dry out faster) so they remain juicy through a longer cooking process. Try brining before cooking your turkey in your regular oven next Christmas or Thanksgiving – you'll thank me.

WARNING: you're going to cook a whole turkey on a barbecue. This is a challenging recipe. Don't worry, you can do it. It's not difficult, there are just a lot of steps, but trust me – it's worth it. Just make sure you read the ENTIRE recipe three times first. Figure the whole thing out in your head and then go for it.

1 fresh turkey, 12–14 lbs (5.5–6.3 kg)

Brine

2 quarts cranberry juice (2 litres)

2 quarts orange juice (2 litre)

2 small garlic heads, cloves crushed
*   but not peeled*

1 cup kosher salt (250ml)

4 star anise

1/4 cup coriander seeds (60ml)

1/4 cup whole fennel seeds (60ml)

4 ounces fresh ginger, thinly sliced (120gr)

6 bay leaves

1 tbsp pepper corns (15ml)

2 cinnamon sticks

1 quart water (1 liter)

Rub for turkey

1 tbsp lemon zest (15ml)

1 tbsp cracked pepper (15ml)

2 tsp chilis (10ml)

2 tsp fresh thyme (10ml)

1/2 cup brown sugar (125ml)

2 tsp cinnamon (10ml)

1 tbsp kosher salt (15ml)

To make the brine:

- In a large stockpot, combine the brine ingredients and bring to a boil over high heat until salt dissolves. Remove from the heat. Allow to cool completely.

- Remove the neck and giblets and any excess fat from the turkey and discard. Rinse the bird inside and out, under cold water, drain, and place in the brine and make sure the turkey is completely submerged. Cover and refrigerate for 24 hours.

- Remove turkey from brine an hour before cooking and pat dry with paper towels. Discard the brine.

To make the rub:

- In a bowl, evenly combine lemon zest, cracked pepper, chilis, fresh thyme, brown sugar and cinnamon.

- Rub the mixture vigorously all over the turkey.

- See? That wasn't hard. So far, so good.

Prepare the bird:

- To the cavity of the turkey add lemons, chopped onion, the orange, apple, garlic and thyme.

- Next, truss the turkey and pin the neck skin flap to body using small trussing needles. Place the turkey on a baking sheet.

- Prepare three smoke pouches (see page 5).

Stuffing for turkey

1 whole lemon, cut in half

1 medium sized onion, chopped

1 whole orange, cut in half

1 whole apple, cut in half

1 whole head of garlic, cut in half

6 sprigs of fresh thyme

Drip pan

1 bottle of white wine

Basting Butter

1/2 cup of unsalted butter (125ml)

1/4 cup lemon juice (60ml)

1 tbsp Dijon mustard (15ml)

1/4 cup maple syrup (60ml)

1 tbsp fresh thyme, chopped (15ml)

Salt and pepper to taste

12 cups of hickory wood chips

Make the basting sauce:

- In a skillet over medium heat melt the butter.

- Add lemon juice, Dijon, maple syrup, thyme and salt and pepper. Stir.

Cook the bird:

- Prepare the barbecue for indirect grilling. Preheat the barbecue to high heat. Place the smoke pouch directly over the heat source and a drip pan under the grill on the side that is off. Pour some white wine into the drip pan. Close the lid and wait for smoke.

- Once barbecue is smoking reduce the heat to 220F/110C and place the turkey on the side of the barbecue without direct heat.

- Smoke the turkey over indirect heat for approximately 3–4 hours or until the internal temperature reaches 170F/77C in the breast and 180F/82C
  in the thickest part of the thigh.

- Replace the smoke pouch and add more wine to the drip pan each hour through the cooking time. Baste the bird when you replace the smoke pouch.

- When fully cooked, transfer the turkey to a cutting board or platter, loosely cover the whole bird with foil, and let rest for 40 minutes before carving.

Serves 8

PORT MARINATED SMOKED CHICKEN

Port is a fortified wine with a rich deep flavor. You get a wickedly complex yet simple marinade when combined with the rosemary, mustard, garlic and shallots. Try experimenting with different types of wood chips to get the flavors you enjoy the best. In fact, throw extra rosemary twigs right on the flames for a double flavor punch.

Marinade

1/4 cup plus 1 tbsp olive oil (60ml plus 15ml)

1/3 cup ruby port (75ml)

1/4 cup red wine vinegar (60ml)

1/4 cup fresh lemon juice (60ml)

1/4 cup whole grain Dijon mustard (60ml)

3 tbsp rosemary, finely chopped (45ml)

1 tbsp coarsely cracked black pepper (15ml)

1 tbsp garlic salt (15ml)

2 tbsp shallots, minced (30ml)

Directions:

- Rinse the chicken breasts under cold water and pat dry. Place in a sealable plastic bag.

- Combine all of the marinade ingredients (reserving 1 tbsp olive oil) in a non-reactive bowl. Mix together and pour into the bag overtop of the chicken. Seal the bag and place it in the fridge to marinate for 1 hour.

- Place 1 handful of wood chips into water to soak for 30 minutes.

4 chicken breasts, bone in, skin on

Salt and pepper

3 handfuls cherry wood chips

- Prepare the barbecue for indirect cooking by oiling the side the chicken will go on. Crank the other side up to high heat and leave the oiled side turned off.

- Build smoke pouch (see page 5). Place directly over heat source of the grill, close the lid and wait for smoke.

- Drain the chicken from the marinade and scrape off the excess liquid. Rub the chicken with the remaining 1 tbsp of olive oil and season with salt and pepper.

- When smoke starts to billow out, reduce the heat to 200F/100C.

- Quickly lift the lid and place the chicken on the cool side of the barbecue. Close the lid and leave to smoke for 1 hour.

Serves 4

GRILLED CHICKEN BREAST WITH BALSAMIC & HERBS

Herbes de Provence is a classic combination of basil, lavender, marjoram, rosemary, sage, savory and thyme. Those French know a thing or two about cooking. You can find this combo in most major grocery stores these days. Sprinkle a handful over the flames just before you toss the chicken on the grill for a nice smokey burst of flavor.

4 boneless, skinless chicken breasts
 (8oz/ 240g each)

2 tsp herbes de Provence (10ml)

2 tsp Dijon mustard (10ml)

1 tsp onion powder (5ml)

1 tsp garlic powder (5ml)

1/4 cup olive oil (60ml)

1 tbsp balsamic vinegar (15ml)

Pinch of salt

Pinch of pepper

Directions:

- Place chicken breasts into a sealable plastic bag.

- In a small bowl combine herbes de Provence, Dijon, onion powder, garlic powder, oil and balsamic. Mix to combine evenly. Add the salt and pepper.

- Pour the marinade over the chicken. Seal the bag and shake gently to coat the meat thoroughly. Place in refrigerator to marinate for 20 minutes.

- Preheat barbecue to medium heat.

- Remove chicken from the marinade and pat lightly with paper towel to remove excess moisture. Season with salt.

- Oil the grill and place chicken directly over heat.

- Cook for about 6 minutes per side or when the juices run clear when pierced with a fork in the thickest part of the breast.

- Remove chicken from the heat and cover with foil.

- Let rest 5 minutes before serving.

Serves 4

GRILLED CHICKEN IN A WHITE WINE TARRAGON SAUCE

Tarragon has this crazy almost licorice thing going on that's also got a hit of lemon to it. Amazing. It is a classic pairing with white wine (also fruity) and chicken. What makes this recipe so amazing is how few ingredients there are to get such a big taste. Try it once and it will become part of your weeknight go-to recipe file.

6 chicken breasts on the bone

2 tbsp olive oil (30ml)

Juice of 2 lemons

1 cup white wine (250ml)

2 tbsp tarragon, freshly chopped (30ml)

Sauce

3 tbsp shallots, finely diced (45ml)

1 cup white wine (250ml)

2 tbsp tarragon, freshly chopped (30ml)

4 tbsp cold butter (60ml)

Salt and pepper to taste

Directions:

- Place the chicken breasts in a sealable plastic bag.

- In a bowl mix the olive oil, lemon juice, wine and tarragon. Pour over the chicken and seal the bag. Toss to ensure the chicken is well coated. Place in the fridge to marinate for 2 hours.

- Preheat the grill to medium high heat.

- A half hour prior to cooking time, remove the chicken from the fridge and allow the meat to come to room temperature. Remove the chicken from the marinade and pat it dry. Discard the marinade.

- Oil the grill liberally to help avoid sticking.

- Place the chicken breast-side down on the grill. Leave to cook for about 10 minutes and flip. Continue to cook for another 5 minutes.

- Meanwhile, in a saucepan, sauté the diced shallots until translucent but not browned.

- Add white wine and bring to a boil. Reduce heat, add tarragon and leave to simmer and reduce for 10-15 minutes.

- Strain the sauce into a bowl and discard the discolored tarragon.

- Add the butter one knob at a time and whisk until it is all incorporated.

- Season with salt and pepper and drizzle over finished chicken.

Serves 6

GRILLED LEMONADE CHICKEN

Check out the ingredients. The tart concentrated lemonade paired with the salty soy and the hot sauce zing gets a bump from the garlic and fresh mint. This recipe calls for chicken legs which gives you the tastier dark meat and added flavor from cooking "on the bone."

8 chicken legs, bone in

6oz can frozen lemonade concentrate, thawed

1 tbsp soy sauce (15 ml)

A dash of hot sauce

1 tsp celery salt (5 ml)

2 fresh garlic cloves

1/4 cup fresh mint

Salt to season

Pepper to season

Olive oil to coat

Directions:

- Place chicken legs in a large sealable plastic bag.

- Pour the lemonade concentrate into a medium glass bowl.

- Add soy and hot sauces, celery salt, garlic and mint. Mix. Pour the marinade into the plastic bag, coating the chicken. Reserve some marinade for basting.

- Seal the bag and place in the refrigerator to marinate for 2 1/2 hours.

- Half an hour before cooking, remove the chicken legs from marinade and pat dry with paper towel.

- Season the chicken with salt and pepper, drizzle with oil to prevent sticking.

- Preheat the barbecue to medium-high heat 350F/175C. Oil the grill.

- Place the chicken on the grill bone-side down. Sear the meat, then lower the temperature and grill with the lid up for 15 minutes per side.

- Baste the chicken with reserved marinade during the last 10 minutes of cooking.

- Remove the chicken from the grill and tent with foil for 5 minutes before serving

Serves 8

GRILLED STUFFED CHICKEN BREASTS

You can get away with dried oregano for this one but the basil must be fresh. The combo of roasted garlic, lemon and maple syrup will drive everyone at the table nuts.

4 large, whole, boneless, skin on chicken
breasts (each 10oz) (each 280g)

1/4 cup chopped fresh basil (60ml)

1/4 cup chopped fresh oregano (60ml)

1 cup goat cheese, crumbled (250ml)

1 tsp chopped lemon zest (5ml)

1 tbsp pure maple syrup (15ml)

2 tbsp toasted pine nuts (30ml)

1 whole head roasted garlic (see note)

Coarse salt and pepper to taste

3 tsp olive oil (15ml)

Directions:

- In a bowl combine crumbled goat cheese, basil, smashed roasted garlic (see directions below), oregano, zest, syrup, pine nuts and salt and pepper.

- Wash and pat the chicken breasts dry and then cut a pocket lengthwise in each.

- Stuff the mixture into the pocket. Not too much. Secure the opening with toothpicks. Coat the chicken with oil.

- Preheat barbecue to medium low.

- Oil the grill.

Roasted garlic

1 head of garlic

1 sprig of fresh thyme

1/2 tsp cracked black pepper (2.5ml)

1 tsp olive oil (5ml)

- Place chicken skin-side down and grill for about 7 minutes or until the skin is golden brown and crispy. DON'T play with it. Let the grill do its job.

- Flip chicken and continue to cook the other side for 7 minutes. Remove from grill. Cover with foil and allow to rest for 5 minutes.

To roast garlic:

- Preheat barbecue to 300F/150C keeping one side off to prepare for indirect cooking.

- Cut the top of a head of garlic.

- Place the garlic onto a sheet of foil, drizzle with oil and cracked pepper and top with a sprig of thyme. Fold in sides of the foil and make a package ready for the grill.

- Place the garlic on the side of the grill with no heat under it. Close lid and cook for 30 minutes or until soft. Remove from grill to cool.

Serves 4

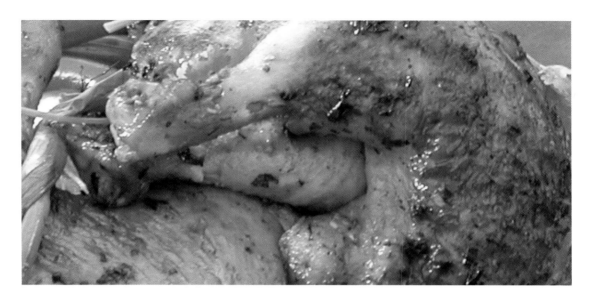

SPICY BARBECUED CHICKEN LEGS

This one has a bit of an Asian thing going on with the lemon juice, fish sauce, ginger and garlic. Delicious. You can find fish sauce in most major grocery chains these days. If your store doesn't carry it then it's time to change grocers.

6 whole chicken legs (drumsticks with
thigh attached)

Marinade

1/4 cup vegetable oil (62ml)

1/4 cup green onions, finely sliced (62ml)

3 tbsp lemon juice (45ml)

1 tbsp fish sauce (15ml)

1 tbsp sugar (15ml)

2 tsp garlic, minced (10ml)

3 tsp ground ginger (15ml)

1 tbsp hot sauce (15ml)

Directions:

- Combine all marinade ingredients in a non-reactive bowl.

- Place chicken legs in a sealable plastic bag and pour marinade mixture over chicken legs; close bag tight and marinate in refrigerator for 4 hours.

- Preheat barbecue to medium high

- Remove the chicken from the marinade and pat dry.

- Lightly brush the legs with oil and season with salt and pepper.

- Oil the grill and place the chicken skin-side down on grill. Cook until golden brown, about 7 minutes. Flip and season other side and continue cooking for another 7 minutes.

- Tent with foil for 5 minutes before serving

Serves 6

GRILLED CHICKEN BURRITOS

This is a great dish for one of those lazy Sunday evening barbecue buffets where everyone gets to load up their own plate and sit around yakking and laughing. Pork also works really well with this recipe.

1 lb boneless and skinless chicken breast
  (500grams)

2/3 tsp garlic, minced (3.5mL)

1/2 tsp cumin (2.5mL)

1/4 tsp chili powder (1.25mL)

1/3 tsp salt (2mL)

1 tbsp lime juice (1mL)

4 large flat flour or corn tortillas

1 cup Salsa (250mL) (see Smoked
  Salsa recipe on page 225)

1 cup sour cream (250mL)

1 cup shredded Monterey Jack cheese (250mL)

1 cup shredded iceberg lettuce (250mL)

1 cup canned black beans, mashed (250mL)

Directions:

- Preheat grill to medium heat.

- Combine garlic, cumin, chili powder and lime juice. Rub chicken with mixture evenly on all sides. Wrap seasoned chicken in a tight foil package and cook on the grill for 20 minutes.

- Remove chicken from foil and grill over open flame for 2 to 3 minutes on each side. Remove chicken from grill and let stand for 5 to 10 minutes.

- Warm tortillas by placing a piece of foil on barbecue and tortillas on top of the foil. While tortillas are warming, slice grilled chicken into 1/2-inch pieces.

- Place a portion of beans, chicken and cheese in the center of each tortilla. Fold each end over the filling and grill until brown.

- Once burrito is grilled on both sides serve seam-side-down with lettuce and sour cream and top with salsa. Serve and enjoy!

Serves 4

GRILLED CHICKEN SKEWERS

Here's one with an Indian twist that comes from the garam masala and the yogurt. Play around with the quantities to get the spice level you like.

*6 lb (3kg) boneless, skinless chicken
    thighs cut into 1-inch cubes*

Juice from 4 limes

1 tbsp salt (15mL)

1/2 cup plain yogurt (125mL)

1 tbsp freshly grated ginger (15mL)

7 cloves of garlic, chopped fine

3 tsp garam masala (15mL)

1/2 tsp freshly ground pepper (2.5mL)

1/2 tsp cayenne (2.5mL)

Extra virgin olive oil

Bamboo skewers

Directions:

- Combine chicken, lime juice and salt in a large bowl and toss until the chicken is well coated. Place the chicken and the liquid into a large, sealable plastic bag.

- In another bowl, combine yogurt, ginger, garlic, garam masala, pepper and cayenne. Mix well and pour over the chicken in the bag. Toss and coat the chicken with the mixture. Seal the bag and refrigerate for 4 hours to overnight.

- Soak bamboo skewers in water for 30–45 minutes.

- Remove the chicken from the refrigerator 1/2 hour prior to cooking time to come to room temperature

- Preheat the grill to medium-high heat.

- Place two or three pieces of chicken on each bamboo skewer. Oil the grill grate and place the skewers on the grill, with the ends off the heat.

- Cook with the lid up for 7 to 8 minutes per side. Serve and enjoy!

Serves 12 appetizer portions

HICKORY SMOKED TURKEY LEGS

I love turkey legs. They have way more flavor than the breast and you get to pull a Fred Flintstone when you eat them. Sage and thyme are classic go-with herbs for turkey and the Cajun spice adds an extra flavor boost to the rub. Plus, you get to put bourbon in this one. No bourbon? No problem. Try using a dark rum or whiskey.

Rub

1 1/2 tsp salt (7.5ml)

1 tsp freshly ground pepper (5ml)

1 tsp fresh sage (5ml)

1 tsp dried thyme (5ml)

1 tsp Cajun spice (5ml)

Grated zest of 1 lemon

4 turkey legs

2 tbsp (30ml) of bourbon

3 handfuls of hickory wood chips

Directions:

- Combine the rub ingredients in small bowl.

- Rinse the turkey legs and pat them dry.

- Apply even amounts of the rub to each leg. Place the legs into a sealable plastic bag and refrigerate for at least 1 hour up to 6 hours.

- Remove from the fridge 30 minutes before cooking

- Preheat the barbecue to high on one side and oil the grill. On the other, leave the heat off.

- Place smoke packages directly over heat source.

- Close the lid and wait for smoke. Reduce heat to 200F/100C.

- Place the turkey legs on the cool side of the grill and close the lid. Smoke for about 2 hours.

Serves 4

LEMON GRASS SMOKED DUCK

Unlike turkey or chicken breasts, duck has beaucoup fat . . . which is a good thing. We like fat. We love fat. "Fat cap" refers to that nice slab of fat you'll find on top of the breast (or on a cut of beef or pork or anything, including maybe your neighbor). By the way, star anise has a licorice sort-of flavor to it and is a nice counterpoint to the sake in the rub. Sorry, no substitute for sake.

Check out the smoke pouch for this one: black tea, lemon grass, more star anise, raw rice (helps with the smoke) and coriander. Bet you've never done anything like this before, huh?

4 duck breasts, scored fat cap approximately
*   9-10 oz each*

Rub

1/4 cup sake (60ml)

2 tsp kosher salt (10ml)

1 tbsp fresh minced ginger (15ml)

4 whole dried star anise

1/4 cup vegetable oil (60ml)

2 green onions, coarsely chopped

2 tsp coarsely ground black pepper (10ml)

1 tbsp minced garlic (15ml)

Directions:

- Score fat cap on the duck breast by gently making a diamond pattern in the fat. Ensure you only pierce the fat and not the flesh.

- In a bowl, combine sake, salt, pepper, oil, garlic, green onions and ginger.

- Place the star anise in a coffee grinder and pulse until a light powder is achieved, add to mixture.

- Mix together using a whisk until all ingredients are evenly combined.

- Combine the rub and the duck in a sealable plastic bag and put in the refrigerator to set up overnight.

Smoke pouch

6 tea bags (black tea)

1 whole lemon grass stalk – bashed with
  knife and halved lengthwise (this is
  done just to release the flavor)

4 cups raw rice (600g)

2 tbsp whole coriander seeds (5ml)

6 whole star anise pods

- Remove duck from refrigerator and take out of the baggie about 30 minutes before cooking.

- Make yourself a smoke pouch (see page 5).

- Prepare the barbecue for indirect grilling. Turn one side on high and leave the other side off. Once you've got some heat going, place the smoke pouch right on the flame and close the lid.

- Once smoke is achieved, turn the heat down to low and let the temperature slip to 220F/110C, then quickly place the duck breast on the side of the barbecue that is off.

- Close the lid and slow-smoke the duck breasts over indirect heat for 50 minutes (note this is for medium rare).

- Remove duck from grill when desired temperature is reached, cover with foil and rest for 10 minutes.

- Slice duck breasts thinly and serve with plum sauce.

Serves 4–6

MARMALADE DUCK

Yes, that's right . . . marmalade. Tangy, tart marmalade with a bit of licorice from the star anise and some heat from the dried chili peppers works amazingly well with the rich duck meat. Cranberry jam or chutney works really well too. Serve the duck with the mango-orange sauce featured along with an arugula salad (arugula is peppery so it'll stand up to the duck) and some grilled sweet potatoes. Two things: PLEASE don't overcook the duck. It ain't no chicken – it's meant to be devoured medium to medium rare. Also, you can remove the remaining fat AFTER the duck is cooked and has sat under foil for 5 minutes. Trust me on this. Wine? Think Zinfandel or Shiraz.

4 whole boneless duck breasts

Marinade

2 star anise

1/2 cup dry white wine (125ml)

1/3 cup orange marmalade (75ml)

1 tbsp canola oil (15ml)

1 garlic clove, minced

1 tsp ground summer savory (5ml)

1/4 tsp of freshly ground pepper (1ml)

1 tsp of dried chili flakes (5ml)

1/4 cup of brown sugar (50ml)

Directions:

- Combine marinade ingredients in a small bowl.

- Put duck into a clear plastic bag and pour in marinade.

- Refrigerate for at least 4 hours and as long as overnight.

- Remove the duck from the marinade and discard plastic bag.

- Score duck skin fat in crisscross pattern with a sharp knife. Ensure you don't cut into duck flesh.

Mango Orange Sauce

1 ripe mango

1/2 cup orange juice (125ml)

1/4 cup liquid honey (50ml)

1 tsp chopped ginger root (5ml)

1 tsp orange peel (5ml)

1/4 tsp salt (1ml)

1/8 tsp white pepper (0.5ml)

- Preheat grill to 350F/180C. You're going to cook with indirect heat here so leave one side off.

- Place duck on oiled grill rack on the side that's turned off. Close the lid and cook for about 10 minutes fat-side up.

- Remove the duck from grill and tent with foil for 5 minutes.

- Fan duck slices on warm plates and garnish with Mango Orange Sauce

Sauce Directions:

- Combine mango, orange juice, honey, ginger root, peel, salt and pepper into a small saucepan. Bring to a boil, reduce heat and cook for about 5 minutes or until fruit is soft.

- Remove from heat and cool slightly.

- Place in a food processor and puree until smooth.

- Return to saucepan to keep warm

Serves 4

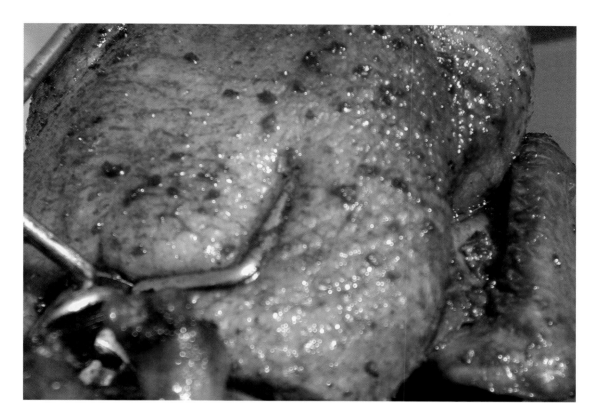

PEKING STYLE SPIT-ROASTED DUCK

There's a lot of fat on a good duck. Slow roasting on a spit will allow the fat to melt off through the meat leaving it moist and juicy with a nice crispy skin.

1 duck, 4 1/2–5lb (2.25–2.5kg)

3 tsp five-spice powder (15ml)

4 tbsp soy sauce (60ml)

3 tbsp sesame oil (45ml)

2 1/2 tbsp rice vinegar (37.5ml)

2 1/2 tbsp fresh ginger, peeled and chopped (37.5ml)

5 large cloves garlic, finely chopped

3 whole star anise

Sweet-and-sour sauce

Enough water to fill a drip pan halfway

Directions:

- Rinse the duck, inside and out, and pat it dry. Remove and discard any excess fat.

- Using your fingers and starting at the tail cavity, carefully loosen the skin of the duck over the breast and thighs. Rub the five-spice powder under the skin spreading it as evenly as possible.

- In a bowl stir together the soy sauce, sesame oil, vinegar, ginger and garlic. Place the duck in a large sealable plastic bag, pour the marinade in the bag, reserving half for later. Add the star anise.

- Seal bag and refrigerate for at least 4 hours, up to 24 hours.

- Remove the duck from the marinade, pat it dry, then return it to the refrigerator uncovered for 30 minutes to dry the skin further.

- Remove the duck from the refrigerator 30 minutes before grilling.

- Prepare the barbecue for rotisserie roasting over low heat, 200F/100C.

- Truss the duck on the spit according to the manufacturer's instructions.

- Place the water filled drip pan underneath the duck. Depending on your barbecue, the pan might not have enough clearance to fit under the duck, in which case you turn off the heat in the middle, remove the grill and put the pan on the burner.

- Spit-roast the duck, brushing every 1/2 hour with the reserved marinade, until it is a rich golden brown, 1 1/2–2 hours.

- To test for doneness, insert an instant-read thermometer into the thickest part of the thigh away from the bone; it should register 170F/77C. The temperature will rise another 5–10 degrees while the duck is resting under foil for 20 minutes.

- Transfer the duck to a cutting board and slice away. Serve the duck with a warm sweet-and-sour sauce.

Serves 4

ROTISSERIE GAME HENS

You're in for a treat if you've never had a game hen before. This is not white-flesh chicken so be careful not to overcook or you'll end up with something very dry and chewy (that would be a bad thing by the way). You can find them frozen these days in most grocery stores and any decent butcher will either have fresh ones on hand (usually in time for the weekend) or will order you some if you call in advance. You can use dried oregano and sage in a pinch but only fresh rosemary or thyme please. The first gets bitter I find and the second just fades away. Experiment with different mustards in the rub for your own personal touch.

4 game hens about 1 1/2 lbs each, cleaned
   and patted dry

Rub

1 tbsp fresh oregano chopped roughly (15ml)

2 tsp fresh sage chopped roughly (15ml)

1 tbsp fresh rosemary chopped roughly (15ml)

2 tsp fresh thyme chopped fine (10ml)

1 shallot, chopped fine

Directions:

- For the rub: Chop the herbs and mix them in a bowl with the shallots, pepper, Dijon, lemon zest and olive oil.

- Place the cleaned birds in a shallow pan. Rub mixture all over the birds including inside the cavity. Cover with plastic wrap and allow to marinade in the refrigerator overnight.

- Remove the birds from the refrigerator and truss then place them on to a spit, remembering to balance them. Sprinkle all over with kosher salt.

Pepper to taste

1 tbsp Dijon (15ml)

Zest of 2 lemons

1/4 cup olive oil (60ml)

Kosher salt to taste

Drip pan

2 cups of white wine (500ml)

4 sprigs of fresh thyme

- Prepare the barbecue for indirect grilling. Preheat grill to medium high heat.

- Remove center grill and add a drip pan. Add the white wine and fresh thyme to the pan.

- Mount the spit containing the birds to the rotisserie.

- Grill for approximately 40 minutes with the lid up or until skin is golden brown and crispy and juices run clear when pieced with a knife.

- Remove the birds form the barbecue and then form the spit. Tent with foil.

- Let them rest for 10 minutes before plating.

Serves 4–6

SMOKED RASPBERRY CORNISH HENS

Cornish hens are the perfect one-per-person size and these ones are both smoked *and* stuffed. Frozen berries work just as well for a marinade as fresh ones because you don't really care about the consistency. The taste combo of the tart berry, sweet sugar and fresh mint makes for a very interesting marinade.

4 Cornish game hens 1–1 1/2 lbs (500–750 g)

Marinade

1 cup red raspberries (250ml)

1/2 cup rice wine vinegar (125ml)

1 tbsp white sugar (15ml)

Juice of 2 limes

3 cloves garlic, crushed

3 tbsp chopped fresh mint (45ml)

3/4 cup olive oil (190ml)

Salt and pepper to taste

Directions:

• Make 2 smoke pouches.

• Rinse the game hens under cold water and pat dry. By the way, you do this to get rid of gunky stuff and it helps make the skin crispy.

• Combine the marinade ingredients in a medium size non-reactive bowl. Set aside 1/2 cup (125ml) of marinade for basting.

• Place the game hens in 2 large sealable bags. Divide the marinade between the 2 baggies and toss to coat the games hens completely.

Stuffing

2 small white onions

4 stalks of celery

1/2 cup mint leaves (125 ml)

2 lemons sliced thin

Salt and pepper to taste

Butcher twine

6 cups (1250ml) mesquite wood chips

- Place the birds in the refrigerator to marinate for 4 to 6 hours.

- Chop onions and celery into small 1/2-inch (8 mm) pieces. Chop the mint. Slice lemons thin and combine all the stuffing ingredients in a bowl.

- Remove hens from the marinade and pat dry.

- Season the cavity and outside of the bird with salt and pepper.

- Stuff the cavity of the hens loosely with the stuffing. Bind the hens securely with butcher twine.

- Prepare the barbecue for indirect cooking and oil the grill. Preheat to 400F/204C with one side on and the other off. Place the smoke pouch directly over the high heat source and close the lid. Wait for smoke. Once smoke is achieved reduce temperature to 225F/107C or low heat.

- Place hens on cool side of the grill and close lid. The hens will take 1 1/2– 2 hours to cook. Change the smoke pouch halfway through cooking time and baste the hens with reserved raspberry marinade. When hens have 10 minutes cooking time left, baste again. Remove hens from the barbecue and place on a tray.

- Loosely cover with aluminum foil and let rest 10 minutes before serving.

Serves 4

GRILLED MISO CHICKEN

3 tablespoons light soy sauce (45ml)

3 tablespoons of Sake (45ml)

3 tablespoons of Mirin (45ml)

3 tablespoons light miso (soy bean paste) (45ml)

2 green onions, crushed and silvered

2 teaspoons of ginger root, minced (10ml)

3 garlic cloves, minced

3 boned chicken breasts

Directions:

- Blend soy sauce, Sake, Mirin, miso, green onions, ginger root and garlic in a bowl.

- Place chicken in a large sealable plastic bag.

- Pour marinade into bag coating chicken with mixture.

- Marinate for 4 hours or refrigerate overnight

- Preheat grill to 375°F.

- Shake marinade off chicken and pat dry.

- Place skin-down on hot grill for 4-5 minutes

- Flip chicken and grill for 4 to 6 minutes or until golden brown and done inside.

Serves 3

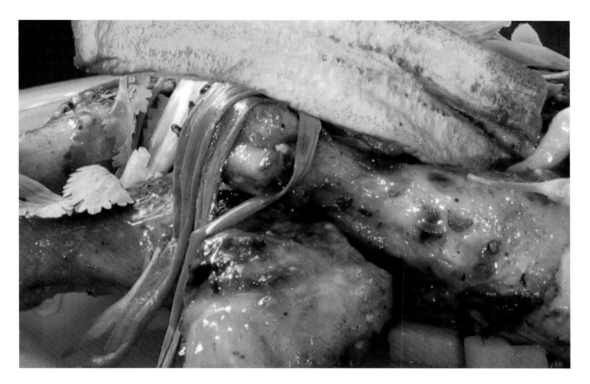

LEMON GINGER DRUMSTICKS WITH MANGO MUSTARD SEED GLAZE

Who would think that mixing mint with mango and mustard would be good? I did, that's for sure – it's not only just good, it's fantastic. If your recipe calls for you to rinse or brush off your marinated chicken, try putting it in a colander or on a wire rack in the sink. This will help make clean-up easier.

16 chicken drumsticks

Marinade

1/4 cup fresh grated ginger (60mL)

2 tbsp garlic, minced (30mL)

1 tsp chili powder (5mL)

Juice and zest of 2 lemons

1/4 cup chopped fresh mint (60mL)

1 tsp cracked pepper (5mL)

Directions:

- Using a sharp knife cut 1/4-inch deep diagonal slashes on each side of the drumstick (approximately 3 slashes per drumstick).

- Place slashed chicken into a large sealable plastic bag. Combine marinade ingredients in a small bowl. Pour the marinade over chicken. Seal the bag and refrigerate for a minimum 1 hour and up to 4 hours.

- Preheat grill to 350F (175C) or medium heat.

- Oil grill. Remove chicken from marinade and brush off excess liquid. Season chicken with salt and pepper to taste.

- Place chicken on grill and cook for a total of 12 minutes, basting with Mango Mustard Seed Glaze every few minutes. Turn the chicken legs every three minutes.

Mango Mustard Seed Glaze

> 1/2 cup commercial mango chutney (125mL)
>
> 2 tbsp mustard seeds (30mL)
>
> Salt and pepper to taste

Glaze Directions:

- To prepare glaze, strain the mango chutney with a fine sieve into a small saucepan and warm the liquid over low heat with 1 tablespoon (15mL) water. Mix in mustard seeds and season with salt and pepper.

Serves 8

LEMON PEPPER CORNISH HENS

Whatever you do, don't overcook these delicious birds. They dry out really quickly. Follow the recipe times closely and then make sure you tent the birds with tin foil after cooking for about 15 minutes so the meat will relax and the juices flow back into the entire hen.

4 Cornish game hens, 1.5 pounds each (680g)

2 lemons and zest

2 tsp red pepper flakes (10mL)

1 tbsp chopped garlic (15mL)

1 tbsp Worcestershire sauce (15mL)

1 tsp dry mustard powder (5mL)

1/4 cup vegetable oil (60mL)

Salt and pepper to taste

8 x 14-inch (35cm) flat metal skewers

Directions:

- In medium bowl mix together garlic, Worcestershire sauce, dry mustard, red pepper flakes and vegetable oil.

- Zest the lemons and add to the bowl of marinade ingredients. Peel lemon, remove the white pith from lemon and discard. Chop the peeled lemon into small 1/2-inch pieces (8 mm) and add to the bowl.

- Remove backbone from game hens using poultry scissors.

- Flatten hens by pushing a skewer horizontally through the wings and breast. Push another skewer horizontally though the thighs. Repeat with remaining hens. Place the chicken on a large baking tray.

- Pour marinade over hens turning to coat. Cover and refrigerate for 3 hours.

- Preheat barbecue 250F (125C) or medium high heat and oil grill.

- Season the hens with salt and pepper to taste.

- Place hens skin-side-down on grill and cook for 15 minutes or until the skin is crispy and golden-brown in color. Flip the hens using the skewers as an aid. Continue to cook a further 10 minutes or until there is no trace of pink at the bone.

- Remove from barbecue and tent loosely with foil. Let meat rest 10 minutes.

- Remove skewers and carve the hens into desired portions.

Serves 6

MUFFIN TIN BBQ EGGS

Breakfast on the barbecue! Pair this up with some smoked Canadian back bacon, a side of grilled hash browns and some strong coffee and you've got the perfect summertime backyard brunch.

12 eggs

Non-stick cooking spray

1/2 cup shallots, finely chopped (125mL)

1/2 cup red pepper, finely diced (125mL)

1/3 cup finely diced chives (75mL)

Salt and pepper to taste

Directions:

- Preheat the grill to medium-high heat. Spray a 12-cup muffin tin with non-stick spray, being sure to coat each cup.

- Crack a single egg into each muffin cup. Sprinkle the egg with finely diced shallots, red pepper and chives.

- Season lightly with salt and pepper, cover loosely with foil, place the tin on the grill and close the lid. Cook for approximately 2–4 minutes until desired doneness. Serve hot.

Serves 6

ORANGE TEQUILA CHICKEN BREASTS

Orange juice and tequila not only make a great summertime drink, they work really well together in a marinade. Throw in some chili flakes, a bit of vinegar, lime juice and mint and you've got a killer barbecue dish that takes no time to prep or to grill.

10 large chicken breasts, skinless and
*   boneless*
1/3 cup brown sugar (75mL)
1/3 cup unseasoned rice vinegar (75mL)
1 tsp dried chili peppers (5mL)
Zest and juice of 4 oranges

Directions:

- In a medium bowl, whisk together the sugar, vinegar and chili pepper and add the remaining ingredients.

- Rinse the chicken in cool water and pat dry.

- Place chicken breasts in a large sealable plastic bag. Pour all but 1/4 cup (60mL) of the marinade over the chicken. Seal the bag ensuring the chicken is well coated. Refrigerate for 3–6 hours.

3 tbsp tequila (45mL)

1 1/2 tsp fresh lime juice (7.5mL)

1/2 cup olive oil (125mL)

1 1/2 tsp fresh mint leaves, chopped (15mL)

1/4 tsp salt (1.25mL)

- Preheat one side of the grill to 375F (190C)or medium-high heat. Leave other side of the grill off.

- Oil the grill. Place chicken over the direct heat and sear chicken until golden brown char marks are achieved on one side only (about 2 minutes). Flip the chicken and move over to side of grill without heat, continue to cook for 6–8 minutes, or until juices run clear.

- Remove chicken, cover loosely with aluminum foil. Let rest for 5 minutes before serving.

Serves 10

PEANUT CHICKEN BURGERS

1 pound of ground chicken burger

2 tablespoons of smooth peanut butter (30ml)

2 teaspoons of sugar (optional) (10ml)

2 teaspoons of Tabasco sauce (10ml)

1/4 cup of chicken broth. (62ml)

1 tablespoon of minced garlic (15ml)

1/2 cup of chopped fresh cilantro (125ml)

1/4 cup of chopped fresh mint (62ml)

1/4cup of chopped fresh chives (62ml)

salt and pepper to taste

Directions:

- Combine all of the ingredients in a large bowl.

- Roll out and flatten into equal sized patties and place on a baking sheet lined in waxed paper.

- Place them into the refrigerator for 30 minutes to set.

- Preheat the grill to medium high heat – 3 steamboats.

- Oil the grill and place the patties on the grill. Do not use a spatula to press on the patties.

- Leave them to cook for approximately 5-8 minutes per side depending on thickness.

- Let the burgers rest under a foil tent for 5 minutes before serving

Serves 4 burgers

PECAN AND DIJON-CRUSTED CHICKEN

You can substitute pretty much any hard nut for the pecans if you're so inclined.
This dish also kicks without the Cajun spice.

8 boneless skinless chicken breasts

2 tbsp olive oil (30mL)

Salt and pepper to taste

Directions:

- To make the crust, combine all the ingredients in a food processor. Pulse until well combined and a chunky paste has formed. Set aside until time to grill.

- Prepare barbecue for grilling with indirect heat by preheating one side of the grill to 250F (125C) or medium-low heat and leaving the other side of the grill off.

Crust

1 cup of vegetable oil (250mL)

3 cups crushed corn flakes (750mL)

1 cup toasted pecans (250mL)

1/4 cup Dijon mustard (60mL)

2 tbsp liquid honey (30mL)

2 tbsp Cajun spice (30mL)

2 tbsp fresh chopped thyme (30mL)

- Oil the grill. Drizzle chicken with olive oil and add salt and pepper to taste.

- Place chicken on heated side of grill and sear each side for 1 minute or until nice char marks are achieved.

- Move chicken over to the non-heated side of the barbecue. Coat the top side of the chicken breasts with crust mixture. Close the barbecue lid and cook for 8 minutes per side.

- Remove chicken and serve with spicy mayo and crusty buns.

Serves 8

QUAIL STUFFED WITH COUSCOUS

Ask your butcher to debone the quail for you. It's a lot of work to do yourself, and they're pretty delicate. Remember this is a dark meat bird so you can serve it on the medium side. An overcooked quail is to cry for.

12 quails, deboned

2 cups oak woodchips soaked in water

1 cup dry oak woodchips

24 bamboo skewers soaked in water
  for 1 hour

Marinade

1/2 cup red wine (125mL)

Zest of two oranges

4 bunches thyme, chopped

2 tsp pepper (10mL)

Couscous

1 cup couscous (250mL)

1 cup orange juice (250mL)

2 green onions, chopped

1/4 cup raisins (60mL)

2 tbsp tasted pine nuts (30mL)

Salt and pepper to taste

Directions:

- In a large bowl whisk together marinade ingredients.

- Place the quail in sealable plastic bags. Using 1/2 cup (125mL) of marinade, pour it over the quails and seal. Reserve leftover marinade. Refrigerate quail for 1 hour.

- Place 2 cups (500mL) of woodchips in water and soak for one hour.

- Prepare couscous (see below). Stuff quail with cooled couscous.

- "Spatchcock" or flatten the quail by pushing one skewer horizontally through the wings and breast. Push another skewer horizontally throughout the thighs. Repeat with the remaining birds.

- Preheat one side of barbecue to 230F (110C) or medium-low heat. Leave the other side of the barbecue off.

- To build a smoke pouch, drain wet woodchips and squeeze excess water out. Spread wet woodchips on a large piece of aluminum foil. Place 1 cup (250mL) of dry woodchips on top and mix together. Close the foil around the chips to make a sealed pouch. Use a fork to puncture holes on both sides of the pouch.

- Place smoke pouch under heated side of the grill, close lid and wait for smoke.

- When smoke is billowing from the barbecue, place quail on cool side of grill and smoke for 45 minutes.

- Remove quail from grill and tent with foil. Let rest for 10 minutes. Serve and enjoy!

Couscous directions:

- Heat orange juice over medium heat until almost bubbling.

- Place couscous in large bowl.

- Pour hot orange juice over couscous and stir. Cover with plastic wrap and let sit 10 minutes. Fluff with fork, add green onions, raisins, pine nuts, salt and pepper.

- Allow to cool.

Serves 6

TEA-SMOKED CHICKEN

Regular peppercorns will work in a pinch if you can't get your hands on the
Szechwan variety. Also, substitute rice wine vinegar if you don't have any sake.

4-5 lb whole chicken

4 cups apple woodchips (1000mL)

1/2 cup black tea leaves (120mL)

Directions:

- For the marinade, crush peppercorns in a spice
  grinder or a mortar and pestle. In a small bowl
  combine the remaining ingredients. Put chicken in
  a large, sealable plastic bag. Pour the marinade
  over the chicken and rub the inside cavity of the
  chicken with the marinade. Seal the bag and place
  in the refrigerator. The chicken should marinate for
  24 hours.

Marinade

1 1/2 tsp Szechwan peppercorns, (7mL)

2 tbsp brown sugar, packed (30mL)

2 tbsp sake (30mL)

2 green onions

1 tbsp fresh ginger root peeled and
    minced (15mL)

1 stalk lemongrass, chopped fine

2 tsp salt (10mL)

Tea Glaze

1/2 cup brewed strong black tea (125 mL)

3 tbsp soya sauce (45 mL)

3 tbsp liquid honey (45 mL)

2 tbsp rice wine vinegar (30 mL)

1 tbsp sesame oil (15 mL)

- Prepare 2 smoke pouches. Place 2 cups (500mL) of woodchips into a bowl of cold water to soak for 1 hour (if using a charcoal grill, soak all chips and place over charcoal). On 2 sheets of aluminum foil combine drained wet woodchips with remaining dry woodchips. Combine tea leaves equally between packages. Seal up pouch and pierce multiple times with the tines of a fork, resulting in many holes for the smoke to escape.

- Mix ingredients of the Tea Glaze in a medium bowl.

- Preheat one side of the grill to high heat and place one smoke pouch directly over the heat source. Once bbq is smoking, place the chicken on the side of the bbq without direct heat.

- Smoke the chicken over indirect heat for 2-2 1/2 hours or until meat thermometer reaches 170°F, replacing the smoke pouch halfway through. Baste the chicken three times over the course of its cooking time.

- Remove chicken from the grill and let rest. Serve with Plum Chutney (see page 223).

Serves 4-6

WHITE WINE AND DIJON MUSTARD WHOLE CHICKEN

When making this recipe, remember: for every measure of white wine you put in the marinade – double it for your tummy.

1 whole chicken, 3–4 lbs (1.5–2 kg)
flattened (back bone removed)

Marinade

2/3 cup dry white wine (150mL)
1/3 cup extra virgin olive oil (75mL)
Juice from 1 lemon
4 cloves garlic, pressed
3 tbsp Dijon mustard (45mL)
1 tsp fresh ground black pepper (5mL)
2 tbsp rosemary, chopped (30mL)

Olive oil for rub

Directions:

- Combine the marinade ingredients in a non reactive container and mix well. Place flattened chicken in the marinade, cover and refrigerate for 4 hours.

- Remove chicken from container and discard marinade. Pat chicken dry and rub with olive oil to coat.

- Preheat grill to 350F (175C).

- Once the grill is hot, turn off middle burner and lower the other(s) to medium. Place the chicken, breast-side down over the burner that is off. Close lid and grill for 20 minutes. Turn the chicken over to balance cooking. Cook for another 25 minutes or until the juices run clear.

- Remove from grill, cover with foil and let stand for 10 minutes before carving. This will let the flesh reabsorb its juices. Serve and enjoy!

Serves 4

Dessert Anyone?

Life is uncertain. Eat dessert first.
–AMERICAN AUTHOR ERNESTINE ULMER

Chocolate Fondue with Grilled Peaches and Pears

Cinnamon Toast Fruit Kebabs

Grilled Nectarines with Ice Cream

Grilled Pineapple

Orange Mint & Mango Salad

Watermelon Salad

Roasted Stuffed Pears

Dessert on the grill? Caramelized beef with a cream-based barbecue sauce? No, absolutely not! Grilled fruit and simple sauces make for the perfect ending to a barbecue dinner. Plus, they are an excellent treat . . . even better than grilled veggies – honestly!

"Why should I bother grilling dessert, if I can go down to my local bakery and get a nice pastry, or just dole out scoops of ice cream from the freezer?" Sure, that's simple enough, but there are so many choices of fruits to cook on the grill for a great dessert, and I think you'll be surprised to learn how easy they are to prepare. Remember, your barbecue is nothing if not an alternative heat source to your oven. Don't be intimidated.

Mush, Mush

Avoid mush at all cost. I'm not talking about a team of dog sledders here, or a really sappy movie. I'm talking about pineapple left on the grill for so long that it has to be scraped off. For grilling fruit – pineapple, nectarines, pears and the like – you want to just lightly touch it to the barbecue. Get a few grill marks, heat it slightly and then – perfection!

Top your grilled fruit with a scoop of ice cream or a drizzle of caramel sauce, and maybe some roasted pecans. Yes, I say! For another delicious topping, combine a bit of dark rum (Jamaican is my favorite), with some butter over high heat, boil it down slightly and pour over the fruit. There is nothing better!

Keep It Clean

Most importantly, make sure you clean the grill and oil it thoroughly before you put your fruit on it. You don't want your delicately grilled peaches to taste like buffalo meat. Or maybe you do.

"Stressed" spelled backward is "desserts." Coincidence? I think not!
–AUTHOR UNKNOWN

CHOCOLATE FONDUE WITH GRILLED PEACHES AND PEARS

Now we're talking my language. I love chocolate. I'll wrestle anyone for a chocolate bar or two. This recipe will not disappoint you, my fellow chocoholics – and you know who you are! This is for you. When grilling fruit with skin on it, grill skin-side-up first, then flip. This will help the fruit remain intact.

10 oz of your favorite fondue chocolate,
coarsely chopped (1 1/4 cups)
2 ripe pears, sliced into thick wedges
2 ripe peaches, halved and pitted
Other fruit (bananas, apples, strawberries,
pineapple and plums) can be substituted

Directions:

- Prepare and preheat grill to low heat.

- In a metal bowl set over a saucepan of barely simmering water (bain-marie) melt the chocolate, stirring to ensure that the chocolate does not over cook.

- Once chocolate is melted, remove the bowl from the pan, and transfer to fondue pot. Place over candle or fondue burner.

- Place cut fruit on grill for approximately 1 minute per side. Remove fruit from grill and serve with fondue forks to dip into chocolate. Enjoy!

Serves 2

CINNAMON TOAST FRUIT KEBABS

These kebabs make a great dessert, but why not use the barbecue for breakfast?

1/4 cup sugar (60mL)

1 tsp ground cinnamon (5mL)

1/4 cup butter, melted

8 x 2-inch thick slices of fresh whole wheat bread

1 pint (2 cups) strawberries, cleaned and cut into halves

2 firm bananas, peeled and sliced into even rounds

1 tbsp vegetable oil to grease the grill (15mL)

Bamboo or metal skewers

Directions:

- Preheat the grill to 300F (150C).

- In a medium-sized bowl, combine the sugar and cinnamon.

- If using bamboo skewers soak them in water for 10–15 minutes.

- Cut the bread into 2-inch cubes and brush them lightly with melted butter. Then gently toss the bread cubes in the cinnamon sugar to coat evenly.

- Thread the cubes on to the skewers alternating with the strawberries and bananas.

- Lightly oil the grill with vegetable oil. Grill the kebabs for 8–10 minutes, turning occasionally until the bread is lightly toasted and browned.

Serves 4

GRILLED NECTARINES WITH ICE CREAM

Nectarines are one of my favorite fruits and they hold up really well on the grill.
Leave the skins on to keep them from falling apart. Substitute peaches for the
nectarines, if you like, and whipped cream works just as well as ice cream here.

10 nectarines, halved and pitted

2 tbsp honey (30mL)

juice of 1 lime and 1 lemon

1 pt French vanilla ice cream (500mL)

Directions:

- Preheat the barbecue to 350F (176C) or medium.

- In a small bowl mix together the honey and juice.

- Brush the cut sides of the nectarines with honey-juice mixture.

- Oil grill.

- Place the nectarines cut-side-down on the grill. Cook until the fruit is warm and lightly charred. This should only take 2–3 minutes.

- Remove nectarines from the grill and place on a serving tray.

- Serve hot with a scoop of vanilla ice cream.

Serves 6

GRILLED PINEAPPLE

Maple syrup is not just for pancakes. It is a great substitute for sugar and caramelizes beautifully on the grill. Careful not to leave this one on too high or for too long! You don't want charred mush!

2 pineapples, peeled and quartered
   lengthwise
1 cup maple syrup (250mL)
1 tsp of cinnamon (5mL)
1/2 tsp of ground cloves (2.5mL)

Directions:

- Peel and quarter pineapple and place in a plastic bag. Add maple syrup, cinnamon and cloves. Marinate for 2 hours or up to 24 hours.

- Heat grill to medium-high.

- Place pineapple on grill and cook until nicely brown on all sides, turning every 3 minutes and watching carefully not to burn.

- Serve hot with vanilla ice cream and any remaining marinade drizzled over top.

Serves 8

ORANGE MINT & MANGO SALAD

4 oranges

1 mango, peeled, cut from the pit and cubed

2 bananas, sliced

1 cup sliced fresh strawberries

1/4 cup vanilla yogurt (50ml)

1/2 cup unsweetened, toasted coconut

2 teaspoons finely chopped fresh mint, plus a few sprigs for garnish (10ml)

Directions:

- Peel, seed and slice 3 of the oranges and place the slices in a large bowl. Add the mango, bananas, strawberries and coconut. Set aside.

- Grate 1 teaspoon of the zest from the remaining orange and juice the orange. Place the zest and juice in a small bowl.

- Add the yogurt and chopped mint and mix well. Add to the fruit and mix well. Garnish with mint sprigs and chill for 2 hours and serve.

Serves 4

WATERMELON SALAD

With the vodka and Grand Marnier this is obviously a very grown-up salad. I like to use this as a palate cleanser between courses instead of as a salad at the beginning of the meal. It's light and refreshing and the booze will have your guests dancing on the table. Just keep them away from the pool.

1 8-lb seedless watermelon, (3.6 kg or
    about 16 cups, cubed)
1/2 cup fresh lemon juice (125 ml)
1/2 cup fresh lime juice (125 ml)
2/3 cup sugar (150 ml)
1/2 cup vodka (125 ml)
6 tbsp Grand Marnier (90 ml)
1/4 cup chopped fresh mint (60 ml)

Directions:

- Cut the watermelon out of rind and cube it into 1-inch pieces. Put all watermelon into a big bowl.

- In a separate bowl, squeeze the lemons and limes. Add sugar and stir until it is dissolved.

- Add the vodka and Grand Marnier.

- Pour mixture over the watermelon and add fresh mint; stir gently to combine.

- Put the salad in the refrigerator for an hour to set up. Don't leave it any longer than that or the watermelon will get all mooshy.

Serves 8

ROASTED STUFFED PEARS

Barbecued pears for dessert? Smoked and stuffed and served with a very grown-up whipping cream on top. You can prep the pears in advance and store in the fridge until you need them. Just remember to take them out 30 minutes before smoking so they can return to room temperature.

6 firm-flesh Bartlett pears

5 tbsp unsalted butter, softened (75ml)

5 tbsp gingersnap cookies, crumbled (75ml)

2 tbsp brown sugar (30ml)

2 tsp chopped lemon zest (10ml)

1/2 tsp cinnamon (2.5ml)

1/4 tsp nutmeg (1ml)

Directions:

- In a bowl, combine room temperature butter and crumbled gingersnap cookies. Add brown sugar, lemon zest, cinnamon, nutmeg, cloves, orange liqueur, scraped vanilla seeds and mix.

- Slice a bit off of the bottom of each pear so that they stand up on a plate.

- Remove the tops and core each pear using a melonballer.

1/2 tsp ground cloves (2.5ml)

1 tbsp orange liqueur (15ml)

1 vanilla bean, scraped

1 lemon cut into wedges

Apple wood smoking chips

Whipping Cream

1 cup 35% cream (250ml)

Splash of orange liqueur

1/2 vanilla bean, scraped

1 tbsp icing sugar (15ml)

- *Tip – dampen a tea towel and place on countertop to hold the bowl in place while whipping*

- Rub the pears with lemon wedges to stop discoloring.

- Stuff the pears with the mixture – not too much – then put the tops back on.

- Butter a perforated barbecue baking sheet and add the pears.

- Make a smoke pouch (see page 5).

- Prepare the barbecue for indirect smoking. Crank the heat on one side and place the smoke pouch directly on the burner. Close the lid and wait for smoke. Once the barbecue is smoking, reduce the heat to 220F/110C.

- Place the pears on the unlit grill side. Close the lid and smoke the pears for approximately 30 minutes.

- Remove from heat and serve warm with this whipping cream:

Whipping Cream Directions:

- Place a large stainless steel bowl in the freezer and chill for 20 minutes.

- Take the cream out of the refrigerator and the bowl out of the freezer.

- Add a splash orange liqueur, vanilla seeds and icing sugar.

- Using a large balloon whisk, whip until soft peaks are achieved.

Serves 6 for dessert

Odds and Sauces

A well-made sauce will make even an elephant or a grandfather palatable.
– ALEXANDRE BALTHASAR LAURENT GRIMOD DE LA REYNIÈRE,
   THE WORLD'S FIRST RESTAURANT CRITIC

Cilantro Radish Relish

Cucumber Dip

Hot Mint BBQ Sauce

Homemade Smoked Ketchup

Golden Mustard Barbecue Sauce

Hot Chili Barbecue Sauce

Maple Mango Barbecue Sauce

Tomatillo Salsa

Banana Salsa

Plum Chutney

Lemon Honey Sauce with Garlic

Sweet & Spicy Mint Sauce

Passion Fruit Applesauce

Pernod Butter

Sweet & Sour Barbecue Sauce

Hot Tomato-Based BBQ Sauce

Mango Cucumber Salsa

Martini Relish

Mustard BBQ Sauce

Peach Chutney

Plum Chutney

Smoked Guacamole

Smoked Salsa

Spicy Vinegar-Based BBQ Sauce

Tarragon Mayonnaise

Tomato BBQ Sauce

A homemade sauce or marinade can turn an ordinary piece of meat into a masterpiece on the grill. And the same cut of meat can taste entirely different – savoury, citrusy, spicy, sweet or a combination of some or all of these flavors – depending on the marinade used in preparing it.

Salsas, chutneys and relishes add a little extra flavor to those succulent dishes you've cooked on the grill. "Fresh" is the key word here – always buy fresh ingredients when you can. For many of us, barbecue season coincides with the summer harvest, so finding fresh cucumbers, tomatoes, herbs and fruits shouldn't be a problem. If you're lucky, you might even have your own garden with all the makings for a delicious salsa. For large quantities, or if barbecuing in the "off-season," certain canned ingredients are perfectly acceptable – like canned tomatoes for instance. In the height of the season, though, tomatoes fresh off the vine are a slice of heaven.

Why not skip the condiment aisle at the grocery store and try some of these recipes for barbecue sauces, relishes and salsas instead? There is nothing like a sweet Plum Chutney on Tea-Smoked Chicken or a Cilantro Radish Relish on fish off the grill. Mmmm . . . I'm starting to get hungry.

Never trust a skinny cook
–UNKNOWN

CILANTRO RADISH RELISH

1 bunch fresh cilantro

1 bunch of radishes

1 large white onion

2 tbsp honey

2 tbsp white cider vinegar

Directions:

- Rinse cilantro under cold running water, blot dry with paper towels and pluck the leaves from the stem. Coarsely chop leaves.

- Rinse and trim radishes and cut them into 1/4-inch cubes. Cut onion into 1/4-inch cubes.

- Combine the honey and vinegar in a serving bowl. Add cilantro, radish and onion, and toss to mix. Relish is best served within 2 hours of preparing.

Serves 8

CUCUMBER DIP

Refreshing cucumber mixed with fresh garlic and yogurt. Put that over just about anything – I even love it as a chip-dip substitute. The mint in this recipe gives it a decidedly Middle Eastern flare.

2 cucumbers, peeled and seeded

2 tsp sea salt (30mL)

6 tbsp fresh mint leaves, finely chopped
    (90mL)

3 cloves garlic, minced

1 tsp sugar (5mL)

1 1/2 cups plain yogurt (regular or low fat)
    (375mL)

3 tbsp chives, finely chopped (45mL)

Directions:

- Peel the cucumber completely and cut into quarters. Use a spoon to scoop out the seeds. Dice the cucumber into 1-inch cubes. Place the cucumbers in a strainer and sprinkle them generously with sea salt. Place a bowl underneath the strainer to catch the liquid. Leave to drain for 15–25 minutes.

- Meanwhile, combine the mint, garlic, sugar and yogurt in a medium-sized bowl. Set aside in the refrigerator until ready to use.

- Drain the cucumber and rinse well. Pat the cucumber dry with paper towel and add to the yogurt mixture. Add the chives and mix gently. Leave in the fridge to let the flavors combine until ready to serve. This will keep in the fridge for up to 2 days. Serve cold.

Yields 1 cup

HOT MINT BBQ SAUCE

1 cup store bought barbecue sauce
(250mL)

1/2 cup mint jelly (125mL)

1 tbsp hot sauce (15mL)

1 tbsp lemon juice (15mL)

1 tbsp lime juice (15mL)

1/4 cup fresh cilantro, chopped (60mL)

Salt to taste

Directions:

- In a medium saucepan combine all ingredients except the cilantro and salt. Bring to a gentle boil over low heat.

- Allow sauce to simmer for 5 minutes. Remove from heat and stir in the cilantro and salt to taste.

Yields 2 cups

HOMEMADE SMOKED KETCHUP

Hey, why buy ketchup when you can make your own? We snuck into the Heinz plant under cover of night and stole their secret recipe. Kidding. Smoking the tomatoes with hickory wood chips ensures that this tastes nothing like any ketchup you've ever had before. Ketchup or catsup (depending on where you're from) has been around for at least 300 years and is said to have originated in China. Seriously. This time I'm not kidding.

2 lbs tomatoes, halved and seeded

3 tbsp olive oil (45ml)

1 tbsp white sugar (15ml)

garlic cloves, peeled (one for each

    tomato half)

1/2 cup sweet onion, finely diced (125 ml)

3 tbsp cider vinegar (45ml)

2 tbsp brown sugar (30ml)

1 tsp ground allspice (5ml)

1/2 tsp ground cumin (2.5ml)

1/4 tsp ground nutmeg (1.25 ml)

1 tsp Worcestershire sauce (5ml)

Hickory wood chips for smoking

Directions:

- Make a smoke pouch (see page 5).

- Place the tomatoes on a perforated barbecue baking sheet and drizzle with 1 tbsp of oil until well coated. Sprinkle with sugar.

- Place a garlic clove into each of the tomato halves.

- Prepare the barbecue for indirect grilling. Crank the heat on one side and place the smoke pouch directly on the burner. Close the lid and wait for smoke. Once barbecue is smoking, reduce the heat to 220F/110C.

- Place the tomatoes on the side of the barbecue where there is no direct heat. Close the lid and smoke the tomatoes for 1 1/4 hours.

- Once fully smoked, put the tomatoes and garlic in a blender and blitz.

- In a saucepan set over medium heat, sauté the onions in oil until tender but not browned.

- Add the pureed tomato and garlic to the saucepan.

- Add vinegar, brown sugar, allspice, cumin, nutmeg and Worcestershire sauce.

- Simmer over medium heat for 30 minutes until thickened.

- Season to taste and leave to cool.

- This will keep for up to 1 week covered in fridge.

GOLDEN MUSTARD BARBECUE SAUCE

1 cup white vinegar (250ml)

1/2 cup prepared yellow mustard (125ml)

1/4 cup Dijon mustard (60ml)

1/2 medium onion, minced

1/3 cup water (83ml)

1/4 cup tomato paste (60ml)

1 tbsp paprika (15ml)

2 tbsp brown sugar (30ml)

7 cloves garlic, minced

2 tsp celery salt (10ml)

1/2 tsp cayenne (2.5ml)

1/2 tsp freshly ground black pepper (2.5ml)

Directions:

- Place all of the ingredients into a non-reactive heavy-bottomed saucepan over medium-high heat and bring to a simmer.

- Reduce heat to low and cook for 25 minutes, simmering until the mixture thickens and the onions are tender. Serve warm or cold.

- This will keep for 2 weeks covered in the refrigerator.

Yield: 2 1/2 cups (625ml)

HOT CHILI BARBECUE SAUCE

This recipe calls for four different types of chili peppers. Not only do different peppers have different heat quotients, they also have different tastes. Combining them brings depth of flavor to your sauce and every Barbecue Master (or Mistress) is known for his hot barbecue sauce, so don't mess around. Try and use at least 3 of them if you can't find all four. If your local grocer doesn't have chipotles, it's time to get a new grocer.

1 small poblano pepper, seeded and diced

1 serrano chili, seeded and finely diced

1 Thai chili, finely diced

1 tbsp olive oil (15ml)

2 canned chipotle peppers in adobo
  sauce, minced

1 small white onion, diced fine

1 tbsp minced garlic (15ml)

1 cup tomato sauce (250ml)

1/4 cup ketchup (60ml)

2 tbsp prepared mustard (30ml)

2 tbsp prepared horseradish (30ml)

1 1/2 tsp ground cinnamon (7.5ml)

3 tbsp molasses (45ml)

1 tbsp Worcestershire sauce (15ml)

1/2 tsp soy sauce (7.5ml)

Salt and pepper to taste

Directions:

- In large skillet heat the oil over medium heat until almost smoking, add the fresh chilies and cook for 2 minutes or until slightly charred.

- Add garlic and onion and sauté until translucent.

- Add the remaining ingredients and bring to a simmer.

- Reduce heat to low and simmer for 30 minutes. Adjust seasoning if necessary.

Yield: 2 cups (500ml)

MAPLE MANGO BARBECUE SAUCE

Maple mango barbecue sauce. Try saying that three times fast. This one is fast and easy and is perfect with pork or chicken.

1/2 cup maple syrup (125ml)

1/2 cup mango chutney (125ml)

1/2 cup ketchup (125ml)

1/2 cup bottled barbecue sauce (125ml)

1/2 cup tomato sauce (125ml)

1 tbsp ginger powder (15ml)

1 tbsp onion powder (15ml)

1 tbsp celery salt (15ml)

1 tbsp lemon pepper (15ml)

2 tbsp hot sauce (optional) (30ml)

Juice of 1 lemon

Directions:

- Place all of the ingredients into a non-reactive heavy-bottomed saucepan. Place over medium-low heat and cook for 20 minutes without letting the sauce boil. Stir occasionally.

Yield: 2 1/2 cups (625 ml)

TOMATILLO SALSA

Tomatillos are also known in some places as Mexican green tomatoes and are not tomatoes at all but rather are related to the gooseberry. Most times you're going to get them when they're green which is a good thing for this salsa because they'll be nice and firm. Tomatillos have a sort of lemony apple flavor (that's not quite it, but it's the closest I can come up with) that makes for a great salsa when combined with the chili, cilantro and red pepper. Nice colors too. Works really well with a big meaty fish or a nice veal chop.

8 tomatillos, husks discarded

2 fresh jalapeno chilies with seeds, chopped

1 cup fresh cilantro leaves, washed well
and spun dry (250ml)

1/4 cup water (60ml)

1 tsp coarse salt (5ml)

2 shallots diced fine

1 medium sweet red pepper, diced fine

Directions:

- Rinse tomatillos under warm water to remove sticky film and pat dry with paper towel.

- Quarter the tomatillos and place in a blender with the jalapeno, cilantro and water.

- Puree in bursts until chunky.

- Pour mixture into a bowl and add salt, diced shallot and red pepper.

- Cover and let rest in fridge.

- Bring salsa to room temperature before serving.

Yield: 1 cup (250ml)

BANANA SALSA

You are going to love this with chicken or red snapper. The chipotles give the salsa some heat and smokiness.

4 ripe bananas, peeled and diced
  (about 2 cups) (500ml)

2 chipotle peppers from a can, finely diced

1/2 medium red pepper, finely diced

1/2 cup finely diced red onion, (125ml)

4 tbsp freshly chopped mint (60ml)

2 tbsp orange juice (30ml)

2 tbsp freshly squeezed lime juice (30ml)

1 tbsp honey (15ml)

Directions:

- Combine all of the ingredients except the banana into a bowl. Toss gently. Add the banana and toss again to coat. Cover and place in the refrigerator for 2–3 hours.

Yield: 3 cups (750ml)

PLUM CHUTNEY

1 lb red plums, ripe but still firm

1 large Gala apple

2/3 cup sugar (225ml)

1 cup water (250 ml)

6 tbsp red wine vinegar (90ml)

1 tbsp peeled and minced fresh ginger (15ml)

1 tsp chopped garlic (5ml)

2 tsp grated orange zest (30ml)

2 tsp nutmeg (10ml)

2 tsp cloves (10ml)

1 tsp cinnamon (5 ml)

Directions:

- Halve and pit the plums. Dice into 1/2-inch cubes and place in a bowl.

- Core and halve the apples leaving the skins on. Dice into 1/2-inch cubes.

- In a saucepan, dissolve the sugar in the water and bring to a gentle boil over medium-high heat.

- Add vinegar, ginger, garlic, diced apples and half of the diced plums.

- Bring mixture to a gentle boil and simmer for 5 minutes.

- Add the remaining plums, orange zest, nutmeg, cloves and cinnamon.

- Bring to a gentle boil and cook for 10 minutes or until thick and syrupy

- Remove and cool.

- Serve at room temperature.

Yield: 2 cups (500ml)

LEMON HONEY SAUCE WITH GARLIC

FIFTEEN CLOVES OF GARLIC!! Trust me, this works. Adjust the number of chilies to suit your heat tolerance.

15 cloves of garlic, minced

1 hot chili, seeded and finely chopped

4 tbsp minced fresh cilantro (60ml)

Juice of 2 lemons

8 tbsp honey (120ml)

1 tsp fish sauce (5ml)

Directions:

- Combine all of the ingredients in a bowl and whisk until fully incorporated. Adjust seasoning as desired and serve immediately.

Yield: 1 1/2 cups (375ml)

SWEET & SPICY MINT SAUCE

The trick is to make it *look* like you spent forever making dinner. This sauce is great with lamb or shrimp.

3/4 cup mint jelly (187ml)

1/2 cup white vinegar (125ml)

1 red Thai chili, split, seeded and finely diced

1/4 cup chopped fresh mint

Directions:

- Combine all of the ingredients in a saucepan and bring to a boil.

- Reduce heat slightly and simmer for 3 minutes and serve immediately.

- If the sauce becomes too thick, add a tsp of water at a time until you reach desired consistency.

- Add chopped fresh mint prior to serving.

Yield: 1 1/4 cup (310ml)

PASSION FRUIT APPLESAUCE

2 1/2 cups of applesauce (600ml)

1 cup strained passion fruit sauce,
    pulp or nectar (250ml)

1 tsp vanilla extract (5ml)

3 slices peeled and minced fresh ginger
    (1/4 inch think)

1/4 cup dark Jamaican rum (60ml)

3 tbsp honey (or more to taste) (45ml)

1 cinnamon stick

1 tsp allspice (5ml)

Directions:

- Combine all of the ingredients in a heavy-bottomed saucepan and bring to a boil.

- Lower the heat and simmer for 15 minutes.

Yield: About 4 cups (1L)

PERNOD BUTTER

Pernod is a French licorice-flavored liqueur and makes for a great compound butter to be served with fish or shellfish.

1/4-lb unsalted butter, softened

3 tbsp Pernod (45ml)

1 tsp pepper

Directions:

- Mix all of the ingredients together in a bowl.

- Scrape the butter into a piece of plastic wrap and roll into a log shape.

- Place in the fridge to set.

Yield: 1/4 lb of butter (450g)

SWEET & SOUR BARBECUE SAUCE

1/2 cup bottled plum sauce (125ml)

3 tbsp soy sauce (45ml)

3 tbsp rice wine vinegar (45ml)

2 tbsp sesame oil (30ml)

1 tbsp fresh ginger, grated (15ml)

3 garlic cloves, finely diced

Pinch of dried chili flakes (optional)

Splash of Tabasco sauce

Salt and pepper to taste

Directions:

- Combine ingredients in a small saucepan and bring to a simmer for 5 minutes.

- Let stand for at least an hour to mellow and blend.

Yield: 8 servings

HOT TOMATO-BASED BBQ SAUCE

3 tbsp vegetable oil (45mL)

1 medium onion, minced

4 cloves garlic, minced

1/2 cup ketchup (125mL)

1/2 cup tomato sauce (125mL)

1 cup water (250mL)

3 tbsp cider vinegar (45mL)

3 tbsp Worcestershire sauce (45mL)

2 tbsp of fresh lemon juice (30mL)

1 tsp of your favorite hot sauce (5mL)

1/2 tsp of liquid smoke (2.5mL)

3 tbsp of firmly packed dark brown sugar
    (45mL)

3 teaspoons of dry mustard (15mL)

1/2 tsp of freshly ground black pepper
    (2.5mL)

1/3 cup of apple sauce (75mL)

Salt to taste

Directions:

- Heat oil in a large saucepan over medium heat, add onions, and garlic and sauté over low heat until soft and translucent.

- Stir in ketchup, tomato sauce, water, cider vinegar, Worcestershire sauce, lemon juice, hot sauce, liquid smoke, sugar, dry mustard, apple sauce and black pepper and bring to a boil. Reduce heat to low and simmer uncovered for approximately 15 minutes or until the sauce has thickened.

- If the sauce becomes too thick add a tablespoon of water.

- Remove from heat and season with salt and pepper, sugar and a splash of vinegar to taste. This sauce will keep for several weeks when covered tightly and stored in the refrigerator.

Yields 3 cups

MANGO CUCUMBER SALSA

I love to cook with mangos. They are such a versatile fruit. Even when they're not ripe, they're great!

2 cups mango, peeled and chopped (500 mL)

2 cups cucumber, peeled and chopped (500 mL)

1 1/4 cup chopped red bell pepper (315 mL)

1/2 cup red onion, diced (125 mL)

1/3 cup chopped fresh cilantro (83 mL)

3 tbsp lime juice (45mL)

1 jalapeno pepper, seeded and minced

Salt

Freshly ground black pepper

Directions:

- In a large bowl mix the mango, cucumber, red pepper, shallots, cilantro, lime juice and jalapeno.

- Season to taste with salt and pepper. Serve and enjoy.

Yields 5 cups (1250mL)

MARTINI RELISH

1/2 cup kalamata olives, chopped and
   pitted (125 mL)

1/2 cup nicoise olives, chopped and pitted
   (125 mL)

1/2 cup Sicilian stuffed olives, chopped
   and pitted (125 mL)

1/2 red onion, chopped fine (125mL)

1 tbsp olive oil (15mL)

1 tbsp red wine vinegar (15mL)

5 leaves fresh basil, chopped

1 tsp fresh thyme, chopped (5mL)

2 tbsp vermouth (30mL)

Fresh pepper to taste

Directions:

- Combine all ingredients in a medium-sized bowl.
  Stir well. Cover and refrigerate for 2–3 hours.

- Serve with crusty bread.

Yields 2 cups

MUSTARD BBQ SAUCE

1/2 cup Dijon mustard (125mL)

1/2 chipotle pepper, chopped

3 tbsp honey (45mL)

1 tbsp cider vinegar (15mL)

1 tbsp grainy mustard (15mL)

Pinch of tumeric

Pepper to taste

2 cloves garlic, roasted

Directions:

- In medium sized bowl whisk together all ingredients but garlic.

- Squeeze 2 cloves of roasted garlic on to a board and mash into a paste with the side of a knife. Add to sauce and mix.

- Cover with plastic wrap

- Let mixture rest for at least 2 hours before serving.

Yields 1 1/2 cups

PEACH CHUTNEY

Peaches have such a short growing season. Such a shame! Grilled, fresh, pureed, frozen, canned, over ice cream, under ice cream – they are sheer perfection!

8 peaches, pit removed and halved

Juice of 1 lemon

1 tsp ginger, minced (15mL)

1 onion, sliced

1/4 tsp allspice (1mL)

1/4 tsp cinnamon (1mL)

1 tbsp cider vinegar (15mL)

1/4 cup white wine (60mL)

1 tbsp olive oil (15mL)

Marinade

1/2 cup bourbon (125mL)

1 tbsp honey (15mL)

1/2 cup pure maple syrup (125mL)

1/4 tsp fresh nutmeg (1mL)

1 tsp fresh black pepper (5mL)

2 tbsp sugar (30mL)

Cedar planks soaked in water for 1 hour

Directions:

- Combine marinade ingredients in a saucepan and simmer for 10 minutes or until mixture thickens

- Squeeze lemon juice over peach halves and brush peaches with marinade. Cover peaches in plastic wrap and refrigerate for 3 hours.

- Preheat grill to 375F (190C).

- Place cedar planks on grill, close lid and wait until the edges of the planks start to char and smoke.

- Reduce heat to 325F (162C). Place peaches cut-side-down on planks. Grill for 5 minutes. Remove and let cool.

- Chop grilled peaches and place in bowl.

- Preheat skillet to medium. Add onion and ginger. Sauté until onion is slightly softened. Add cinnamon, cider vinegar and white wine.

- Remove from heat and add to chopped peaches. Serve with pulled pork.

Serves 8

PLUM CHUTNEY II

1/2 lb each of yellow and red plums,
*   ripe but still firm*

1 large gala apple

2/3 cup honey (225mL)

6 tbsp white wine vinegar (90mL)

1 tbsp minced peeled fresh ginger (15mL)

1 tbsp chopped garlic (5mL)

2 tsp grated orange zest (30mL)

2 tsp nutmeg (10mL)

2 whole cinnamon sticks (10mL)

Directions:

- Halve and pit the plums. Dice into 1/2-inch cubes. You should have 3 cups (750mL) of diced plums. Place into a bowl.

- Halve apple. Dice into 1/2-inch cubes. You should have 1 cup of diced apple.

- Place water and honey in a saucepan. Stir to dissolve and then bring to a boil. Add vinegar, ginger, garlic and half of the diced plums and the diced apple.

- Bring mixture to a boil and cook for 5 minutes.

- Add the remaining plums, orange zest and spices. Bring to a gentle boil and cook for 10 minutes or until thick and syrupy.

- Remove from heat and let cool. Discard cinnamon sticks. Serve with Tea Smoked Chicken (page 201).

Yields 2 Cups (500mL)

SMOKED GUACAMOLE

2 large red bell peppers

4 smoked Serrano chilies

1/2 small red onion finely chopped

1/2 cup finely chopped fresh cilantro
  (125mL)

1 tsp of salt (5mL)

1/2 tsp black pepper (2.5mL)

Juice of 1 lime

3 large, ripe avocados

2 cups dry hickory woodchips

1 cup hickory woodchips, soaked for
  30 minutes

Directions:

- Remove grill from barbecue and preheat to a medium heat.

- Prepare a smoke package. Squeeze the excess water from the soaking woodchips and place in the center of a large piece of tin foil. Add the dry chips to the wet and mix them together. Fold the foil around the chips to create a well-sealed package. Using a fork, poke holes on both sides of the smoke package. Set aside.

- Half and remove the seeds from the peppers and chilies. This will remove some of the heat from the hot peppers.

- Place the woodchip package directly on top of the flame where the grill grid has been removed. Turn the other burners off. Place the pepper and chili halves on the grid over the burners that are off.

- Close barbecue lid. Smoke the peppers and chilies for approximately 10 minutes, or until the flesh is charred.

- The skin can now be removed easily. Once skin has been removed and discarded. chop peppers and chilies well and add to a bowl. Add onion, cilantro, salt, pepper, lime juice. Combine mixture well.

- Pit and peel avocados. Add to mixture and mash until incorporated but still chunky. Cover and chill until ready to use, but return to room temperature when ready to serve.

Yields 4–6 serving portions

SMOKED SALSA

You can make a salsa out of just about any fruit or veggie. This combination reminds me of a night on the ranch, with a smokey fire and the sting of the peppers.

6 large tomatoes

4 smoked Serrano chilies

1/2 cup water (125mL)

2 tbsp balsamic vinegar (30mL)

Salt to taste

3 tbsp dried cilantro (45mL)

Mesquite and hickory woodchips soaked
*   in cold water for 30 minutes*

Directions:

- Remove grill from barbecue and preheat to a medium heat.

- Half and remove the seeds from the tomatoes and hot peppers. This will remove the bitter taste from the tomatoes and some of the heat from the hot peppers.

- Drain mesquite and hickory woodchips and set aside.

- Place tomato and hot pepper halves on to the grill. Once the barbecue reaches a medium heat place grill on barbecue along with damp woodchips and close barbecue lid.

- Process will only take approximately 10 minutes, or until the flesh of the tomatoes and peppers are charred.

- Once charred, the skins of the tomatoes and peppers can be easily removed.

- Dice up tomatoes and peppers; add to blender with water, balsamic vinegar and salt. Pulse to a desired chunkiness, add dried cilantro (or fresh, if available) and voila! Serve and enjoy!

Yields 4–6 serving portions

SPICY VINEGAR-BASED BBQ SAUCE

2 cups cider vinegar (500mL)

1 1/4 cups water (310mL)

1/3 cup brown sugar (83mL)

6 tsp salt, or to taste (30mL)

5 tsp hot red pepper flakes (25mL)

2 tsp freshly ground black pepper (10mL)

Directions:

- Combine ingredients in a stainless steel bowl and whisk until sugar and salt are dissolved.

- Taste for seasoning, adding sugar or salt as necessary. The sauce should be hot but not sour.

Serves 4

TARRAGON MAYONNAISE

1 cup white wine (250mL)

3 sprigs of fresh tarragon

1 cup mayonnaise (250mL)

2 drops of Tabasco, or to taste

Directions:

- In a saucepan combine white wine and tarragon sprig. On medium heat reduce to 1/4 cup. Strain and chill.

- Mix the chilled reduction with mayonnaise and add 2 splashes of Tabasco sauce. Refrigerate until time to serve.

Yields 2 cups

TOMATO BBQ SAUCE

1/2 cup ketchup (125mL)

1/2 cup sugar (125mL)

3/4 can crushed tomatoes (175mL)

1 tbsp paprika (15mL)

1 tbsp dry mustard (15mL)

1 tsp cayenne pepper (5mL)

5 cloves garlic, chopped

1/2 onion, chopped

Directions:

- Add ingredients to a pot and simmer over low heat for 20 minutes.

- Refrigerate mixture overnight before serving.

Yields 2 cups

INDEX

Market location photography:

Taryn Manias, *McArthur & Company*
Linda Pellowe and David Szolcsanyi, *Mad Dog Design Connection*